Bringing Value to Healthcare provides a clear picture of the future of healthcare delivery in the United States—a system that is less burdensome, is more efficient, and produces better care at lower cost by rewarding the quality, not quantity, of services provided. It is a system that is centered around the consumer, helping people live healthier, happier, and longer lives. This important work gets to the heart of the debate unfolding across the country and should serve as a blueprint for healthcare companies seeking to remain relevant in this ever-changing landscape.

Mark T. Bertolini
Chairman and Chief Executive Officer
Aetna

In their newest book, Rita and Michael give an incisive evaluation of what is needed from healthcare leaders today. They outline many of the specific steps organizations must take and the competencies that need to be developed. But in the end, lasting change is really a matter of leadership. In this book, Rita and Michael describe the knowledge and actions needed from the board chair to the department head and outline why such actions have not been taken before and why some organizations and leaders may not be up to the challenge.

Joe Mott
Vice President, Population Health
Intermountain Healthcare

Change requires that we dismiss the familiar and venture out of our comfort zone. For the healthcare industry, the demand for change is not arbitrary, but absolute. An evolving regulatory environment, a confusing competitive landscape, nonstop radical changes in technology, and drastically different public demands have dove-tailed to compel transformations in the healthcare industry. Combining these factors with the rapidly changing roles of the players in this industry—the healthcare providers, the healthcare product companies, the payers, the hospitals, the clinic, the pharmacies, the wellness centers, and the new reality that "patients" are no longer passive but active participants in their healthcare—has created the equivalent of a 5000-piece jigsaw puzzle without any picture for guidance.

No one can examine, investigate, study, discuss, and research the myriad forces and role-players in the healthcare arena than the team of Rita Numerof and Michael Abrams. When you combine their vast experience with their profound ability to lay out a clear and understandable hypothesis to approach this exploding transition to a new system, you end up with a masterpiece for all stakeholders to read. It's called *Bringing Value to Healthcare: Practical Steps for Getting to a Market-Based Model.*

Robert Z. Gussin, PhD
Retired Vice President for Science and Technology and Chief Scientific Officer Johnson & Johnson

If you want to transcend conventional thinking on the emerging transformation of healthcare, Numerof and Abrams will illuminate the irresistible market forces that are finally taking the lead for the future of healthcare.

Consumers move markets; consumers demand and obtain information they value; consumers drive competition, and competition accelerates efficiency, better quality, and better price, all of which will raise the tide in the healthcare harbor.

On a parallel track to all the resistance to change in healthcare, information tools have disrupted every market. And all of the healthcare consumers have become very facile in using those tools throughout; obtaining information; making complex decisions; and being accountable for their lives. They demand no less from healthcare, as is revealed in this book. See the bright future for healthcare... but do not look to government, insurance companies, or oligopolists... look to the consumers and their information partners.

Stephen B. Bonner
Member, Board of Directors
Former President and Chief Executive Officer
Cancer Treatment Centers of America®

Americans should expect the unexpected. The Affordable Care Act of 2010, though centralizing control in the federal government, may turn out to be a catalyst for disruptive market-driven change. Private insurance exchanges, defined contribution financing, and direct physician payment arrangements are emerging. Convenient and efficient walk-in clinics and ambulatory care centers are flourishing. Big hospital systems face new pressures from new players, promising value to patients. Open and transparent healthcare markets are not only possible but also likely. And personal choice and real competition—not bureaucracy and regulation—will drive that transformation. Health policy experts Rita Numerof and Michael Abrams explain what is happening and why.

Robert E. Moffit, PhD
Senior Fellow
Center for Health Policy Studies
The Heritage Foundation

Bringing Value to Healthcare presciently describes a future where healthcare is hugely changed—and how we are going to get there.

Every industry produces the product that its customers buy. In healthcare, the buyers all buy pieces of care. Piecework has defined the care industry and has been the source of cash for all care providers (with a few notable exceptions). So providers produce and sell pieces. Buyers need to change what they buy to make that reality different.

In this book, Rita Numerof and Michael Abrams describe the powerful changes that took place in the healthcare system once buyers stopped paying for some hospital mistakes. This simple change had a major impact, with lessons for how we replicate the experience across the industry.

Buyers should reward provider behaviors that lead to better outcomes and should buy care by the package whenever possible. Bundles are good; capitation is better. Long-term health is too hard to define and impossible to reward in relevant care team context, but short-term health improvement milestones, like blood pressure control, can be measured and lead to better health.

The authors are right. A golden age for care delivery is possible, once buyers are focused on buying the right products in intentional ways.

George C. Halvorson
Chair of the Institute for InterGroup Understanding
Retired Chairman and Chief Executive Officer
of Kaiser Permanente

The blunt force of the Affordable Care Act is upending healthcare business models across the industry, but no sectors have more to lose—or gain—from increased consolidation and cost-cutting pressures than pharmaceuticals and medical devices. The growing prevalence of at-risk provider contracts, treatment protocols, and government-funded CER all threaten to slow the pace of innovation in these sectors as evidence requirements mount for demonstrating real-world efficacy and cost effectiveness.

Numerof and Abrams argue—eloquently and correctly—that the siloed, cost-plus, physician-centric business models of the past won't cut it in the post-ACA environment. Innovators must focus on delivering enhanced value to payers, providers, and consumers through superior understanding of targeted disease spaces that allow them to identify pipeline candidates that have the greatest potential to meet unmet medical need and/or drive cost savings across the entire treatment continuum, including prevention. Cost effectiveness has to become a paramount R&D consideration, allowing firms to design registration trials that generate both clinical efficacy data and cost-effectiveness data, and then boldly embrace pay-for-performance contracts based on real-world data in stratified patient populations.

Bottom line: innovators need to think beyond products, and towards systems of care where product and service wraps can be disruptive across the entire clinical space. This will require hand-in-glove collaboration among providers, payers, innovators, and patients who utilize data to target new technologies to the greatest advantage in an increasingly competitive and cost-sensitive landscape driven by an aging global population. U.S. policymakers can and should accelerate this transition by driving competition and transparency efforts, but it will all be for naught if industry doesn't develop proof of concept paradigms showing that it can work. In a growing era of precision medicine and business model disruption, this book is a must read for C-Suite healthcare executives who want to know how to survive and flourish when the payment models of the past are becoming increasingly obsolete.

Paul Howard, PhD
Director and Senior Fellow
Center for Medical Progress
Manhattan Institute for Policy Research

In their book *Bringing Value to Healthcare: Practical Steps for Getting to a Market-Based Model,* Rita Numerof and Michael Abrams provide a map to the future of healthcare with helpful instructions to assist healthcare executives navigate the tricky terrain in front of them.

Michael O. Leavitt
Founder and Chairman, Leavitt Partners
Former Secretary of the U.S. Department
of Health and Human Services
Three-Term Governor of Utah
Co-Chair of the Financial Review Panel for The Global Fund

In *Bringing Value to Healthcare: Practical Steps for Getting to a Market-Based Model*, Rita Numerof and Michael Abrams offer a clear-eyed, unsparing analysis of the healthcare system we currently have and present an inspiring vision of the consumer-centered, value-driven system that might be. The book makes an important contribution to the national conversation over health policy, pointing out in rich detail how the status quo lacks accountability and effective incentives to provide value instead of volume, and how consumers are kept at arm's length from healthcare decision making.

I would recommend this book to all of those who craft and influence healthcare laws and regulations. A system that fully utilizes data, emphasizes wellness and prevention, and relies upon consumer choice to drive value is achievable in the foreseeable future. The Numerof and Abrams book provides intellectual fuel to jump-start this progress.

Mary R. Grealy
President
Healthcare Leadership Council

As Walt Disney enabled us to envision a better way to deliver family entertainment, so have Rita and Michael who enabled us to envision a better way to deliver health and healthcare. It is a system that has at its core a market-based approach delivering on the promise of improved clinical value for both outcomes and cost with the consumer as the driver of choice! The road-map they provide for the reader is one that is mastered only by those with new competencies for innovation and results in accountability to the consumer and the recognition that competition will come from not-in-kind organizations but those outside the traditional healthcare structure. They boldly remind us that we are either part of this transformation or a memory from the past. Sounds a lot like the market disruption that was the Disney formula of success.

Esther Emard
Adjunct Instructor, The George Washington University
Former Chief Operating Officer,
National Committee for Quality Assurance

Rita Numerof and Michael Abrams have written a compendium on the state of American healthcare that is at once a timely snapshot of a dynamic industry, a critical analysis of the forces that are shaping change, a series of important practical strategic questions for each of the industry's stakeholders, and a reasoned, passionate call to action to assure that the trajectory of change in healthcare results in the hope for benefits—assured access, affordable cost, and high quality. This volume's remarkably broad scope of analysis and vision is accomplished through writing that is clear and to the point. Numerof and Abrams are advocates of change, but worried that the current trajectory is off-course. They are believers in choice and free markets, guided by government policy, as the best ways to drive change, and critical of top-down bureaucratic approaches. Their spot-on descriptions of current issues and their cogent recommendations will be thought-provoking for all who read their work—regardless of one's own policy or political preferences. Among much good advice, there is none better than their closing admonition that "Success (in changing healthcare) requires every one of us to drive real change." By reading their book, one will be much better equipped to be an effective driver of change. I encourage all to do so.

Robert J. Laskowski, MD, MBA
CEO (retired), Christiana Care Health System
Principal, Laskowski Advisors
Professor of Clinical Medicine, Thomas Jefferson University

The authors bring their vast experience and knowledge of organizations and public policy to advocate for important structural changes in our healthcare system. Insiders have been unable to address the systemic change needed to provide access, affordability, and high-quality healthcare to all our citizens. The perspective of managing costs through transparency, as proposed by Numerof and Abrams, empowers the consumer, introduces fiscal accountability for providers, and approaches healthcare reform in a very commonsense way. Perhaps the fact that this hasn't been done gives truth to the notion that "commonsense isn't so common after all."

Ellen Harshman, PhD, JD
Former Provost, Academic Affairs
Saint Louis University

Valuable insights on the major issues facing the medical industry and the country on healthcare! The authors do a terrific job of explaining and simplifying the dynamics created for all stakeholders when incentives are not aligned. The status quo is unsustainable and unacceptable for patients, and this book breaks down the issues and provides options and solutions that are needed to define a more efficient and effective system that can bring affordable healthcare to the United States.

Gary P. Fischetti
Company Group Chairman
DePuy Family of Companies

Numerof and Abrams effectively drive home the point that executives, including those leading major pharma companies, need to think more critically about the changes they need to make in order to survive in the future healthcare environment that is evolving very quickly. Indeed, "good science" is a given but it won't be sufficient going forward.

Elizabeth J. Fowler, PhD, JD
Vice President, Global Health Policy
Johnson & Johnson

[Numerof and Abrams offer a] fresh and critical view of healthcare reform that all providers, payers, and policymakers should have as "a must read" on their list. [The book presses] for a more enlightened view of the true nature of the healthcare market and the fallacies inherent in the current reform approaches, and practical suggestions for smarter alternatives are all here for those with an open mind. There is some redundancy in the chapters, but the ideas are well articulated and this is an "easy read." Some of my pet ideas are here...

I love the notion of moving to an individually purchased health insurance model where the defined contribution is used for a true free market purchasing selection, and patients are free to choose wisely or poorly, and face the consequences themselves...

Bruce M. Gans, MD
Executive Vice President & Chief Medical Officer
Kessler Institute for Rehabilitation

Bringing Value to Healthcare

*Practical Steps for Getting to
a Market-Based Model*

Rita E. Numerof, PhD
Michael N. Abrams, MA

· ·

Foreword by David B. Nash, MD, MBA

CRC Press
Taylor & Francis Group
Boca Raton   London   New York

CRC Press is an imprint of the
Taylor & Francis Group, an **informa** business
A PRODUCTIVITY PRESS BOOK

CRC Press
Taylor & Francis Group
6000 Broken Sound Parkway NW, Suite 300
Boca Raton, FL 33487-2742

© 2016 by Numerof & Associates
CRC Press is an imprint of Taylor & Francis Group, an Informa business

No claim to original U.S. Government works

Printed on acid-free paper
Version Date: 20151211

International Standard Book Number-13: 978-1-4987-3514-8 (Hardback)

Library of Congress Cataloging-in-Publication Data

Numerof, Rita E., author.
  Bringing value to healthcare : practical steps for getting to a market-based model / Rita E. Numerof and Michael Abrams.
    p. ; cm.
  Includes bibliographical references and index.
  ISBN 978-1-4987-3514-8 (hardcover : alk. paper) I. Abrams, Michael N., author. II. Title.
  [DNLM: 1. Delivery of Health Care--United States. 2. Private Sector--United States. 3. Health Care Reform--United States. 4. Marketing of Health Services--United States. W 84 AA1]

RA771.5
362.1'0425--dc23   2015030339

Visit the Taylor & Francis Web site at
http://www.taylorandfrancis.com

and the CRC Press Web site at
http://www.crcpress.com

Contents

Foreword

Bringing Value to Healthcare: Practical Steps for Getting to a Market-Based Model

The transition from Blockbuster to NetFlix and the rise of Uber, Airbnb, and countless others are evidence that the American economic engine is in high gear. Our creativity is the envy of the world. The rise of the consumer in all aspects of his interaction with the environment is central to the growth of our gross domestic product (GDP), and yet our healthcare system seems mired in 1995 rather than in the future in 2025. Yet, there is hope. Numerof and Abrams are astute observers of seismic shifts affecting our industry. They have a keen ear for hearing those hoofbeats in the distance. They have overcome what I have previously called "mural dyslexia"—the inability to read the handwriting on the wall. In fact, Numerof and Abrams are the translators and interpreters for the future. That future has arrived!

Bringing Value to Healthcare: Practical Steps for Getting to a Market-Based Model is long overdue, in my view. In each chapter the reader will be treated to pragmatic advice that can be implemented from an organizational perspective tomorrow. The vision that they lay out in Chapter 1 is compelling and I could not wait to transport myself to the world that they describe. I hope I live to see it!

In *Healthcare at a Turning Point: A Roadmap for Change,* these same authors confronted unpleasant truths and they exploded mythology that was widely embraced by so-called thought leaders across the country. Previously, they exploded myths about accountable care organizations, product lines, and hospitals as the focus of our efforts to implement wellness programs.

In this new book, they go beyond exploding myths with a real blueprint for action. For example, I was very impressed by Chapter 6 and the roadmap they describe for competing in a world of bundled payment. I embrace their definition of value and I know the reader will as well. When the world is going in one direction, somehow Numerof and Abrams are able to steer readers in a different and more productive direction.

Chapters 8 and 9 tackle areas not often seen in books like this—namely, the pharmaceutical and device industries. Since together they comprise more than 10% of the healthcare GDP, how could we continue to ignore their impact? Numerof and Abrams paint a really eye-opening portrait of the market-based model of the future. They cleverly weave the needs of consumers into both of these chapters as well.

Concluding Chapter 11 is a nice bookend for the introductory chapter. By the time you reach this chapter, you are now ready to appreciate seismic changes like new collaborations, reprising the role of the consumer, understanding the power of choice, and, ultimately, both creating and sustaining a brand new business model for our industry.

This book is not for everyone. For persons who are happy to sit on the sidelines and watch our industry transmogrify, I recommend that you stay away. For leaders who want to embrace the power of the market, which is indeed the most powerful economic force on our planet, this is your mantra.

Once again, kudos to my good friends, Numerof and Abrams, for bringing us *Bringing Value to Healthcare: Practical Steps for Getting to a Market-Based Model.* I applaud their courage in helping our reluctant industry to enthusiastically embrace the tenets of the future marketplace. I know that I will continue to turn to them for advice and I am confident that many readers will, as well.

David B. Nash, MD, MBA
Dean
Jefferson College of Population Health
Thomas Jefferson University
Philadelphia, Pennsylvania

Acknowledgments

As was true for our last book, the list of whom to thank or acknowledge along the journey to writing this book was very long. We continue to be touched by people who challenge our thinking, agree with and extend our ideas. The amount of turbulence that's occurring in the healthcare sector has been intense—new businesses starting up, massive consolidation, some businesses failing with many hurt along the way. There is no one who can say with any degree of credibility that change isn't happening.

Relatively few, however, know how to conceptualize and then embrace a different business model for what continues to be in our view one of the most important sectors in our society. As a result there is still significant resistance to bringing about a new business model that reflects more value—a business model characterized by greater transparency and accountability for outcomes that matter to all of us. Imagine a time when hospitalization and nursing home stays generally reflect the healthcare system's failure to help us stay well and active. We remain committed to a new business model and hope that this book reinforces the views of like-minded people, challenges the assumptions of those holding onto an untenable past, and gives others a common language and set of tools to advance critically needed changes in a nonideological manner.

At the top of our list of those to thank has to be our dedicated team at Numerof & Associates. Each member of this bright, hard-working, dedicated, and enormously talented group of professionals has continued to be subjected to and participate in spirited discussions about the state of the health-care sector and its implications. Many of these discussions became part of the firm's thought leadership, finding their way into papers with some of them ultimately being incorporated into the book.

Healthcare is an industry in transition, and it is core to our work. So this book, like others before it, is informed by our practice, by our clients, and by the firm's writing. It is also informed by confidential discussions with congressional and administrative leaders and their staffs who have remained open to our challenges and have engaged us to think about solving problems in new ways.

Kim White, a senior member of Numerof's consulting team who worked tirelessly with us on our last book, *Healthcare at a Turning Point: A Roadmap for Change*, once again led our efforts to secure our publisher's support for this work and guided the development of another winning proposal.

This time it was Christen Buseman who masterfully guided the research efforts and managed the tight timeline that allowed us to stay on track, bringing the manuscript to the publisher within weeks of the original promise date. Always with a smile, she raised questions for us to consider, and took responsibility for fact-checking critical developments that often changed in the course of our writing. We are indebted to Christen for her commitment and dedication to the project.

As before, Vicki Mertz, a key member of our operations team, deserves our special thanks. Her dedication is noth-ing short of amazing—working long hours to meet deadlines, maintaining version control, and making sure the manuscript was clean. Her attention to detail has been incredibly valuable. Commas are in place, and references are where they belong because of Vicki.

On the research side, we also want to thank Mike Kuchenreuther for helping to ensure that our citations were up to date and for searching out key, but often illusive, facts to illustrate points we wanted to drive home.

At the end of our journey to publication was our manuscript review team comprising Eric Abrams, another key member of the consulting team, Kim White, and Christen Buseman. They each made sure that our points were clear and compelling. They did heavy lifting to ensure that questions at the end of relevant chapters covered the right ideas to provide practical guidance for next steps. Their commitment to this effort made late night reviews and proofing sessions fun—not a small feat!

Beyond the Numerof team special thanks go to Bob Gussin, Steve Bonner, and Bob Laskowski for their long-standing support for our vision and its possibilities. We are privileged to count David Nash as friend, partner, and colleague, as well as George Halvorson, who has been at the forefront of a different vision for healthcare for decades. With Peter Bach, Marty Makary, and Andy von Eschenbach there have been spirited discussions around value and the business as well as political implications of realizing it. We are indebted to Paul Howard with the Manhattan Institute and Bob Moffit with the Heritage Foundation for their continued support, encouragement, and willingness to engage in spirited discussion about the subject of healthcare. Many thanks go to Emily Kressaty and Simon Lam of 2e Creative for their original cover artwork.

Introduction

Embarking on the Journey

The journey to the prequel to this book, *Healthcare at a Turning Point: A Roadmap for Change*, began in the summer of 2008 in the run-up to the presidential election. As committed voters, we watched the debates and listened intently to the political speeches of the Democratic and Republican hopefuls. Our ears perked up when the subject turned to healthcare, and it frequently did. Given that it was a subject we both knew quite a bit about—we'd been consulting across the industry globally for almost two decades—it was disturbing when we heard solutions being proposed that we knew didn't have a snowball's chance of fixing the serious, underlying problems that *had* to be addressed. We knew that healthcare delivery was fragmented, confusing, opaque, expensive, and sometimes downright dangerous—anything but consumer centric. While it made sense that information technology (IT) would be seen as playing *a* role in any ultimate solution, it was outrageous to suggest—as most of the hopefuls did—that IT was *the* solution. It was, however, an appealing cry that wouldn't likely offend anyone; in that regard it was politically "safe" and unlikely to alienate potential voters—safe but misleading.

From our perspective the real underlying issues weren't being addressed, in large part because the right questions weren't being asked. Since IT was being offered as the solution to an expensive, broken healthcare system in this country, then one basic question would have to be, why the industry didn't introduce IT to help modernize itself and create more efficiencies just like other industries did. The short answer is that it didn't matter, in large part because the root problem wasn't IT; it was a more fundamental one—it was about payment: who pays, how, and what gets paid for. Ironically, healthcare delivery organizations used technology well when it came to ensuring that they got paid. It mattered there. But, to coordinate care and to drive improvement in outcomes and lower cost, technology wasn't used. Even in those organizations that had invested millions in data warehouses, there was far too often a profound reluctance to meaningfully change behavior. Or the data were available, but people lacked the ability to package it in a way that made it easily accessible to improve outcomes. As we argue here, the reasons for this are multifaceted, but until they're understood, it's unlikely that the fundamental changes we need will take place.

In the fall of 2008 we had just completed a project for a major pharmaceutical manufacturer. It was a time of intense scrutiny of that segment of the industry by Congress, the Department of Justice, and a number of other interested parties, including academic medical centers. The business environment was particularly hostile to pharma; continuing medical education (CME) was in the crosshairs. Subpoenas were issued regularly, and the underlying issue centered on conflict of interest. In a nutshell, the industry was criticized for unfairly influencing physicians to prescribe drugs of "questionable" value. The influence came in the form of payment— often for participation in clinical trials, speakers' bureaus, paid continuing medical education, and the proverbial branded trinkets. Lots of legislation ensued, and manufacturers are now required to report payments to doctors of greater than $10 or more than $100 in aggregate per year. What was often missed in the intense rhetoric were the thinly veiled agendas of players across the board.

Academic researchers and the medical centers that paid them positioned themselves as pure and objective because they are nonprofits, and many wanted to keep manufacturers from calling on doctors at all. And they had a lot to gain in this scenario. Essentially, they were positioning themselves as the gatekeepers for medical information and CME.

It was at this time that Rita had a chance to speak off-line with a pharmaceutical executive who had recently held a senior administrative post in one of the key federal agencies concerned with healthcare. She laid out a picture of the environment she saw unfolding: that the government was headed down a path intended to slow innovation, and moving to get more and more Americans on a government-based single-payer system with the ultimate objective of reducing access. We were, after all, facing the crush of baby boomers and a limited amount of money. Expecting (and secretly hoping) to be told she was just being paranoid, Rita was shocked when the executive's reaction was quite the opposite: that the picture she'd painted was an accurate one and few realized it. Armed with that disturbing piece of insight, we became convinced that we had an obligation to attempt to influence the debate. We didn't like where the train was headed; we knew we needed healthcare reform in this country, and we became committed to trying to make a difference.

By the spring of 2009, Rita had become an advisor to a number of congressional leaders, bringing a strategic and systemic set of solutions—rational insights into what needs to change if we're going to crack the code and fix the underlying problems across this critical industry. We are "equal opportunity critics" and recognize that the business model of the industry needs to change and *is* now changing. We have spoken and written extensively on the subject, advocating for a consumer-driven market model, a position we first articulated more than 20 years ago. The time was right and it still is;

2,700 pages of legislation and thousands more pages of rules aren't the solution, but at least the legislation has forced an important dialogue. Despite the partisan rhetoric surrounding the Supreme Court verdict upholding the constitutionality of the Patient Protection and Affordable Care Act (PPACA), the controversial individual mandate, and the equally intense debates surrounding the subsidies for consumers buying insurance through the federal exchange, we *need* healthcare reform in this country. What it will mean for every segment of this essential industry is the subject of this book.

In the 3 years since *Healthcare at a Turning Point* was originally published, healthcare continues to be a hot topic. The predictions we laid out in that book have been borne out; as the implementation of PPACA moves forward, it is very apparent that there is even greater need for a market-based business model for healthcare.

The journey has been personally exciting, challenging, rewarding, and humbling for each of us. We hope our insights provide perspective. We are all in this together, and together we believe we can bring about the changes needed to improve our nation's health.

Rita E. Numerof
Michael N. Abrams
Saint Louis, Missouri

Chapter 1

A Vision for Tomorrow

Vision of a Fundamentally Different Future

It's the year 2025. It's hard to believe that just a little over a decade ago there was intense debate about healthcare in the United States. Today, we have more options than were ever available before. We spend less on healthcare delivery, and we seem to be generally healthier as a nation. Costs have come down dramatically in some sectors of the industry, and dynamic new businesses have sprung up to meet emerging needs. Traditional businesses have evolved with core components repurposed. Financing mechanisms have changed and, while not perfect, there is better alignment between cost and quality. There is better coordination of care, more personal accountability for health outcomes, more choice and competition, fewer restrictions, and generally less intervention and fewer procedures.

Of course, there have been some business "casualties" across the industry, as those organizations that held on to old models found themselves unable to adapt and therefore unable to compete in a new marketplace.

Medical tourism is up as the United States has once more become the global destination for elective procedures and continues to be the gold standard for complex care. Innovations here have been taken to other parts of the globe as researchers in the United States continue to work collaboratively with their global counterparts to find ways to improve health outcomes. New investments in research and development (R&D) have had big payoffs, as medical interventions have replaced surgery, and, in some cases, minimally invasive surgical procedures have replaced chronic medical treatment. Equally important, non-Western approaches to treatment have gained acceptance as the evidence for their efficacy is increasingly demonstrated. Personal accountability for critical behavioral choices affecting health outcomes has increased and incentives are aligned to reinforce good decisions.

Personalized medicine has become more normative with companion diagnostics and genomic testing helping people manage very serious conditions like cancer as chronic diseases. Scientific advances have even revolutionized how we think about and treat cancer.

Everyone in the United States has access to health insurance. Typically, it's attached to the person like auto insurance, although there are still some sectors of the economy where employer-based healthcare is the preferred option. National access opened up competition. Local providers sprang up, sometimes coordinated with more traditional care delivery organizations, which together built comprehensive or "bundled" approaches to disease management, wellness, and prevention. Whereas fragmentation and inefficiency still characterized healthcare in 2015, coordination and cost effectiveness increasingly characterize the industry. Of course, there are still niche players who are quite successful in their market segments.

What's so remarkable is the creativity brought to bear on seemingly intractable problems that some argued could only be fixed by a single government payer. Indeed, the creation of true market-based solutions, with very targeted policy (government) intervention, has enabled this magnitude of change in such a relatively short period of time.

Insurance payment reform enabled interstate access and reduced complicated rules and bureaucratic inefficiency. Member retention, once a major problem for the industry due in part to an overreliance on employer-based benefit coverage, has dramatically increased in recent years. Whereas average member retention was once pegged at 18–24 months, it continues to increase, with some carriers reporting averages of 6–8 years and a positive trend line. Portability is characteristic of all insurance since most individuals hold their own policies, with myriad design options for consumers to choose from: long-term care, full coverage including vitamins and over-the-counter (OTC) products, basic catastrophic coverage, and specialty options including 10-, 20-, and 30-year life support.

Pooling and tax incentives have leveled the playing field and made this a reality. True competition has lowered costs and increasingly put consumers in the driver's seat. Employers, where they do provide coverage, have almost entirely moved to defined contribution approaches. Employers get to make the determination of what the contribution will be—not the insurance provider or the government. For insurers still in the business, the model has moved to a retail individual-dominated market.

On the delivery side, things are very different. Fundamental to change has been a shift in a basic assumption of the industry: that volume (or at least a certain type of volume based on payer and procedure) is good. In the world of the healthcare continuum—prevention, early diagnosis, intervention, and rehab—traditional hospitalization volume represents a cost, not revenue! Not wanting to repeat the mistakes of capitation in the 1980s, innovators committed to short- and long-term health outcomes.

This required enormous behavioral change on the part of physicians, social agencies, and consumers. It also required new approaches to metrics and the generation of evidence. Increasingly, healthcare delivery institutions are focused on optimal outcomes: the right treatment(s) in the right amount, administered in the right way, at the right time and the right place for the right patient. Hospitals are less frenetic for caregivers, and they tend to focus more on the things they do best: acute, complex intervention, often in specialty institutions. They are less likely to attempt to be "all things to all people."

Nurses who had previously focused on getting through the shift without hurting anyone now focus on the bedside—on consumer and family education, on rehab, on care management, coordination, and health outcomes—and a smooth transition back into the home and community.

Hospital-acquired infection rates, while never reaching zero, have been dramatically reduced; medication errors also are down below 1%. No longer are hospitals generally recognized as unsafe.

Together with the elimination of redundant and unnecessary care, previously estimated at between 30% and 40% at some of the best hospitals, these changes resulted in the savings that enabled innovation and universal coverage without adding cost.

The refusal of the Centers for Medicare & Medicaid Services (CMS) to pay for such error-based *never events* initially forced healthcare delivery institutions to dramatically change practice—or suffer the financial consequences. Similarly, 30-day readmission penalties drove better coordination within the hospital setting and facilitated discharge planning and coordination with community agencies and post-acute-care settings. Discharge planning now starts at preadmission except in the case of emergent situations, and even there, it begins at the time of admission. Commercial insurers, not surprisingly, followed CMS's lead.

On the physician front, frightening trends in primary care have been reversed. With balanced payment increasingly recognizing the enormous contribution and broad system expertise of primary care physicians and a decrease in compensation for narrow *specialty* care, more physicians have been going into primary care medicine as a specialty, thus reversing earlier trends. Where there had been significant shortages projected for primary care physicians for 2025, now more than 20% have selected this specialty area. Contrary to what was anticipated, the small business model for independent physicians continues, despite a period of massive consolidation between 2010 and 2015 as primary care and specialty physicians attempted to "take shelter" in the face of escalating costs, crushing regulation, and massive hospital consolidation. The use of nurse practitioners has become routine in physician practices; some have even opened their own offices, backed up by real-time telehealth physician consults and approved computerized decision support systems. Integrated cross-specialty practice models have emerged to offer their customers comprehensive healthcare solutions accessible to local communities. Increasingly, consumers get the care they need in their homes, at retail clinics, and sometimes at the office ... when they need it.

The problem of defensive medicine, historically offered as a major contributor to the problem of overutilization, has been dramatically reduced. Essentially, physicians and hospitals had felt as though they needed to leave no stone unturned in diagnosis and treatment to protect against potential legal liability. Some patients, unencumbered by the need to actually pay for the services, would likewise demand that no stone be left unturned, even when the downside risk outweighed the upside potential. Clinical judgment was painted as a prisoner of the legal system, and tort reform became the obstacle to rational resource utilization. How things have changed in just a few short years!

Today, increased transparency, reliance on evidence, increased patient financial exposure to nonstandard costs, and the redefinition of the consumer's role in healthcare decisions have dramatically changed the picture. Patients are more likely to collaborate with their physicians, especially primary care providers, and evidence is used to determine which tests need to be done and when.

In the midst of this change, some hospitals have repurposed bricks and mortar, turning low-occupancy beds into assisted living, long-term care (LTC), and long-term acute care hospitals (LTACHs). Still others have created temporary residences for families visiting sick relatives receiving needed treatment and rehabilitation. And some communities, in partnership with social service agencies, have created residential living centers for vulnerable populations, including the homeless and those suffering from severe mental illness. Finally, on the acute care side, specialty hospitals within hospitals have grown, sometimes catering to ethnic groups with unique preferences and treatment needs.

New players that were not in the traditional healthcare space created dramatic disruption by taking advantage of the industry's inability to see itself in a fundamentally different business model. The movement of primary care to walk-in clinics in retail settings that had begun slowly around 2010 picked up speed dramatically over the next decade. More and more people focused on convenience and began to trust non-traditional settings for blood pressure and other screenings, flu shots and other immunizations, and even nonurgent care.

Screenings have led to earlier diagnoses and referrals to specialists. Industry leaders, including Walmart, Walgreens, and CVS, shook up the industry. Capitalizing on location, they brought the health clinic into the retail space, tying in low-cost access to generic prescription medications and store-brand OTC products. Their enormous success also disrupted traditional pharmacy benefit managers (PBMs) who, in retrospect, have been a bridge between the old and new model of healthcare.

It's truly a different world!

Seeds of Disruption

Getting to a new future isn't easy. But if it can't be envisioned, then it can't be realized. Typically, the move to anything radically different is sparked by a catalyst. But for the catalyst to work, the environment for change has to be prepared. The Patient Protection and Affordable Care Act (PPACA) served as the catalyst.

The PPACA legislation of 2010 reflects the largest appropriation of power from the individual to the administrative branch in our country's history. It has provoked phenomenal controversy in an industry that has been loath to change. It has accelerated industry *transition*—that painful process that forces market leaders to rethink their business models and allows new entrants, unencumbered by "the way we've always done it before," to become the market leaders of the future. The seeds of disruptive innovation are around us, beckoning to the truly innovative and threatening those wedded to the past. Fortunately, healthcare isn't the only industry to undergo fundamental transformation, and there are important insights to be learned from the experience of others.

Healthcare Isn't the First Industry in Transition

Some of the best insights can be learned from the experience of IBM, now a global leader, with nearly $100 billion in sales and approximately 380,000 employees. But in the late 1980s, IBM was close to bankruptcy.

In the early 1980s, IBM was dominant; it focused on mainframe computing, the "big iron" purchased by large corporations. The company enjoyed approximately 50% gross margins on mainframes and the lion's share of worldwide industry profits. It had a bullish future. Long-term projections were pegged at over $200 billion in sales. The company also enjoyed a stellar reputation and strong brand position— "Nobody ever got fired for buying IBM." In 1985 the company was, in the words of its new CEO, John Akers, "successful beyond [its] wildest expectations."

However, in just a few years, IBM flirted with bankruptcy and, between 1991 and 1993, reported over $24 billion in restructuring charges. IBM ignored the warning signs that the market was moving away from mainframes, holding on to the belief that the business computer was, and always would be, the mainframe. Their assumption was that PCs were for small businesses and home computing—at the desk and in the kitchen. As IBM saw it, mainframes had great margins and proprietary technology and IBM had solid customer relationships and market-leading products. PCs, on the other hand, were a niche invention, with "upstart" companies coming onto the scene.

As we all know, the PC wasn't just a niche product. It was the business model of the future. Even though IBM was widely credited with inventing the PC, the company didn't fully appreciate the shift in the market. IBM wound up nearly bankrupt and endured a painful and difficult restructuring.

When hardware sales tanked, IBM's survival strategy was services, which had been the sweetener in its mainframe heyday. Ironically, services became the bread and butter of the company's business model and the bridge to its PC-based business. The IBM case demonstrates the need to know what's happening in the market and *in adjacent spaces*, understand the implications, and take the right actions to protect market leadership. Most important, it demonstrates the risk inherent in organizational arrogance, too frequently the blind spot of market leaders who erroneously believe they can't be unseated because they're so dominant. The need for continued market vigilance is underscored by analysts' criticism in October 2014 of IBM's failure to invest in cloud computing, which most industry experts see as technology's future.

Perhaps less dramatic, but nonetheless painful for those involved, have been recent disruptions in the travel and real estate industries. Travelocity and Expedia, both created in 1996, offer a window into an industry disrupted by technology. Travelocity, a subsidiary of Sabre Holdings, which is a division of American Airlines, revolutionized consumers' ability to compare and purchase tickets directly, without going through travel agents or brokers. It was the first website that allowed consumer access to Sabre's schedule and fare information, becoming more popular once AOL's travel portal became associated with the Travelocity brand in 1999. At the same time, Expedia, another online booking site that revolutionized how consumers researched and booked travel more generally, was launched by Microsoft. A small division in 1996, it was spun out in 1999, becoming a publicly traded company on NASDAQ. It has grown dramatically since 2002, following InterActiveCorp's acquisition of a controlling interest in the company, and it remains the world's leading online travel company, successfully disintermediating the traditional travel agent.

In real estate a similar dynamic has unfolded. The introduction of *for sale by owner* has taken a bite out of the profits of traditional real estate brokers. The model is attractive in that commissions are in the 1%–2% range, not the traditional 6+% range that real estate brokers historically commanded.

In the publishing, music, and photography industries the dynamic is similar. Amazon disrupted the retail book sales world, while Apple continues to disrupt through the creation of smart devices—replacing phones, cameras, calendars, and so on with smartphones.

In healthcare delivery disruption isn't entirely new, but the impact hasn't really been as well understood as it needs to be. Traditional hospital moneymakers have been dislodged and moved to other settings. Over the last 15 years, entrepreneurial physicians and administrators, enabled by the emergence of new technology, have created free-standing specialty ambulatory care centers characterized by efficiency, convenience, and a consumer-centered model. Hospitals, struggling with silos and bureaucracy, have long recognized that they couldn't compete successfully with these more nimble enterprises and, in some cases, exited these specialty niches altogether.

Conflict-of-interest charges brought against some of these entrepreneurs have significantly restricted what these groups can and can't do. Nowhere has the question of hospitals' vested interests in this really been in the public spotlight, maybe because they've been seen as "too big to fail" or perhaps another "third rail." In many areas around the country, hospitals have become the dominant employers; other business leaders sit on their boards and their employees are an important part of the electorate. As the move to a consumer model in healthcare takes shape, coupled with increasing concerns about cost, all players in the industry should take note of what this means.

Where Are We Currently?

Popular discontent with the healthcare system has grown so significantly that legislators and regulators have responded with new laws, new mandates, and additional coercive controls, unfortunately not recognizing that sometimes *less is more.* The 2010 healthcare reform legislation included broad experimentation, new payment methods, and new market mechanisms that could profoundly alter market dynamics for healthcare delivery and all other segments of the industry, but not necessarily in a positive way.

Federal and state regulations are moving toward greater disclosure of clinical metrics, based on the premise that consumers should be able to evaluate quality as part of their decision-making process. New organizational structures have been promoted—for example, accountable care organizations (ACOs)—almost as a desperate attempt to fix the looming challenges we face. The inherent problems with this are discussed in Chapter 5. New payment methods are also evolving that attempt to link payment to more specific and robust quality measures, cost efficiency, and patient outcomes. As an example, the 2012 Center for Medicare and Medicaid Innovation (CMMI) bundled-pricing demonstration projects laid out a series of guidelines and different models that attempted to align physician and hospital charges, improve outcomes, and foster integration across the continuum of care.

CMMI added new rules in 2013 and 2014, at great expense to taxpayers, as some participants dropped out of its programs citing bureaucracy and untenable risk–reward ratios, even as new ones entered. Committed to its vision, CMS continues to tweak the rules, sometimes diluting efforts to connect payment to meaningful outcomes, typically under pressure from powerful lobbying groups representing organizations resistive to fundamental change.

This shows, in part, the inability of government to legislate real improvements in health or in the delivery of healthcare services. That said, the federal government has been a catalyst for change. Transparency, a key ingredient of a market-based model, is in the air—sparked in part by CMS and its requirement that hospitals post prices. While the posting requirement has little bite in terms of penalties for noncompliance, it is a green-shoot for a market-based model. It has forced some delivery organizations to dramatically lower their posted charges to reflect a more realistic price structure.

Providers are under increasing pressure to improve quality and deliver care in new ways. At the heart of the problem is fee-for-service (FFS) payment, now broadly recognized as creating perverse incentives for hospitals and physicians to offer more treatments and more options than may be medically necessary. FFS doesn't currently reward efforts that would improve quality or prevent unnecessary utilization, like chronic disease management for diabetics to reduce emergency room visits for low-blood-sugar reactions. A shift from FFS to a more accountable care model would mean a shift of responsibility for outcomes, increased sharing of risk for healthcare costs, and increased gain sharing as improvements are realized.

New delivery approaches are being piloted, like patient-centered medical homes and ACOs, but the current excitement obscures the fact that many organizations lack the resources and capabilities to successfully implement them. Furthermore, CMS rules covering ACO governance models are enormously complicated and resource intensive, and they rest on a faulty set of assumptions. Since treatments must be paid for, insurers and their network of providers have to work in tandem to implement new care delivery and payment models. Working in tandem requires collaboration and that, in turn, requires trust. Unfortunately, that's a commodity that's been in precious short supply as we will discuss in Chapters 6 and 7. And at the end of the day, consumers need to behave differently. In the chapters that follow, we explore how the industry got here, define the implications for each of the major industry segments, and offer a plan for moving forward.

Chapter 2

Whose Agenda Controls Your Healthcare?

Why a Market-Based Model for Healthcare Is a Good Thing

In the fury of the healthcare debate, most people have come to realize that we spend a lot of money on healthcare in this country. It's also generally recognized that we aren't getting our money's worth. "Better health outcomes at lower cost" has become the common theme for efforts to reform healthcare.

Better outcomes at lower cost is the rallying cry because spiraling healthcare cost inflation has reached a tipping point—threatening to overwhelm federal, state, and personal budgets, while eroding U.S. competitiveness and financial viability. At the same time, health outcomes, measured against comparably developed economies, are mediocre at best.

So, why is this? It's partly because neither the physician nor the hospital—the critical decision makers in the equation—has historically had accountability for cost and quality outcomes.

Unlike other markets, third parties negotiate for and pay the costs of healthcare—businesses through the mechanism of benefits and insurers through paying the bills. While it's generally understood that rising costs for healthcare benefits have had a dampening effect on wages, the concept is theoretical to most, generally because we have limited visibility to how this really works in practice. Nor do we understand how this dynamic impacts our purchasing power in the form of higher prices for goods and services in other markets— essentially a double whammy.

In every other industry, advancing technology has generally resulted in lower costs and improved products and services. It hasn't worked that way in healthcare.

Until we create a true market-based approach to the healthcare industry, we won't be able to crack rising costs in any meaningful way. Transparency, increased accountability, and a consumer-centered model for healthcare will be table stakes to achieve the goal of better health outcomes at lower cost.

How Did We Get into This Mess?

At the heart of the problem is the reality that *how we pay for healthcare drives what we get*.[1] This is how any market works—or doesn't.

So, how did we get to this point? During World War II employers began offering benefits such as health insurance to attract and keep employees in response to price and wage controls. Then, in 1954, Congress passed a law making employer contributions to these health plans tax deductible, without making the health benefits taxable to employees. This innocuous tax benefit not only encouraged the spread of catastrophic insurance, but also unintentionally encouraged the use of healthcare insurance for all expenses. The snowball continued to gain momentum when Medicare and Medicaid adopted the comprehensive insurance model as the basis for their payments. As a result, today many believe we need comprehensive health insurance for *all* care, and that even routine care is too expensive for us to handle on our own.

As healthcare insurance became widespread, two results followed. Demand for care ballooned, reflecting the elimination of cost to patients that had previously served as a damper. As a result, cost increased, reflecting that demand. For hospitals and physicians, the more services they provided, the more they made. The stage was set for spiraling costs and, with them, insurance premiums.

As long as increasing costs could be passed along in higher premiums, private payers were fine with the situation. Indeed, higher premiums meant bigger margins. As a booming medical research sector made it possible to diagnose and treat a wider range of ills with drugs, devices, and procedures, patients developed confidence that medicine could "fix" their health issues; their own responsibility to manage their health never came into focus.

One of the most critical reform success factors, then, will be the proper alignment of payment with results: providing incentives for the right provider *and* consumer behaviors in order to achieve measurably better health outcomes. We need a new business model in the industry.

Any realistic effort to create an improved business model must comprehensively address the extraordinarily complex array of multiple stakeholders involved. In particular, this includes drug, device, and diagnostics manufacturers; hospital and physician providers; and ourselves as consumers and payers (including the government). *Every one of these stakeholders is "at fault" for our current situation, including the consumer.*

Beyond these primary dynamics there were numerous business practices that stakeholders developed in order to maximize their own profitability. Each of them has played a role in getting us to the current situation—for example:

■ Manufacturers have focused on clinical value or equivalence as required for regulatory approval and otherwise largely ignored economic value in their innovation of new drugs, medical devices, and tests. In every other industry, new technology has resulted in *more benefit at lower cost.* In healthcare, this has not been the case, as payments have not been tied to evidence of economic and clinical value.

■ Providers have assumed a production mentality that has resulted in overutilization, uncoordinated care, and deteriorating quality. In the absence of payment tied to quality and cost management, the healthcare delivery industry is notably unique in its inability (or unwillingness) to change how it provides care in order to improve. Despite the industry oversight and accreditation of Joint Commission on Accreditation of Healthcare Organizations (JCAHO), most hospitals have not meaningfully improved quality or their value proposition. Nor have they taken a lead in coordinating care in their communities.

■ Consumers are demanding drugs and procedures whether their physician says they need them or not. Over time, employer-based healthcare insurance has eroded any expectation that consumers make cost–benefit decisions on their own behalf, displacing this with a sense of entitlement for any service they desire. Direct-to-consumer advertising by drug and device manufacturers has taken great advantage of this lack of accountability, encouraging patients in droves to "talk to your doctor" about any real or imagined ailment for which there is a product. And, too often, physicians have found it easier to acquiesce than to risk patient ire.

■ In their interest to control costs, payers (especially the government) have devised a payment system that lacks any alignment with either better care or reduced costs. Worse, they have created a new administrative cost burden with a cost-accounting approach to payment that has spawned a new industry just to deal with the minutiae of billing—totally disconnected from any outcomes that healthcare is supposed to achieve.

■ Finally, both the Centers for Medicare & Medicaid Services (CMS) and private payers, by virtue of their choice of payment rationale and business practices relative to providers, have contributed to a deterioration in the ethical standards of the entire healthcare sector.

CMS has chosen to underpay providers by 15%–20% relative to market rates and the actual cost of care delivery as its way of managing costs. Because of its massive market power, providers have no choice but to accept this compensation, which naturally leaves them feeling abused. CMS also has established the business practice of paying the claims received promptly and relatively uncritically. Combined with a Byzantine pricing scheme, this serves as an invitation to game the system through upcoding, which has become normative, and outright fraud, which has become widespread.

Medicaid reimbursement is even more stingy and delays in payment are rampant.

Private payers have taken the opposite tack. They scrutinize claims—challenging, denying, and downcoding payments. When combined with excessive payment delays, this again leaves providers feeling victimized, setting the stage for rationalization of any tactic they take that allows them to redress the financial humiliation forced on them.

The combination of these dynamics has created a situation in which physicians, hospitals, and even manufacturers more easily find excuses for overutilization of diagnostics and procedures; for devoting resources to building volume for those services that pay, rather than those that are needed; for gaming the system against the spirit if not the letter of the law; and for using their own market clout to exact unreasonable concessions from their suppliers. The pervasive reach of payers and the impact of their respective practices have contributed to the ethical erosion of a profession historically energized by the most noble and ethical motives—a loss that is far more profound than any economic measure can capture.

As a result, the United States is paying more than any other country for healthcare (see Table 2.1), while national epidemics such as diabetes and obesity rage out of control. All stakeholders are contributing to this situation, and all will need to be part of the solution.

A critical requirement for a free market to actually work is accountability for the cost consequences of decisions—in this case the treatment decisions between a physician and a consumer. Across stakeholders, this accountability is actually very difficult to find and more the exception than the rule despite the advent of CMS bundled pricing experiments. As we have described, providers, manufacturers, and consumers are driving unnecessary utilization that represents unnecessary costs. Recently, minor improvements in quality have been cited but hospitals are still largely regarded as unsafe. Moreover, providers have generally expected to be compensated for fixing

Table 2.1   Total Health Expenditure by Country (per Capita)

Country	Population[a]	2009[b]	2010[b]	2011[b]	2012[b]	2013[b]
United States	309.0	$7,687	$7,919	$8,136	$8,389	$8,826[c]
Norway	50.5	$5,115	$5,237	$5,531	$5,881	$6,398
Switzerland	7.8	$5,205	$5,292	$5,671	$6,080	$6,411[c]
Canada	34.1	$4,081	$4,184	$4,273	$4,380	$4,604[c]
UK	61.3	$3,197	$3,064	$3,094	$3,172	$3,338[c]
Spain	46.0	$2,982	$2,946	$2,940	$2,943	$3,118[c]
S. Korea	50.5	$1,801	$1,967	$2,059	$2,186	$2,306
Mexico	108.4	$895	$923	$948	$1,028	$1,095[c]

Source: Compiled from Organization for Economic Co-operation and Development (OECD) Health Data, Organization for Economic Co-operation and Development, http://stats.oecd.org/Index .aspx?DataSetCode=SHA.

[a] Population estimates in millions based on 2010 data.
[b] Numbers are per capita healthcare expenditures based on U.S. dollars.
[c] When data were not available for a specific year, costs were based on the calculated country-specific average annual rate of growth.

problems they've created. And private insurers have followed CMS lead in lockstep to create a payment system that encourages overutilization rather than quality and cost control.

When we remove accountability for the consequences of our actions, we invite unintended negative consequences. The implementation of diagnosis-related groups (DRGs) by CMS in essence removed any organizational or individual responsibility for cost *and* quality decisions. The doctors who make the decisions generally don't have any stake in the cost to treat their patients and often have a positive stake in more procedures. Rare is the hospital that routinely reviews the costs generated for the same DRG across physicians, questioning the decision processes used by physicians who are consistent outliers. This absence of accountability has stimulated a tendency to test more, to treat more, and to consume more health services, with little if any incentive to save costs. Not surprisingly, costs have gone up without any necessary improvement in health outcomes. While there have been pockets of improvement in the last couple of years, they continue to be more the exception than the rule.

The consumers who have had employer-based healthcare coverage also don't have any accountability for costs. They have no real line of sight to how increasing healthcare costs have negatively impacted their salaries, so they don't even know that they should be participating in an informed way to make decisions that balance costs versus outcomes. As a result, they have no meaningful incentive to save costs.

In the last several years there have been moves to change this, but they come with unintended consequences. Ironically, in the push to increase access to healthcare insurance and make it mandatory to buy government approved coverage through federal or state exchanges, individual plans, or employer-sponsored plans, many consumers have opted for the cheapest coverage, leaving them vulnerable to very high deductibles and high copays. So people have highly subsidized insurance but have found themselves unable to pay for physician visits and medication. This may not have been exactly what was planned by the architects of the law, but it was predictable.

If there were incentives for consumers to manage costs, including modifying their own health behaviors, they would demand much better cost and outcome information than the mortality and morbidity data that are still the provider industry norm. Imagine if the auto repair industry competed for customers on such a mortality and morbidity value proposition. Repair shops would run commercials advertising, "Your car is less likely to never run again if you come to our garage," or "Come see us because we're less likely to remove your engine when you come in for a simple oil change"!

A fundamental economic premise has been ignored in the creation of a payment system that has no accountability. When the product is highly desired and associated with real value, *demand curves always go up when the cost of the product is free* or close to free. The solution to payment reform will have to build in this currently lacking accountability across stakeholders if the corrective pressures of a free market are to be unleashed.

End of the Model Year

One of the realities thoroughly ignored by the Obama administration's healthcare reform efforts has been that the fundamental business model of healthcare is driving most of the problems in the system. What we mean by *business model* is the way in which healthcare providers are paid for what they do. It's called *fee for service*. In this model the hospital and physicians are essentially working on a time-and-materials basis—the more services they provide for a patient, the more they make. This and the fact that consumers haven't typically paid directly for their healthcare services have largely contributed to overutilization and spiraling cost inflation, which has averaged just over 5% annually over the last decade.[2-4]

The downsides of fee for service are not news. In fact, this country's largest payer, CMS, has attempted to deal with the problem for decades. In the early 1980s, CMS introduced a new way of paying for healthcare: DRGs. Rather than rely on the "usual and customary" payment method for services that *were* rendered, DRGs ushered in the concept of a fixed price for a defined bundle of services—a "prospective" payment in which highly efficient providers stood to make more on the service (e.g., hip replacement) and inefficient providers lost money. Unfortunately, CMS never connected prospective payment to outcomes and, predictably, quality problems increased along with continuously rising costs.

Outside of healthcare reform legislation, CMS declared in 2008 that it will no longer reimburse providers for so-called *never events* (e.g., falls, hospital-acquired infections, surgeries on the wrong site) and readmissions within 30 days for the same problem for selected conditions. This is clearly an attempt to connect activity and outcomes, another critical aspect of fundamental business model change.

Significant readmissions penalties started with heart failure (HF), acute myocardial infarction (AMI), and pneumonia (PN) in 2012. Penalties started at 1% in the first year, moving to 2% and 3% in each subsequent year. In 2015, three other therapeutic areas were added to the list: hips, knees, and COPD. While the formulas for calculating penalties are very complex, the fact that they also involve external trend comparisons has surprised many healthcare executives. It has clearly been a wake-up call.

Historically, hospitals have actually been paid to fix the mistakes they made! It's like taking your car to the repair shop for an oil change and winding up with a bill for a cracked engine block that occurred in the process. Not surprisingly, CMS administrative change has triggered a new focus on safety. How bold it will be remains to be seen. Our perspective is that increasing awareness by consumers and employers followed by demands for transparency and predictability will be the real levers of change.

What's long been recognized in other industries is that quality and cost must be addressed together, and consumers need to have a line of sight to the value they receive in order to make informed choices. After 25 years, CMS has finally reached the same conclusion. CMS covers roughly half of all healthcare spending in the United States. As for the other 50% of healthcare largely handled by private insurers, the path that CMS has laid down offers some cover. Given the intense level of public dissatisfaction with ongoing premium increases by commercial insurers, they have a vested interest in business model innovation in healthcare delivery that offers the potential to deliver better value. That's good news, because the current model is looking very, very dated.

Understanding Healthcare Reform as Business Model Change

Healthcare is big business. Despite the window dressing, when you get right down to creating change in any industry, it's all about the money—who pays, for what, and how. Economic incentives work in a very nuanced way, consciously and subconsciously, and drive decisions. This fact operates in healthcare across *all* segments.

As you'll recall from Chapter 1, healthcare isn't the first industry to face the need for a fundamentally different business model. All industries go through periods of such transition as a result of significant changes in their regulatory environment, competition, technology, or market expectations. These times of transition are very difficult. They force *all* stakeholders to rethink their business models and challenge fundamental assumptions about their markets—who their customers are, what products and services they offer, and how best to bring them to market.

Rethinking a business model requires a transfusion of fresh thinking, and that requires an *external analysis* of customers—in this case, healthcare consumers and a network of influencers, including payers and providers—to identify *truly unmet needs*. Such analysis, if it's going to be successful, must go well beyond what is understood as traditional market research, which is typically constrained in its design to dimension potential demand for services as *they are defined today*. For example, hospitals study the demographics of the population in the geographic area they serve and project demand accordingly. The real unmet need that's ignored in this approach is the fact that most people don't want to go to a hospital. As one hospital executive put it, "If we're really providing health*care*, we're putting ourselves out of business as we have traditionally known it." Add to this the idea that hospitals have largely been in the acute care business and the challenges to the current business model are even that much more striking.

Underlying the development of a new business model is the need to identify a better value proposition. The healthcare industry has historically been focused on a *clinical* value proposition. New drugs and devices must meet efficacy and safety standards to get approved. The lengthy approval process, governed by the Food and Drug Administration (FDA), follows very specific research requirements that demand significant evidence that a given product works for a specific population and causes no harm (i.e., it's safe and efficacious). Health outcomes in the hospital setting, for the most part, have historically only been measured in terms of gross mortality and morbidity rates associated with given procedures. The industry has experienced a surge of innovation, providing more and better treatment options, but at increasingly higher costs. Now costs have reached an unsustainable level. Missing in the current fee-for-service payment method, which assigns an economic value, procedure by procedure, is any analysis of *total economic and clinical value* over a continuum of care. This is the essence of trying to achieve better outcomes at lower cost, which should be the ultimate objective of any attempt at healthcare reform.

Once unmet needs and new economic and clinical value propositions are identified, they must be operationalized. Creating a new business model requires developing new *infrastructure*—defining new mandates for core functions and developing new capabilities and supporting processes. This is enormously hard work and, not surprisingly, it typically meets with great resistance. Reform efforts have usually recognized this potential resistance and have attempted to structure work to include all stakeholders in some type of business model redesign. The problem is that each stakeholder comes to the party to protect his or own interests first. Change is fine, as long as it happens to someone else! And, without an overarching integrated strategic approach to the problem—in other words, a new design—reform efforts are doomed to tweak "what is" at the margins, with horse trading the norm and no real change the unfortunate result.

Effective new business model implementation requires an integrated approach that brings to the surface and resolves sources of resistance as well as unintended consequences. Every segment of the industry—from pharma, to device and diagnostics manufacturers, to payers, providers, employers, and consumers—will need to come to terms with the fundamental changes that will be required, or we face the real possibility of destroying what works in the industry and going broke in the process.

Central Role of Payment Reform

There is increasing awareness that the healthcare financing mechanisms in place today do not align with the goals of disease prevention, improved health outcomes, and reduced costs.[5] Changing these mechanisms starts with different and better answers to four key questions:

1. Who pays?
2. How does the payment exchange occur?
3. What gets paid for?
4. And, at the end of the day, is it worth it? (Are we getting value for what's delivered?)

The answers to these questions must take a systematic approach that considers the agendas of and impact on all stakeholders, including payers, providers, manufacturers, employers, government, and consumers. Ultimately, each of these segments must make changes in an orchestrated, coordinated, and integrated manner, or the changes won't be effective.

Whenever change is introduced, there are *always* unanticipated and unintended consequences. Uncoordinated "islands" or "siloed" approaches to change increase the likelihood of such unintended consequences. As change is introduced in one area, there are ripple effects as the change begins to impact other areas. There are two examples that clearly illustrate this point, and they are central to understanding the healthcare fix we're in today.

Unintended Consequences: The Hospital Example

Paying for Volume, Not Results

Hospitals today are paid on a production basis reflecting what they *do* to people. There is no incentive to keep people out of the hospital. They are only paid when people are admitted to the hospital. Increasing volume is good in this business model. The more patients and the more procedures, the more they make. Hospitals are clearly in the *sickness* business, not the prevention or wellness business. As one hospital CFO said,

"I'm not investing one dime in wellness; it doesn't pay the bills. And I don't think it ever will!" Coming from an acute care, sickness business model, he can't conceive of anything else. So success for hospitals has meant more procedures. Since someone else was paying, a third-party insurer or employer in most cases, increasing costs didn't really matter—until recently.

Real Impact of CMS on Quality of Care and Costs

It's ironic that the first time the healthcare delivery industry took costs seriously was when CMS introduced DRGs as an alternative to the traditional retrospective method of usual and customary rate (UCR) payment. This was a well-intended attempt to impose cost controls in a situation that CMS recognized more than 30 years ago wasn't sustainable.

Hospitals were given incentives to improve their *efficiency*, since any difference between their actual costs and their DRG reimbursement was *profit* or *loss*. Few anticipated that the way in which they would choose to lower costs would result in many of the serious quality issues and increased costs we face today. Hospitals created a *production environment* focused on increasing demand and capacity to handle more procedures to offset lower revenues per procedure. Investments in new technology—like imaging equipment, for example—have added pressure to make these purchases pay for themselves. Combined with consumer interest in having the latest test (especially when a third party pays), limited awareness of their associated risks, and providers' reliance on technology to offset perceived threats of malpractice, there have been steady pressures to build volume. As a result, many hospital executives in private conversations estimate that 30%–40% of the "care" delivered today isn't clinically necessary! And these estimates are from people managing some of our nation's best institutions.

CMS introduction of DRGs as a means to control costs was based on an assumption that hospitals would *ensure quality* as part of any change. Unfortunately, that hasn't proven to be the case, a point we predicted at the time. As noted in the cover story of the September 2009 issue of *Consumer Reports*,[6] hospitals aren't as safe or as sanitary as they should be—something insiders have known for years. In a side-by-side survey of nurses and patients, two very different perspectives emerged:

- Twenty-eight percent of nurses saw problems with hospital cleanliness, while only 4% of patients saw problems.
- Thirty-eight percent of nurses said that care wasn't coordinated properly, compared to 13% of patients.
- Twenty-six percent of nurses said that hospital staff sometimes didn't wash their hands, while only 5% of patients observed this.

In their efforts to cut costs, during the late 1980s and 1990s, many hospitals partially dismantled the infrastructure they needed to ensure quality. They slashed the ranks of first-line and middle management, seriously compromising their capability to build, monitor, and correct quality processes as an inherent part of doing the work. As a result, an *unintended consequence* of CMS effort to control costs is that consumers now face a significant risk of getting sicker, rather than better, in a hospital.

This unintended consequence of the DRG approach to cost control has more recently led to yet another Band-Aid. As noted earlier, CMS has informed the industry that it will no longer pay for never events—medical problems that the hospital created or should have avoided, such as hospital-acquired infections, medication errors, or falls. Putting responsibility back on hospitals for fixing their mistakes is a belated attempt to reconnect cost and quality—something that was decoupled by CMS when DRGs were first introduced.

The premise is that if hospitals are responsible for paying for their errors, they'll make sure that errors are prevented.

Another new wrinkle to attempt to get to accountability for outcomes is the idea of refusing to pay for 30-day readmissions for the same diagnosis, as described earlier in this chapter. The intent is to force better discharge planning and coordination with community services, which was once the service hallmark of many healthcare delivery organizations under usual and customary rates, but not cost effective under DRGs. However, unless the fundamental business model changes, it will be very difficult to transform healthcare delivery.

Imagine buying a new flat-screen television and being expected to pay to fix the manufacturer's quality problems! Not surprisingly, one of the most transformative actions in recent years has been CMS decision NOT to reimburse providers for the so-called never events noted before, and it didn't require an act of Congress to create the change. If the basic rule of *follow the money* was actually followed, we'd see that payers' propensity to pay for volume without regard to quality drives volume without regard to quality.

While directionally well intended, CMS recent efforts— readmissions penalties and sanctions for never events—miss the mark largely because the fundamental business model hasn't changed. Let's take a real example to illustrate the point.

A newly formed integrated delivery network comprising several systems in adjacent geographies merged under a common umbrella. The chief executive officer (CEO) of one of the merged entities had a clinical background and was committed to excellence in patient care. Close to retirement, he declined the offer to lead the new organization but did accept the challenge to lead the transformation to a new business model and introduce population health management. He envisioned a new delivery and corresponding payment model focused on the care continuum. He was committed to moving to risk.

The new system CEO was previously chief financial officer of the other entity. His organization had the benefit of little competition in the market and he was able to squeeze significant concessions from his commercial book of business.

His mantra was "heads in beds" followed quickly by another telling directive, "lock up the doctors." He bought practices in an attempt to control revenue streams and referral patterns. Despite compelling evidence showing that these practices didn't perform, his behavior continued. Outpatient services were a necessary but totally separate (and non-revenue-producing) line of business. Doing high-end procedures was what kept the machine running, and he'd made a lot of money doing it.

So, was it any surprise when the new vice president of population health, an MD and ostensibly accountable for leading the transformation effort, guided his team with the following: "Readmit wherever and whenever you can, but make sure it's after day 31!"? Imagine the whiplash for the staff truly committed to a new model of care delivery focused on the right care at the right time and place for the right person.

The story illustrates the problem of attempting to change the healthcare business model with siloed, piecemeal approaches to delivery and payment. It also highlights how deeply ingrained the culture is in support of the existing business model.

Lost in the series of CMS Band-Aids is the fact that healthcare payment is mired in minutiae that in and of themselves are contributing to the cost problem. The implementation of DRGs was a cost-accounting approach that has actually spawned a whole new industry to help providers figure it out in order to get paid. Care providers spend a considerable amount of time coding their interventions for maximum reimbursement, time that could be spent with patients. In addition to introducing complexity that has significantly increased administrative costs, this payment method has also completely disconnected payment from outcomes, which is what the money is supposed to be achieving in the first place. A sub-industry devoted to maximizing reimbursement per case has also been spawned as providers learn to upcode in an effort to maintain revenue—life support for a dying business model.

The unanticipated consequences of DRGs illustrate what can happen when changes are introduced as isolated actions rather than as a series of integrated steps across stakeholders. This has only been exacerbated with the additional regulations and changes to regulations since the Patient Protection and Affordable Care Act (PPACA) was introduced. Instead of controlling costs, this change in payment has triggered additional administrative costs, a deluge of unnecessary care, and an erosion of quality of care—all unintended consequences that have significantly added to the costs of healthcare rather than reducing them.

Unintended Consequences: The Primary Care Example

Consider the circumstances of an independent primary care doctor we interviewed. He's an internist who takes great pride in his ability to help his patients manage their chronic diseases—asthma, diabetes, various cardiac problems, and so on. The more complicated the case is, the more he gets to serve as medical "detective." His patients appreciate him because of his thoroughness and because he so effectively diagnoses and helps them manage their conditions, in contrast to their previous physician experiences. As a result, they maximize their quality of life, avoiding complications, unnecessary hospital visits, and multitudes of specialists.

He takes the time to ask questions and diagnose the root cause(s) behind his patients' symptoms, utilizing expensive diagnostic tests only when necessary. He uses visits to educate his patients, guiding them to better manage their health to avoid preventable healthcare interventions if their condition progresses. He coordinates care among needed specialists to whom he refers his patients when he has determined that he really needs their consultation.

Discouraging the Type of Care That Results in Better Outcomes

Unfortunately, he's penalized in our current payment system, although his behavior is exactly what's needed to lower costs and improve outcomes! His time to educate patients isn't reimbursed. Or, if he codes for an extended visit to recoup his legitimate time spent, his claim is much more likely to be flagged by an insurer as an outlier and will either be rejected outright or result in delayed payment. Unfortunately, his behavior is not typical of primary care today. It's a much easier path for the primary care doctor to pass his patient on to a specialist, reducing his liability and, in the process, increasing costs to the system.

Once again, approaching the work of primary care physicians on a piecework basis has resulted in the unintended consequences of both increased costs and reduced quality. To sustain a viable income, primary care physicians have focused on maximizing the number of patients they see rather than spending the amount of time necessary to guide their patients and orchestrate their necessary care. As a result, more expensive specialists are utilized unnecessarily. Care is fragmented and uncoordinated between doctors, increasing the likelihood of errors and the redundant use of expensive tests.

Critics of this argument might suggest that CMS has recently begun to recognize the value of primary care and is now paying for patient education and care coordination. As an example, CMS has begun to pay for care coordination. Doctors we've interviewed clearly point to an uncomfortable truth: It's not as rosy a picture as the government suggests. The amount that CMS reimburses is relatively small—about $40 per month per qualifying patient.[7] More problematic is that the bureaucratic process and red tape imposed by CMS to justify the additional payment just aren't worth the effort. It leaves a lot of doctors scratching their heads; it's easier to avoid the aggravation by not taking the money. And, not surprisingly, the payment changes reflect a piecemeal approach and continued tweaking of the current broken payment model!

Creating a Critical Shortage of the "Right" Kinds of Doctors

Beyond the negative cost and quality impacts of the way we're paying primary care physicians is an even larger problem. Just as we're realizing the critical importance of primary care to achieve improved outcomes at lower costs, we're facing a severe shortage of primary care physicians. Why does this shortage exist, and why is it currently projected to get worse? Quite simply, the answer is financial. There is little incentive today for graduating medical students to choose careers in primary care specialties. Since primary care doctors are the lowest paid of all physicians, graduating medical students with hundreds of thousands of dollars of school loans are choosing primary care specialties with much lower frequency. Only 14% of internal medicine residency graduates choose to stay in general internal medicine. The rest opt for the more lucrative subspecialties in which they are paid to do procedures such as cardiac catheterization and endoscopies. Medicare and insurance companies pay much more for procedures than for the intellectual capability of primary care physicians to diagnose, provide, and coordinate care, which can often obviate the need for expensive procedures.

As noted by the Center for Payment Reform,[9]

> Payments should create market incentives that foster an adequate supply of clinicians to meet the needs of an aging population and to ensure that all patients have access to high quality and affordable healthcare services. ... Creating market incentives will require more highly valuing primary care functions related to evaluation, counseling and coordination relative to the value of procedural, diagnostic, and interventional care.

Healthcare Is *Big* Business

The hospital and primary care physician compensation examples just described illustrate the failure of uncoordinated, isolated efforts to make improvements and the unintended negative consequences they bring. Any realistic effort to create an improved business model for healthcare must comprehensively address the extraordinarily complex array of multiple stakeholders involved, as illustrated in Figure 2.1.

Successful business model change must anticipate and plan for the fact that each of the stakeholders in Figure 2.1 has an agenda and a vested interest in maximizing it. In such a

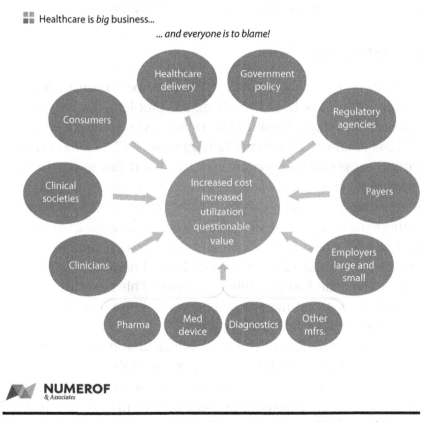

Figure 2.1   Key healthcare stakeholders. (Courtesy of Numerof & Associates, Inc.)

market environment, incentives must be aligned. Creating a new business model to improve care and reduce costs must be approached systemically, integrating changes across and within the parts so that the intended solutions work together.

Considering our current national economic situation and the level that healthcare costs have reached—estimated at approximately one-sixth of the gross national product (GNP)—it's understandable that many want to look for someone to blame. It's certainly politically expedient to single out private healthcare insurers or drug and medical device manufacturers as primary causes of our cost problem. But *looking for a scapegoat* (and forcing change only in that area) is the wrong answer and would just repeat the isolated, Band-Aid approach to fixing the system that we've taken in the past.

Recent Example

Since the U.S. healthcare system has become so convoluted, piecemeal approaches to resolving the problem won't work and tend to exacerbate the situation. Here's a very recent example.

CMS conducted the Acute Care Episode (ACE) Demonstration Project—a government-sponsored pilot effort that tests whether delivering certain medical services at a fixed price can yield cost savings without compromising quality. In the pilot, for example, orthopedic surgeons were encouraged to find ways to lower the cost of a typical knee replacement. One of the common solutions was to standardize on a more limited number of artificial knee joints than had typically been used. This meant eliminating the highest cost manufacturers of joints and working with a smaller selection of possible products.

The key motivator of this activity was that the surgeons were promised a check for some portion of the money saved. This is where the story gets interesting. The Department of Justice is actively pursuing investigations of manufacturers who did essentially the same thing. They said to surgeons, "Use our products and we'll find a way to compensate you." Yet just because a surgeon held a patent on a product or spoke on behalf of the product didn't mean that the product wasn't optimal for the patient. In any case, the Department of Justice has collected millions of dollars in fines to settle such cases of alleged and real impropriety. The core principle is that personal gain by the physician shouldn't be allowed to bias his or her clinical decision. So why is it a great idea when CMS signs the check and a criminal offense when the check is signed by a manufacturer? Someone's agenda always controls decisions that affect your healthcare.

Even in the absence of agendas by CMS or manufacturers, doctors under the current fee-for-service system generate more income when they provide more service. On the face of it, the scenario is no different from a patron in a restaurant: The more you order and the more expensive the meal is, the more the owner makes. The big difference is that at the restaurant, you know what you're ordering and you know what the cost will be. In healthcare you have no line of sight to the costs and limited information with which to evaluate the quality of what you're buying.

The real issue in the healthcare debate is what it will take to make your agenda count. No one is really talking about this.

Creating a Competitive, Functioning Market

Many voices in our current national debate are advising against too much government intervention and the preservation of a natural market. While this is directionally the right approach, it implies that a functioning market has been at work in the past. Nothing could be farther from the truth!

There Is Little Accountability in the Current System

As we noted at the beginning of the chapter, a functioning market requires accountability for the cost consequences of decisions. In the case of healthcare, these costs reflect the care decisions between physicians and their patients. Across the industry, this accountability is very hard to find and, unfortunately, more the exception than the rule. As we've described, providers and consumers are driving unnecessary utilization that in turn drives unnecessary costs. Quality has slipped but providers have been compensated for fixing the problems they've created. And private insurers have followed CMS lead in lockstep to create a payment system that encourages over-utilization rather than quality and cost control.

As our hospital and primary care physician examples illustrated, when we remove accountability for the consequences of our actions, we realize unintended negative consequences. Any solution to payment reform will have to build in this currently lacking accountability *across* stakeholders if the corrective pressures of a natural, competitive market are to be unleashed.

There Is Little Information Available on Which to Base Responsible Care Decisions

Assuming that consumers had incentives to manage costs, including modifying their own health behaviors, they would demand much better information than the mortality and morbidity outcome data that are typically available.

As the Health Quality Alliance steering committee noted, it's hard to tell which providers are doing a good job and which aren't.[8] They, too, recognize that in contrast to most well-functioning markets, there is a lack of consistent information about our fragmented healthcare system that can be used to improve outcomes while keeping costs down. They argue for a "nationally consistent, technologically sound, and efficient approach to make performance information widely available," recognizing that under no circumstances can you improve something you can't measure.

Our bias is that clinical societies, in concert with others, have the opportunity *and* responsibility to define performance measures for routine, predictable procedures. We will have to be more cautious and flexible with complex situations, where diagnosis is difficult and disagreements on courses of care can be expected. There is danger in formulaic approaches to all care needs, but this should not preclude establishing standards for more routine, predictable care.

Another critical requirement of a free market is an industry's ability to self-monitor and -correct. To this point, the health-care delivery industry has demonstrated an inability to do this. When hospitals had the money to invest in information technology in order to improve efficiency and effectiveness, they didn't do it. Now the industry is playing catch-up with a government mandate to implement electronic medical records.

Providers have historically just passed increasing costs on to payers, rather than cultivate a culture focused on continuous efficiency improvement—until payers pushed back. But the pushback wasn't a collaborative effort to determine new approaches to care that were more effective and efficient. It was just the dictate of an arbitrary discounted price like any buyer with muscle pushes on its suppliers.

And consumers, encouraged by their employers and insurers long ago, now have a warped sense of entitlement, viewing healthcare insurance as free unlimited care rather than protection against catastrophic financial costs. The solution to payment reform must make the necessary information available and align incentives for all stakeholders to self-monitor, make decisions, and act accordingly.

There Is Already Enough Money in the System

Part of our national debate on healthcare reform is whether or not we can afford it. In fact, it's possible to ensure coverage for all without increasing cost, without increasing taxes, without creating increased debt, and without introducing yet another government solution.

Based on a report from UnitedHealth Group's Center for Health Reform and Modernization, "the federal government could save $540 billion in healthcare costs over the next 10 years *if existing, proven programs* and techniques that have improved healthcare quality and slowed the growth of medical spending *are applied more broadly* ..."[9,10] (emphasis added).

A broader look at the entire industry promises even greater savings potential if common errors and unnecessary services can be reduced. With the proper incentives, we've estimated that we can easily find $500 billion annually that we're unnecessarily spending—for starters:

- According to the Agency for Healthcare Research and Quality (AHRQ), medication errors cost $5.6 million per hospital annually. Across 5,000 hospitals, that represents *$28 billion* of annual unnecessary cost. (In a recent *American Hospital Association News* article, one hospital was praised for reducing medication errors from 20% to 8%, ignoring the larger question of how an 8% error rate was acceptable in the first place!)[11]
- Projects to reduce length of stay (LOS) at top hospitals in areas of medicine conservatively estimated an annual cost of $75 million per hospital for unnecessary LOSs. Considering that there are over 5,000 hospitals in the United States,[12] *better care coordination* and corresponding *reduction in LOS* can easily produce $420 billion in annual savings.
- Leading hospital executives estimate that 30%–40% of the care they are providing is *clinically unnecessary*. Considering that over $650 billion of care is annually provided by hospitals,[13] eliminating 15% of that care (vs. 30%–40%) represents an annual savings of *$100 billion*.

The United States already spends more money on healthcare than other developed countries on a per-capita basis, so spending even more on top of that defies basic logic! *The problem isn't that we're not spending enough; it's that we're not spending it appropriately.* As we've illustrated, there is at least $500 billion per year that can be redeployed. And this is before we deal with the fraud and abuse in the system.

There Is a Solution, and It's Closer than Some Think

In the process of creating the real change we all desire from healthcare reform, we need to be *really clear* about *what* we're changing and *why*, and what the impacts are likely to be, both intended and unintended. If we introduce change but don't address the underlying causes of inefficiency, duplication, and error, we won't solve the problem!

This will require a yet-to-be-developed, integrated strategy and corresponding set of solutions that rest on an understanding of the drivers of our current problems. This integrated strategy must effectively align and implement change across all stakeholders. Isolated Band-Aids haven't fixed anything and have actually exacerbated the problem. Successful reform will require the planned and coordinated creation of a fundamentally new business model for healthcare that aligns the financing mechanisms of the industry with the goals of prevention, improved quality, and reduced costs.

There is an important role for government in this new business model creation, but it isn't legislating the new model. We do need legislation to enable more healthcare insurance competition, as we lay out in Chapter 10. And we have enough money in the current system to cover *all* Americans without new taxes or more debt.

Finally, we need to make certain that consumers are at the center of our new business model. They need to have meaningful outcome information in order to make good cost–benefit choices and ensure that they are receiving real economic and clinical value. And they wouldn't have to be dependent on their employers for insurance if we eliminate barriers in healthcare insurance and create a truly competitive market space.

Endnotes

1. Rita E. Numerof. "Practical Strategies for Healthcare Reform." *Medical Progress Today.* November 2009. http://www.medical progresstoday.com/spotlight/spotlight_indarchive.php?id=1830.
2. Kaiser Family Foundation. "Average Annual Percent Growth in Health Care Expenditures per Capita by State of Residence." http://kff.org/other/state-indicator/avg-annual-growth-per-capita/.
3. Organisation for Economic Co-Operation and Development. "Health Expenditure Since 2000." http://stats.oecd.org/Index .aspx?DataSetCode=SHA.
4. Centers for Medicare and Medicaid Services. "National Health Expenditures 2013 Highlights." http://www.cms.gov/Research -Statistics-Data-and-Systems/Statistics-Trends-and-Reports/National HealthExpendData/downloads/highlights.pdf.
5. Rita E. Numerof. "Healthcare Reform: Strategy, Myths and Solutions." *Medical Progress Today.* November 2009. http:// www.medicalprogresstoday.com/spotlight/spotlight_indarchive .php?id=1830.
6. "Patients, Beware: 731 Nurses Reveal What to Watch Out for in the Hospital." *Consumer Reports.* September 2009. http://www .consumerreports.org/health/doctors-hospitals/hospitals/over view/hospitals-and-nurses-ov.htm.
7. Lauran Neergaard. "Medicare Begins Paying Doctors to Coordinate Chronic Care for Seniors." Associated Press, *PBS NewsHour.* January 2015. http://www.pbs.org/newshour/run down/medicare-begins-paying-doctors-coordinate-chronic-care -seniors/.

8. Quality Alliance Steering Committee. "Charting the Course to High-Value Health Care." March 2009. http://www.rwjf.org/content /dam/farm/reports/issue_briefs/2009/rwjf37223.

9. Center for Payment Reform. "Payment Reform Principles." April 2009. http://www.centerforpaymentreform.org/uploads/CPR _Detailed_Principles0909.pdf.

10. UnitedHealth Group. "Federal Health Care Cost Containment: How in Practice Can It Be Done?" UnitedHealth Center for Health Reform & Modernization, working paper 1. May 2009. http://www .unitedhealthgroup.com/~/media/UHG/PDF/2009/UNH-Working -Paper-1.ashx.

11. UnitedHealth Group. "UnitedHealth Group Identifies More Than $500 Billion in Specific Health Care Costs Savings to the Federal Government over the Next 10 Years." May 2009. http:// www.unitedhealthgroup.com/newsroom/articles/news/united health%20group/2009/0527costsavings.aspx.

12. American Hospital Association. "Fast Facts on US Hospitals." Health Forum LLC. 2015. http://www.aha.org/research/rc/stat -studies/fast-facts.shtml.

13. American Hospital Statistics. "2009 Profile of US Community Hospitals." http://www.aha.org/research/rc/stat-studies/Studies .shtml.

Chapter 3

In the Eye of the Storm: The Role of Consumers and Employers

Introduction

When consumers hear about healthcare reform, they ask three questions: Why should I care? What am I going to lose? What's in it for me? As much of the current healthcare debate has focused on changes to systems and processes, it doesn't translate well to the individual, so consumers typically aren't interested in following the debate. Yet, when changes are discussed, consumers become concerned with what they may lose and automatically assume that any changes will be a detriment to them. When they're presented with options, like high-deductible health plans (HDHPs) and health savings accounts (HSAs), consumers want to know what the benefit of engaging in these will be and how they will affect their current state.

Regardless of the situation, consumers know that they need information in order to make good choices. But they run into some interesting problems in the process.

It is extraordinarily difficult for consumers to get information about cost, quality, and outcomes in healthcare as the necessary information isn't readily available. Even after they've undergone a procedure and are looking at the explanation of benefits sent by their insurer, consumers aren't always sure what services they received, how much those services really cost, or what if anything they owe!

And when consumers do ask questions, the questions aren't universally welcomed by providers. This could be a result of the providers not having information because *they* don't know what the true costs of care are. And why is this? It's because cost hasn't mattered since someone else always pays the bill. As a result, critical discussions about cost, quality, and outcomes that should take place between physicians and patients don't.

But it can also reflect the fact that questions represent changes to the traditional roles of physician and patient: The doctor prescribes and the patient follows the prescription. Patient questions in this model represent, for at least some physicians, an affront to their fundamental authority, rather than the legitimate engagement of the patient-consumer as an active participant in his or her own care and well-being. How deeply ingrained this is culturally is seen in recent guidance offered by *Consumer Reports* that makes a point of warning patients to be very careful about how to frame questions so as not to offend their caregivers!

In too many situations we receive only the information that our doctors choose to give us. There has generally been a lack of information publicly available, but perhaps equally troubling is the lack of a requirement for doctors to provide more. In any other industry, there is some requirement of disclosure. If a patient receives a drug, it comes with information pamphlets—not because the pharmacist chooses to give them, but rather because the manufacturer and the pharmacist are both required to provide them. New cars have stickers with information in a uniform format so that you can compare the price of one car to that of another—because the sticker is required. Food packages have nutrition facts and ingredient lists for the same reason. But we are expected to make decisions about what kind of surgery to have without so much as a common format to guide us.

Worse yet, all too often we hear stories of doctors who get annoyed when patients try to behave like informed consumers. Doctors often assume that adverse events, many which go unreported, simply come with the territory. Instead of a culture of transparency, we have a culture of opacity.

While there are exceptions, this situation must change. Doctors should consider educating their patients to be a legitimate and required activity, not an unnecessary burden. Patients should participate in their healthcare decisions. And employers and insurers should motivate consumers to behave like consumers—providing education about what to expect, what questions to ask, and what kinds of answers are acceptable. By changing expectations, we can change accountability across the board and actually set up the conditions needed to get better health at lower cost.

A Personal Example

One of us recently encountered an experience that drove this last point home. Michael had a small lump in the palm of his hand that occasionally became tender. The internist, after feeling around without insight, recommended a hand surgeon. At the appointment 3 weeks later, the hand surgeon did the same "feel around," reiterated the obvious ("you have some kind of mass"), and recommended an x-ray, conveniently located on the premises. Michael's not a clinician, but even he knows that x-rays don't adequately show soft tissue, which this mass surely was. But he followed the doctor's instruction and had the x-ray.

To no one's surprise, the x-ray was uninformative. "It's almost certainly benign, but I need more information before

I can tell you what it is." The surgeon suggested that Michael get an MRI at the hospital's outpatient radiology department, "because it's convenient and the results come up on this screen, right here." Two weeks later, Michael was filling in the same paperwork he'd filled in for the surgeon (how "convenient") when he read the small print that said the MRI would cost a minimum of $1,300, possibly more. He gagged.

That's when he realized several things. First, that he didn't care that much about a condition that was a minor irritant. And second, that whatever it was, the next conversation with the surgeon (after the charge for interpretation of the MRI) would likely go like this:

Surgeon: "Well, Michael, it looks like a (your choice of technical term)" or "I'm still not clear about what you've got there, but whatever it is, I could cut it out, assuming that's what you want me to do. Recognize that no surgery is without risk. So the question for you to decide is how troubling this is and whether it's worth it for you to undergo surgery."

Since Michael already knew the answer to that last question, he left the imaging center, vowing to ask better questions at the start.

Michael realized that he hadn't asked what difference the MRI would make when it was recommended. If he'd been talking to an auto repair shop and they recommended a $1,300 test, he would have asked that question. We've all been conditioned to accept physician recommendations without much examination. Michael's HSA-mediated consumer experience prompted him (better late than never) to ask why: Why do I need this? What will be learned? How will it make a difference?

The operative assumption behind our easy acceptance of physician recommendations is that they're always in our best interest. With the many changes going on in healthcare, there are too many other potential agendas out there to count on that any more. As patients, we need to approach the purchase of healthcare services in the same way that we purchase any other service, whether we have an HSA or not.

When it comes to healthcare, we need to stop thinking like patients and act more like consumers. That's not always easy. When we're at a physician's office, we often find ourselves dressed in a paper gown that barely covers us, stripped of our identities and dignity for our "well-being." Being dressed like this creates a feeling of vulnerability and helplessness, with a desire to get back to our street clothes as quickly as possible. When the physician comes in, we seldom ask questions and accept the diagnosis and treatment with minimal discussion. If the office hasn't already collected it, we pay our copay and leave. But when we're in the market for a new television or automobile or even insurance—important and expensive purchases—we become consumers. We ask lots of questions about product features and benefits, comparison shop for the best value for our money, and negotiate payment terms to get the best deal. So why don't we universally apply these same skills to healthcare in decisions regarding our most precious possession: our health?

As the example at the beginning of this section shows, consumers in most other markets make their decisions with their wallets and their feet.

At a spring 2012 program sponsored by the Heritage Foundation, Senator Tom Coburn, a physician from Oklahoma, described an exception to this behavior. He believes that the Amish in his community are the best purchasers of healthcare and provided compelling examples to illustrate his point. The Amish don't buy health insurance. And when they seek medical help, they ask for a list of all anticipated costs. They ask lots of questions about the *need* for a given treatment or procedure, and they look for the provider willing to give them the best price. Once a decision to move forward is made, they actively and respectfully negotiate deals and ask questions like, "If I pay in advance, do I get a discount?" From our perspective, this should be normative. Unfortunately, not all healthcare delivery organizations welcome this active advocacy!

Shopping for Cancer Care: An Illustration

The problem of opacity isn't just a problem of doctors not conveying information. Lack of transparency has been the default for hospitals across the industry. The following example, based on market research our firm recently conducted, illustrates just how culturally ingrained this attitude is.

We were engaged to conduct "mystery shopper research" to evaluate pricing and transparency regarding a cancer treatment: stem cell transplant (SCT). We were in effect putting ourselves in the role of a relative of a patient who'd been told he needed this procedure and who wanted to know beforehand what to expect regarding the course of treatment and its cost. We targeted top-rated national and regional cancer institutions to benchmark our client against "the best" regarding available information on:

■ Cost
■ Treatment scope (what services were included, and whether any were offered at a fixed or bundled price)
■ Outcomes
■ Patient experience

We approached our research as any consumer would—with a review of web information that would be expected to be credible, followed by phone calls to fill in what we couldn't learn from what we found on the web. We investigated:

■ Major payers
■ The National Marrow Donor Program (NMDP)
■ The provider institutions themselves

We supplemented our web research with phone calls and completed our research with calls to the individual provider organizations, positioned as an information-seeking call on behalf of a relative who needed the procedure (the "mystery shopping" call). The following is what we learned.

Payer Websites and Information

We learned through our research that some large payers had designated select providers as "centers of excellence" or the like, based on volume and quality criteria. Unfortunately, we were unable to get specifics on those criteria from any of the payers we contacted, and websites were equally vague. We also learned that some large payers had established bundled payment arrangements with select providers, but again, this information was unavailable on websites or by phone. Such arrangements might have made a difference in the copay due from a hypothetical patient, but those arrangements were considered proprietary and closely held. Payers would not even share what elements might be included in a bundle, and the existence of any bundling is not transparent to the consumer who may be inquiring about treatment.

National Marrow Donor Program

NMDP's principal activity is finding bone marrow donors matched to the recipient who needs the transplant. So it was not surprising that, for most facilities that perform SCT in the United States, NMDP reported standardized 1-year survival data and limited volume statistics on such transplants that allow comparison across institutions.

This is useful information in that patients can generally compare one institution's outcomes against another's, but data are often not broken down by stage or cancer type—two important variables—and completeness of procedure volume data was spotty.

Provider Websites

The quality and availability of information regarding SCT on these centers' websites varied. Most websites predominantly focused on disease-related patient education information;

some were more engaging and informative than others. Those that had been designated by various payers as "centers of excellence" made that clear, and call centers were offered as the next step for prospective patients. But *none of the web-sites provided any information on what exactly was included, outcomes, or cost; clearly, if we wanted to know what we were getting into, we'd need to have a conversation.*

Mystery Shopping

Through mystery shopping our staff were able to speak with the stem cell transplant representatives at half of the institutions. At another third of the institutions we spoke with call center representatives. Surprisingly, we were unable to speak to anyone at 12% of the facilities, despite multiple attempts to reach them.

For each call we made, we announced that our purpose was to research care options on behalf of a relative trying to decide where to be treated based on the outcomes, cost, and the experience of interacting with these providers. The minimum patient details were provided, and then we asked questions about the care process, out-of-pocket costs, and why someone should choose that institution over others.

While representatives were sympathetic and able to describe the care process in general terms, none **were able to provide any data that would assist in making a decision based on outcomes and price**. In most cases they were focused on the need for insurance information both as a determinant of price and eligibility for treatment. The idea that a patient would or could pay for treatment outside a health plan was often laughed off!

Clearly, a patient's insurance carrier determines which facilities are considered "in network" and thus might limit the number of facilities from which a patient could choose to get treatment at in-network rates. Nevertheless, a patient would most likely still have a number of hospitals to consider. However, we found that the hospitals do not provide data on price and outcomes to help the patient make that choice:

> It's a lot of work to put together a quote; you need to be more committed to coming [here] first.

Most facilities were unwilling to be specific about the costs of treatment until after they had performed an evaluation. While this is understandable due to many unknowns (cancer type, staging, protocols, health status, etc.), patients who want to make a decision about where to be treated prior to evaluation would be frustrated. As it is unlikely that a patient would choose a separate institution for his or her treatment once he or she had been evaluated, this compounds the importance of making the best choice from the start.

Of those facilities that were willing and/or able to discuss cost, none were able to explain what might be included in the rough figures they quoted. Typically, a wide range was given, couched in "disclaimers," and the representatives did not appear to have any great confidence in their numbers:

> I don't want to quote you a price. What if I told you it was a maximum of $1 million and then something happened and it was $3 million?

It is not surprising that discussions about cost were focused on the insurance carrier because most patients' outlay will be dependent on their deductible; however, it is surprising that there is no information concerning outcomes. **No facility was able to discuss outcomes in any quantitative manner.** Those that asserted that they were superior had no evidence to support their claims. One actually represented the region as the rationale for getting care at the facility:

> [This city] is Mecca for excellent cancer care.

Some institutions claimed various accreditation programs and volume of transplants as indicators of quality. Many hospital representatives were able to discuss the core treatment process and how long it might last, but not all were able to provide such basic and critical information when called.

Clearly, when it comes to moving to a market-based, consumer-centric model of healthcare delivery, this scenario illustrates just how much work still needs to be done! There is a good news angle in the story, however. As so little information is available, **leading organizations have an opportunity to differentiate themselves** if they can provide transparent information about cost and quality, including outcomes of interest to patients (e.g., length *and* quality of life). They can further differentiate themselves by moving forward to offer fixed price options to payers and, ultimately, to consumers. And, as consumers shoulder more and more of the cost burden, this information will be critical in their decision making about where to seek treatment.

A Glimpse of the Business Model of the Future[1]

There are a number of areas in healthcare that exhibit very different market dynamics than most areas of healthcare delivery. As discussed in previous sections, healthcare is usually paid for by a third party on a fee-for-service basis. In contrast, where patients pay directly for services, providers compete based on cost and quality. These providers demonstrate the power of a market-based, consumer-centered model based on delivering value.

Future Model

LASIK surgery and cosmetic dermatology demonstrate the potential of a new business model focused on value. These procedures usually are not covered by payers, which means that more traditional market dynamics consistent with other consumer industries are at work. Unlike the usual healthcare situation in which the patient has no line of sight to costs and little or no information about quality, patients are told what the price is for these elective procedures. They also are able to compare providers and their services to find what they consider to be the best quality at the lowest price. One impact is that competition and technology lead to demonstrable improvements in both cost and quality. Corrective eye surgery (radial keratotomy) cost approximately $8,000 15 years ago. LASIK surgery, using newer laser technology, has improved patient outcomes, reduced recovery time, and now costs approximately $2,000 per eye.

LASIK surgery and cosmetic dermatology providers must compete for patients' business and, as a result, these providers typically offer greater convenience, lower prices, and innovative services unavailable in traditional clinical settings. In addition, these providers are transparent about their fees; patients can compare prices before treatment, and the price usually covers an entire set of services, unlike prices for other healthcare services. These providers demonstrate how a transparent payment model tied to outcomes that consumers value creates incentives for providers to deliver better care at lower cost and engages consumers in the process in very different ways.

Whose Agenda Controls Your Healthcare? Another Look

One of the hotly debated issues that continues to surface *and resurface* is the question about conflict-of-interest concerns when it comes to physicians and their relationship to manufacturers and specific products. In a nutshell, critics argue that physicians should have no monetary relationship to the products they use, recommend, or prescribe in the treatment of their patients. Their only concern should be their patients' well-being, and a financial tie to testing or products puts that focus at risk. Taken at face value, this seems like a reasonable position. But is it?

Imagine an experienced orthopedic surgeon who decides he has a better idea for a surgical implant in the treatment of lower back pain, especially degenerative disk disorder, than what's on the market. He builds a prototype, gets a patent, and takes it to a manufacturer who likes the concept, agrees to invest in clinical trials, and successfully gets Food and Drug Administration (FDA) approval and commercializes the product. The manufacturer has a royalty agreement with the physician-inventor and both parties make a lot of money as the market realizes the superior value of the product based on legitimate objective outcome data. So what's the problem? If the inventor believes in his product and thinks it's in the best interest of his patients to use it, why should he be penalized for using it, and since he invented it, why shouldn't he be compensated for it? Based on some policy positions, this isn't a good thing.

To illustrate the point, let's walk through an analogy. Imagine you're in the market for a device that allows you to listen to all your favorite music anywhere without bothering anyone else around you. After talking to your friends, doing some research on the Internet, and looking at product ratings, you approach—you guessed it—the local Apple store in your favorite mall. Apple sells its products in Apple stores; it doesn't offer consumers brand choice (i.e., Apple vs. non-Apple), but it has a deep product line to meet lots of diverse consumer needs. The consumer shops, gathers information, and makes the decision to buy the Apple product. The consumer makes the judgment on the perceived value of the product—its features and benefits—rather than on the basic components in the device.

Clearly, deciding to have surgery, picking the surgeon to perform the operation, and determining what product to use are fundamentally more consequential than deciding to buy a personal electronics device. But there's an interesting parallel. The informed healthcare consumer gets referrals, checks available data, talks to the surgeon candidates, gets second or third opinions, explores outcomes, and lands on a decision, ultimately placing his or her most important possession, life, in the hands of that surgeon—extending trust.

Shouldn't the surgeon who is responsible for protecting that trust have the freedom, without legislative barriers influencing (and coloring) his or her clinical judgment, to determine which products will work best for this patient? To do anything less would represent interference of the state in the private matter between physician and patient. So if the surgeon invented the product, believes in it, and uses it, why shouldn't he be entitled to his royalty stream? If he's transparent about the relationship to the product and the patient has done his due diligence in selecting the surgeon, couldn't this also increase the patient's trust/confidence in the outcome?

Let's take this one step further. Let's assume that the surgeon isn't the inventor, but she trained on the product line, trusts the "tools," and believes in the product. Not surprisingly, the manufacturer reaches out, maybe engages the surgeon in clinical studies and asks her to do some workshops on behalf of the line. The manufacturer compensates the surgeon, using a defensible fair market value (FMV) fee. And the problem with this is...? Does the federal government think it wise to tell physicians that they can either practice medicine or they can invent, but that they just can't do both? We don't think so. Having said this, there is a role for government.

Realistically, there are unscrupulous surgeons just as there are unscrupulous individuals and shady characters in every profession and every walk of life. This isn't a new problem; it's been around for thousands of years. Thinking we can legislate trust and integrity or eliminate greed with a law is delusional. And at the end of the day, this is really what it's about: trust, integrity, and greed.

You earn the first; you either have integrity or you don't. Dishonesty, fraud, abuse—often a reflection of unbridled greed and arrogance—can be tempered, and legislation can play a role in this: It can make information available to enable good decisions, recognizing they will always be imperfect. Efforts to report outcomes and increasing focus on transparency in healthcare will enable consumers and independent groups to make informed choices.

You pick the doctor and let the doctor pick the tools that will be best for you, but make sure that the evidence on which that choice is made passes the proverbial smell test.

Perversion of the Concept of Insurance

Too often in the debate about healthcare reform there is no distinction between saying that Americans have *no healthcare* versus saying they have *no health insurance*. We've reached a point where the method of financing healthcare has become synonymous with the care itself.

The need for insurance is obvious. It protects us from catastrophic financial expenses. That's why we buy car insurance, home insurance, life insurance, and personal liability insurance. Certainly there is a parallel need for health insurance, considering that one day we may require urgent, extensive care that would cost far more than the average person could expect to finance. So, some form of catastrophic coverage makes good personal business sense (Figure 3.1).

However, health insurance has become different from other types of insurance. For the most part, we have begun to use health insurance to pay for almost all health-related expenses, not just the catastrophic ones. We expect it to cover regular checkups or an antibiotic prescription for a standard sinus infection. If other insurance worked the same way, we'd expect our auto insurance to pay for oil changes or our homeowners insurance to pay the plumber to unclog a toilet. If

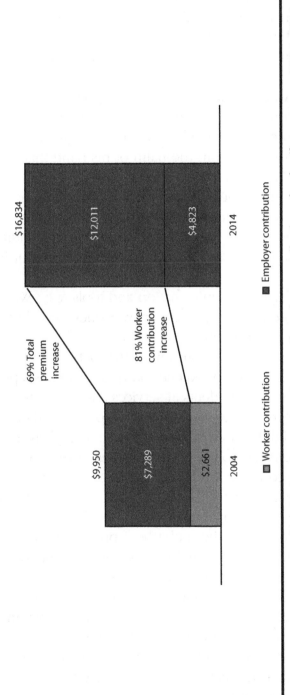

Figure 3.1 Average annual health insurance premiums and worker contributions for family coverage, 2004–2014. (From Kaiser/HRET Survey of Employer-Sponsored Health Benefits, 2004–2014.)

this actually happened, auto and home insurance would cost much more than they do today. To make matters worse, we've become used to someone else (i.e., employers or government) footing the bill and have largely become bystanders in the process.

There is evidence that this is changing. The increasing numbers of consumers with high-deductible health plans are slowly beginning to behave like consumers—just like Michael did with the small lump in the palm of his hand that we described earlier in the chapter. With more and more employers moving from defined benefit to defined contribution health plan subsidies or shifting employees to public and private exchanges with higher deductibles, employees are finding themselves "forced" to make informed decisions about healthcare options.

And they have more information and tools (e.g., WebMD, *Consumer Reports*) to help them answer questions about clinical efficacy, cost, and, ultimately, value.

There is no question in our minds that publishing price information could rein in the enormous range of costs people pay for what are pretty identical services and lower the overall level of prices in general. But, publishing prices by themselves is a tricky and difficult enterprise. Because most delivery organizations haven't had to price their services, many don't know what the true costs are. And, because outcomes haven't been tied to payment historically, what you get for your dollar in terms of service, convenience, accuracy, quality, etc. may not be comparable. Finally, the "published" prices may not reflect actual prices that an individual may pay, in part due to negotiated rates with individual insurance carriers. Some payers and providers, in fact, are uncomfortable with the move to increased public transparency. While they promote transparency in services for their members and have tools to help members navigate their way to lower cost providers in network, these same payers view their negotiated prices as "protected information" that allows them to negotiate better rates for members.

From our perspective, there is an inexorable march toward transparency, sparked in part by the Centers for Medicare & Medicaid Services (CMS) requirement that hospitals post their prices. While some could legitimately argue that the law as written has few teeth, the move has heralded a fundamental change. At least a dozen firms and associations are in the mix, committed to moving the industry toward greater transparency. While we have a distance to travel, ultimately, consumers will be armed with comprehensible, accessible, and comparable information. Even the American Board of Internal Medicine Foundation[2] has promoted open dialogue between providers and consumers through its program "Choosing Wisely." The intent is to focus on medical necessity, avoiding duplication of testing or other care and thus answering the question: Is a given treatment appropriate for a given patient at a given point in time? The program isn't just focused on providers, but encourages the development of a care plan that also reflects costs and challenges conventional wisdom.

The implications will be quite profound as healthcare delivery organizations—whether traditional hospital, ambulatory care center, urgent care clinic, or doctor's office—will need to answer the question, "Why should anyone come to our facility?"

New Sources of Competition for the New Consumer Patient

In the era of high-deductible health plans, consumers are shouldering more of the cost for their care. In response, retailers are making a market appearance in the healthcare space, offering a lower cost and more convenient location to spend your healthcare dollar. Walmart, Walgreens, and CVS are providing primary care, and a Midwestern grocery chain, Schnuck's, has started its own retail infusion center.[3] These new retail options are in addition to the estimated 10,000 urgent care clinics, which already account for about 160 million visits annually. Located on neighborhood corners and in workplaces, shopping centers, and grocery stores, they appeal directly to consumers looking for quality service and unambiguous pricing.[4] LabCorp is following suit, recently announcing that it will let consumers order their own diagnostic tests at its retail locations.[5]

And while retail medicine and diagnostics are on the rise in urban and suburban markets, telemedicine and remote monitoring stand to significantly disrupt and replace much of rural healthcare as it stands today. Advances in telemedicine and remote monitoring will prove to be important tools for improving health as well as new sources of competition for patients who are either unable or unwilling to wait for an appointment. Add this to the convenience offered by expanding retailers as those described earlier and the face of healthcare tomorrow is likely to look very different from what it has been.

In response to these sources of new competition, traditional healthcare delivery providers typically express concern. They publicly worry about the relative quality of care, and they suggest that patients won't receive appropriate feedback and interpretation of test results. While patient safety and quality of care should always be of utmost concern, we think these providers are missing the important point: If they were doing a better job of meeting their patients' needs, then they wouldn't be seeking out these alternatives! Put another way, if a physician is concerned that his or her patients won't get good medical care if they get their lab tests done at LabCorp and their antibiotics at Walgreens, then the physician had better change the way in which the practice is operated so that those options don't look so attractive.

Nearly everyone has a personal story of how a doctor's office failed him or her. Here are some of ours:

■ A colleague needed to get an appointment with her infant son's pediatrician to get a prescription for what was almost certainly another ear infection. The pediatrician's office could not get them in until 4:30 p.m.—the last appointment of the day—even though she called first thing in the morning. Rather than wait all day at home with a sick and miserable baby, she took him to the urgent care clinic down the street. The copay was only marginally higher than a sick visit at their "medical home," and the prescription was in hand more than 6 hours faster than if they had waited. Convenience trumps loyalty when you have a screaming, feverish child!

■ Rita recently called her long-time personal physician to schedule her annual physical, due 6 weeks out. Absurdly, the office did not have an available appointment for nearly 4 months! To complicate the matter, staff were not willing to refill a needed prescription without an office visit. She was given three suboptimal options: Wait to see the doctor and go without the prescription for months, make an appointment with an unfamiliar nurse practitioner (NP), or log on to an online portal to submit a request for a prescription refill since the receptionist stated rather vehemently that the practice didn't call in scripts any more. Thinking herself technologically savvy, Rita opted to try her luck with the online portal, only to find that she had to opt in to "selling" her personal data to a health IT company in order to use the system. It was about 2 p.m. at this point, and she called her practice back, leaving a message requesting that an NP call her to discuss this "urgent" matter. With no response by 4 p.m., she called back, only to get the infamous healthcare delivery voicemail: "We're sorry, the office is closed. If this is a medical emergency, please go to the emergency room immediately." Long story short, Rita eventually talked to an NP and got her prescription filled, but only got the NP's attention because it was thought that she was calling from the emergency room! To a lot of folks, the convenience of a walk-in clinic looks better every day!

Faced with readily accessible competitors, traditional healthcare delivery providers must rethink how they run their practices. The typical physician's office has a long way to go to be consumer savvy and customer responsive. Gone are the obstructive outgoing voicemail messages ("the office is closed for lunch"; "if you're calling past 3 p.m., don't expect to have your call returned until the next day"; "this recording doesn't accept messages"; and, worst of all, "if you have a problem, go to the Emergency Department"). Regardless of whether a practice is designated a "medical home," it will need to operate like one to keep its patients from venturing out.

When outpatient surgical centers became more prevalent, hospitals bemoaned that the "easy patients"—those needing endoscopy, cataract surgery, etc.—were being "picked off." Now physician practices are facing the same situation: Either be the place where your patients can count on care or they'll take their problems elsewhere.

Transparency in Healthcare— Coming to Your Health System Soon![6]

In August 2013, Priority Health claimed the title of first health plan in Michigan to publish specific, regionalized healthcare costs and quality information by procedure, facility, and physician.[7] The company launched this tool so that plan members could review and compare prices and quality for more than 300 of the most common healthcare services. That quality comparisons would be important for patients needs no explanation, but why did Priority Health include price data? It's because the market environment has changed for hospital administrators, and there are now growing demands for transparency, including pricing transparency.

We believe there has been and will continue to be a convergence of trends that drive patients, caregivers, and family members to shop for healthcare in much the same way they purchase other goods and services.

These converging trends include:

■ Growth of high-deductible health plans
■ Adoption of reference pricing
■ Expansion of published quality of care and price data
■ Growth in comparison shopping tools for consumers

It is still early in the process, but we believe that a combination of changing healthcare policy, market dynamics, technology, demographics and cultural trends is converging to drive healthcare delivery to more closely resemble other markets in which purchase decisions are based on the perceived value received.

What Is Driving Demand for Transparency?

Although "transparency" may mean different things to different people, we are talking about a future state in which well-informed patients comparison shop among physicians, specialists, facilities, and treatment options in search of the best value when they need nonemergent healthcare services. This type of transparency and the data needed for effective comparison shopping are essential to empowering patients as healthcare consumers. We have identified four trends that are converging to fuel this demand for greater transparency.

Shift to High-Deductible Plans

One driver of demand for cost data has been the growing popularity of high-deductible health plans that typically incorporate health savings or health reimbursement accounts (HSAs or HRAs). These were created by the Medicare Prescription Drug, Improvement, and Modernization Act of 2003. This class of health plan offers consumers lower monthly premiums in exchange for greater "first dollar" financial responsibility. Consumers can make pretax contributions to their HSA, which they own and which is portable across jobs (Figure 3.2).

These plans reduce the insulation between patients and the costs of care found in traditional health plans. By way of illustration, if a patient has not yet met his or her deductible and a physician orders a CT scan, the patient typically pays the full negotiated rate for that scan. Since the same scan can be performed at multiple locations at different price points (say, $150 at an imaging clinic, compared to $500 at a hospital), the patient has a strong incentive to seek lower out-of-pocket costs (the $150 option).

These plans are becoming more common. According to analysis by America's Health Insurance Plans (AHIP), nearly 17.4 million people were enrolled in high-deductible health plans as of January 2014, up more than fivefold from January 2006. Adoption is still increasing rapidly, at an average of nearly 15% per year since 2010, with large group plans accounting for much of the growth.[8] Recent data on employer-based coverage indicate that high deductible plans accounted for 20% of enrollees in 2014.[9]

The rising popularity of high-deductible health plans means more patients are confronting the costs of care more directly.

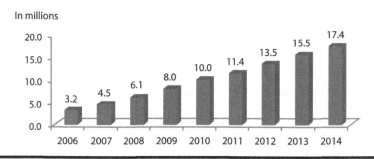

Figure 3.2 Growth of HSA-qualified high deductible health plan enrollment, 2006–2014. (From AHIP surveys; enrollment figures as of January of year noted.)

As a result, they are asking for data on which to base choices among facilities, care settings, physicians, and even treatment options.

Importantly, although high-deductible plans are more common among employed individuals covered under employer group plans, the launch of the state and federal government insurance exchanges has accelerated this trend. Even if millions of consumers eventually purchase bronze, silver, gold, or platinum plans or enroll in Medicaid, the vast majority of these individuals and families will still have significant out-of-pocket expenses to manage and will likely demand cost and quality data to inform their decisions.

Growth in Reference Pricing

Another recent feature of health plan design that is gaining acceptance among employers is "reference pricing," meaning plan terms that limit reimbursement to an established maximum for a given procedure. Patients then have to pay the difference if they opt for a facility that charges above the reference price. If deductibles force consumers to confront costs at the low end of their healthcare expenditures, reference pricing for selected procedures forces a focus on expenditures at the high end. In a pilot project run by WellPoint Inc. and the California Public Employees' Retirement System, this approach enabled WellPoint to reduce its cost for hip and knee replacements by 19%. It's too soon to report on breadth of use of reference pricing, but it's a safe assumption that such results, if they are borne out in further trials, will drive robust adoption.

Reimbursement Tied to Performance Measures

A third trend that is converging with those just mentioned is the availability of quality data, performance metrics, and other useful information that would support comparison shopping. Through CMS "Meaningful Use" incentive program, "Value-Based Payments" initiative, or "Hospital Compare," these programs are making more data publicly available to consumers.

In addition, private insurers have launched similar efforts to tie reimbursement to performance as measured by specific quality of care measures. These efforts have been termed "value-based contracting."[10]

UnitedHealthcare, for example, has launched a relatively sophisticated set of tools to facilitate members' understanding of their benefits and potential treatments they're considering, and to explain differences in quality and cost among options in order for members to maximize their benefits. Packaged as more than an accurate pricing tool (i.e., including copays, deductibles, and out-of-pocket expenses), UnitedHealthcare members are approximately 9% more likely to see a "premium-designated" physician—one who is known for high quality/high efficiency. Their analysis suggests that these same members save approximately 10% on healthcare costs.[11]

For transparency to shift the business model, the price must be tied to outcomes. Consumers need to know what they're getting for their money: It's about value. When states compelled providers to reveal their prices, there was an overall 7% reduction in the cost of common elective procedures, according to a 2013 University of Chicago study.[12] Every state should have transparency requirements, and they need to be effective in giving consumers meaningful information, including quality and outcomes data as well as price.[4]

Better Tools to Communicate Quality and Cost

Another driver is the growth of new tools to communicate the data being made available. These tools include independent websites, such as Healthcare Blue Book, and research firms such as *Consumer Reports* or Leapfrog, which are both compiling and publishing quality data on hospitals across the country. Private insurers are increasingly offering these tools to their subscribers.

As noted earlier in this chapter, one of the weaknesses of many of these tools is the lack of outcomes measures or cost data as a way of comparing facilities, physicians, or treatment options. Also, sites that attempt to provide pricing for typical cases (other than payer-sponsored sites) may reflect list prices, not the negotiated price that insured individuals might pay. Nonetheless, availability of these data is growing, driven by entrepreneurs looking to capitalize on consumer demand and by payers looking for ways to put the brakes on healthcare inflation.

Bottom Line: We Have to Have It

Finally, there is growing recognition among various stakeholders that the ability of patient-consumers to comparison shop for healthcare services remains limited without greater transparency. Fortunately, there are many resources emerging to help consumers navigate the myriad options available to them and make more informed choices.[13]

The recent decision by CMS to make public the rates paid to participating hospitals for the top 100 most common diagnosis-related groups clearly indicates that, from a public policy perspective, competition is regarded as a tool to be used to restrain price growth. Aside from such mandated transparency, other sources are springing up to help consumers evaluate comparative cost and quality for the care they need as described previously. At the state level, the website AZ Hospital Compare allows consumers to compare more than 100 hospitals around Arizona. In addition to reporting outcomes, the site lists what each hospital bills for each of several hundred different medical procedures and it spells out what each hospital reports the procedure actually costs it. Any institution that does not provide such economic and clinical value data—some of which is now mandated by law—risks being omitted from consideration and thus losing out on potential patients. Past reputation will be insufficient unless decision makers (i.e., consumers and employers) can see *data* to support hospitals' claims.[14]

Where Do Employers Fit into the Equation?

So where does business fit into the picture? We are on the cusp of a fundamental change in the business model of healthcare. The industry has reached a tipping point, which is creating changes in the way we pay for and deliver healthcare. As we outline in the following chapters, we clearly can't continue to do what we've been doing or we'll go broke doing it!

Business leaders have an opportunity *and a responsibility* to influence change to ensure that their employees get better health, better outcomes, and greater value. Think about it: Businesses pay directly for care in that they write the checks for healthcare insurance and those checks are getting bigger. Businesses also pay indirectly for healthcare due to absenteeism and "presenteeism" (those who are distracted at the workplace due to health issues and have decreased productivity as a result). Historically, when businesses have tried to influence change in the healthcare model, it's been in the context of the current model. Employers would pressure insurance companies to lower costs, add wellness programs, engage pharmacy benefit managers (PBMs) to move pharmaceutical products to generic drugs, and offer HDHPs. But these efforts haven't brought healthcare cost inflation to heel. It's time to move back toward the original role of insurance: providing a safety net for catastrophic circumstances.

What Can Consumers and Employers Do?

Going forward, employees and employers can have a very powerful voice. There are a few simple steps these groups can take.

Demand Transparency and Accountability

At a bare minimum, patients should think of themselves as consumers. They should know *what* they're getting and *what* the associated costs are. But to make a good decision as to whether or not the treatment is necessary, consumers need more line of sight to outcomes. They should be able to have a dialogue with their healthcare providers about the variety of treatments available to them, the potential outcomes associated with each option, and their related risks and costs. Accepting the physician's word isn't sufficient; consumers must ask for evidence to support the recommendations so that they can gauge the likelihood of the potential outcomes proposed, and that evidence needs to be conveyed in consumer-friendly terms by a clinician you trust.

Large employers are in a position to demand transparency and accountability for outcomes on behalf of their employees. Increasingly, these progressive employers are intentionally selecting providers who demonstrate true transparency and accountability.

Move Conversation toward a Continuum of Care

Currently, most people only see a physician or other health-care providers when they have a problem. Consumers need to move away from these narrow acute episodes and move toward prevention. Cerner Corporation has committed resources to improve the health status of its employees. Building off its success internally, it's taken the approach to the broader Kansas City market, home to its corporate headquarters. Community health competitions have resulted in weight loss and better health management.

Large employers can also use their market clout to force change and reward innovation by demanding bundled, transparent pricing tied to outcomes. Doing so will give them greater line of sight to their costs and help them to anticipate what their costs will be. Companies like Boeing, IBM, Walmart, Lowe's, and a host of others have already begun to move in this direction.

Create/Become Informed Consumers

Businesses can help create informed consumers among employees and within their communities by demanding that insurers and providers arm them with information that's easy for their employees to understand. Like any other market, different providers will offer what appears to be the same service at different costs. Employees need information to understand what their options are and the trade-offs for selecting among them. And employees need to hold their employers accountable for getting this information for them.

Create Incentives for Better Health Behaviors

Employers who offer insurance coverage to their employees can also adopt policies that promote accountability for good health choices and attempts to deter problematic behavior. As an example, Johnson & Johnson's corporate policy clearly discourages smoking. Any employee who wants to engage in tobacco use must go off property to do so. Sometimes, this means getting in your car and driving away. Johnson & Johnson also provides financial incentives for employees to participate in annual health screenings by paying them for completing a health assessment; additionally, the company structures monetary rewards for health maintenance and improvement. Some employers are placing financial penalties on employees who smoke and are therefore expected to utilize as much as 25% more healthcare than nonsmokers. At companies like Home Depot, PepsiCo, and Walmart, cost differentials for smokers range from an additional $240 per year to $2,000 per year more than nonsmokers.[15]

Employers can also encourage employees to take an active role in managing their health expenses by moving to defined contribution plans as opposed to traditional defined benefit plans. A defined contribution consists of a fixed amount of money provided by the employer to the employee for the purchase of insurance that best meets his or her needs.

Change Is Never Easy, But It Is Possible

The challenge of creating informed, accountable consumers should not be underestimated. The healthcare delivery industry struggles to compare the *value* associated with treating at one hospital versus another, focusing primarily on costs *without adequate attention to differential outcomes* and the value associated with care that may be delivered under different cost structures *and* different clinical models.

As we'll discuss throughout this book, it's not *just* about lowering costs; it's about demonstrating economic *and* clinical value. And it's not just about the delivery and insurance sectors; it's about a *fundamentally different model* for the entire industry with a different equation that offers consumers real choice. And it offers our country a pathway to better healthcare and increased competitiveness.

Questions for Employers

- What information am I providing my employees to ensure that they are engaged in the healthcare process?
- What more can I do to make my employees be better consumers?
- To what extent can our insurer (or the providers we contract with) provide a guarantee toward outcomes for certain procedures? Have we even asked for a guarantee?
- What kinds of incentives are we offering employees to engage in healthier behaviors? Am I practicing those good behaviors?

Questions for Consumers

- Am I sufficiently prepared for my next doctor's appointment? In other words, have I prepared questions for my physician about my symptoms, course of treatment, or other areas of interest?
- How well do I understand the rationale/need for the upcoming procedures? Do I understand what I should expect in terms of how the procedure will take place? The outcomes I should expect? What it will cost me to achieve that level of outcome?
- Have I explored other options available to me (like different locations, providers, or alternative treatment and therapy options)?
- Do I acknowledge my role in getting to better care at lower cost? Am I engaging in healthy practices and making good decisions about my health and my healthcare?

Endnotes

1. Rita E. Numerof. "Making the Transition from Volume to Value." American Hospital Association's Center for Healthcare Governance™ Monograph Series. July 2013. http://www .americangovernance.com/resources/monographs/13 -volume-to-value.shtml and http://nai-consulting.com /making-the-transition-from-volume-to-value/.
2. American Board of Internal Medicine Foundation. "Choosing Wisely®." 2012. http://www.abimfoundation.org/Initiatives /Choosing-Wisely.aspx and http://www.choosingwisely.org/.
3. Samantha Liss. "You Now Can Receive Chemotherapy at Schnucks." *St. Louis Business Journal.* November 2013. http:// www.bizjournals.com/stlouis/blog/health-care/2013/11/you -now-can-receive-chemotherapy-at.html?page=all.
4. Rita E. Numerof. "Three Simple Steps to Sustainable Healthcare." October 2014. http://nai-consulting.com/3 -simple-steps-to-sustainable-healthcare/.

5. Cynthia Koons. "The Doctor Is Out: LabCorp to Let Consumers Order Own Tests." *BloombergBusiness.* April 2015. http://www .bloomberg.com/news/articles/2015-04-20/the-doctor-is-out-lab corp-to-let-consumers-order-own-tests.
6. Michael N. Abrams and Daniel King. "Transparency in Healthcare: Coming to Your Hospital Soon!" *H&HN Daily.* February 2014. http://www.hhnmag.com/Daily/2014 /Feb/022014-Abrams-Hospital-Transparency.
7. Paul Fronstin. "Health Savings Accounts and Health Reimbursement Arrangements: Assets, Account Balances, and Rollovers, 2006–2012." *EBRI Issue Brief,* no. 382. January 2013. http://www.ebri.org/pdf/briefspdf/EBRI_IB_01-13.No382.HSA -HRAs.pdf.
8. Center for Policy and Research. "January 2014 Census Shows 17.4 Million Enrollees in Health Savings Account—Eligible High Deductible Health Plans (HSA/HDHPs)." America's Health Insurance Plans (AHIP). July 2014. https://www.ahip.org/2014 /HSA-Census-Report/.
9. Gary Claxton, Matthew Rae, Nirmita Panchal, Anthony Damico, Nathan Bostick, Kevin Kenward, and Heidi Whitmore. "Employer Health Benefits: 2014 Annual Survey." Kaiser Family Foundation and Health Research & Educational Trust (HRET). September 2014. files.kff.org/attachment/2014-employer -health-benefits-survey-full-report.
10. Bruce Japsen. "As Obamacare Looms, Insurers Look beyond Fee-for-Service Medicine, Say Execs at Forbes Healthcare Summit 2013." *Forbes.* October 2013. http://www.forbes.com /sites/brucejapsen/2013/10/10/as-obamacare-looms-insurers -look-beyond-fee-for-service-medicine-say-execs-at-forbes -healthcare-summit-2013/.
11. Dina Overland. "UnitedHealth's Price Transparency Tools Help Consumers Choose High-Quality Docs." *FierceHealthPayer.* September 2014. http://www.fiercehealthpayer.com/story/united healths-price-transparency-tools-help-consumers-choose-high -quality-d/2014-09-16.
12. Hans B. Christensen, Eric Floyd, and Mark Maffett. "The Effects of Price Transparency Regulation on Prices in the Healthcare Industry." University of Chicago Booth School of Business and Center for Health and the Social Sciences (CHeSS). October 2013. http://chess.bsd.uchicago.edu/events/documents /CFMPriceTransparency10913.pdf.

13. A growing list of healthcare comparison resources for consumers includes:
    Consumer Reports Health, www.consumerreports.org/cro/health
    CMS—Hospital Compare, www.medicare.gov/hospitalcompare
    CMS—Physician Compare, www.medicare.gov/physiciancompare
    Fair Health Consumer, www.fairhealthconsumer.org
    Healthcare Blue Book, www.healthcarebluebook.com
    HealthGrades, www.healthgrades.com
    Health in Reach (formerly PriceDoc), www.healthinreach.com
    Hospital Safety Survey (Leapfrog), www.hospitalsafetyscore.org
    New Choice Health, www.newchoicehealth.com
    New Hampshire Health Cost, www.nhhealthcost.org
    Save on Medical, www.saveonmedical.com
    ShareCare, www.sharecare.com
    The Commonwealth Fund, www.whynotthebest.org
    The Joint Commission, www.qualitycheck.org
    Truven Healthcare, www.100tophospitals.com
    U.S. News & World Report, www.usnews.com

14. Rita E. Numerof and Christopher de Wolff. "Building the Value Narrative for Employers and Insurers." *H&HN.* October 2013. http://www.hhnmag.com/Daily/2013/Oct/numerof100313-8200008266.

15. Reed Abelson. "The Smokers' Surcharge." *New York Times.* November 2011. http://www.nytimes.com/2011/11/17/health/policy/smokers-penalized-with-health-insurance-premiums.html?_r=0.

Chapter 4

The Role of Data: Creating an Environment for Change

Comparative Effectiveness Research: An Overview

Until recently, real-world evidence (RWE) and *comparative effectiveness* were terms that only surfaced in conversations among health policy specialists, academics, and other observers of the healthcare marketplace. No longer. The allocation of $1.1 billion to comparative effectiveness research (CER) in the American Recovery and Reinvestment Act (ARRA) of 2009 represented a paradigm shift. It promises to radically alter the level of government involvement in the way in which healthcare products and services are developed, delivered, and paid for. For better or worse, we believe this is a fact.[1]

The United States is a laggard in this arena. Other developed countries, including Britain, Canada, Germany, Australia, France, and the Netherlands, have established infrastructures to serve the same general purpose and for the same reason: They couldn't afford not to. Rapidly aging populations, coupled with rapid advances in technology and aggressive commercialization by manufacturers, made continued ad hoc decision making by providers economically untenable.

That's where the United States finds itself now. With healthcare expenditures at almost 18% of gross domestic product (GDP),[2] our per-capita expense is already more than 40% higher than that of other developed countries, and to make matters worse, our outcome metrics lag peers' substantially. In this context, comparative effectiveness has emerged as a part of the broader challenge of healthcare reform.

Historically, decision making regarding the treatment of choice in a particular case has been the province of the attending physician in consultation with the patient. In situations where the treatment will be paid for by an insurer, which accounts for the overwhelming majority, the prime consideration has been anticipated clinical effectiveness. It's been the physician's role to weigh research and claims made by the manufacturer (subject to Food and Drug Administration [FDA] verification) and by academic and government-sponsored research.

Comparative effectiveness, at least as conceptualized in the ARRA, means more than that. Such research is explicitly mandated to take clinical effectiveness and (for all practical purposes) cost into consideration. And although the legislation implies that research results will be advisory in nature, given the broader economic context, it's hard to imagine such an effort culminating in such an outcome.

We believe a broad range of constituents with a stake in the healthcare marketplace needs to understand this initiative and what it's likely to mean to them.

Drivers of CER

Role of Cost Containment

The most basic impulse behind CER is the desire to control healthcare costs—an inescapable imperative if the Centers for Medicare & Medicaid Services (CMS's) programs are to be saved from insolvency without dramatic tax increases.

The federal government currently spends more than 6.5% of GDP on healthcare through CMS, an amount that already exceeds the payroll taxes intended to pay for it. If costs continue to grow at their current pace, everyone else will have to pay out of pocket while simultaneously footing the bill for CMS.

Ideally, policy makers would like to reduce costs without impacting the quality of healthcare, and CER is seen as one way to get there. By replacing ineffective treatments and standards of clinical care with effective ones, or by replacing more expensive treatments with equally effective but less expensive ones, the cost of care can be brought down, in the words of the Congressional Budget Office (CBO), "without adverse health consequences."

The CBO has consistently pointed to evidence in support of the idea that there are massive savings to be had by changing patterns of clinical practice. The evidence for this comes from several sources. First, other countries have equivalent or better outcomes with much lower costs. Second, an analysis of Medicare spending showed large variations across regions in cost per patient that were not associated with increased illness, higher payment rates, or better outcomes. By some estimates, total Medicare costs could be reduced by 30% if the entire country adopted the clinical practice patterns of the most efficient regions. It has also been estimated that between 30% and 65% of all surgeries that are performed in high-use regions are either clinically inappropriate or of "equivocal" value.

Data like these have raised hopes on the part of politicians that, if only they knew what worked, they could drastically reduce the costs of care while retaining its quality. *What works* is the focus of CER.

Role of Political Expediency

It isn't all about politics, but politics will make itself felt. While CER certainly offers a legitimate, if partial, solution to the real problem of cost containment, it also plays off the perception that pharmaceutical and medical device companies have managed to game the system to extract exorbitant profits, artificially raising the cost of healthcare for everyone.

This perception has been largely created by the very real costs of patented drugs paid by American consumers and the much lower prices of these same drugs overseas. It has been fanned by politicians and interest groups until there is a widespread *misperception* that pharmaceutical costs are the primary reason that healthcare is more expensive in the United States than elsewhere. Yet, prescription drugs only account for 10 cents of every U.S. healthcare dollar!

Hence, an initiative to "find out what really works" has a populist, anti-drug-company flavor that some politicians find appealing.

Why Is the Federal Government Specifically Involved?

The primary argument for the federal government's direct involvement in CER rests on the economic notion that the information developed by such research is a *public good*; like a new highway, it benefits everyone, regardless of whether or not people invested in its creation! And there is a reasonable case to be made that the public-good nature of information has had an impact; in other words, private insurers have been unwilling to invest in CER, despite its potential benefits to them, because it would have equally benefited their "freeloading" competitors. Hence, there's less research than there ought to be to maximize the ability of the healthcare market to produce value. Finally, CMS is the single largest insurer with the most to save, and it doesn't have to fund the effort out of its "profits."

But there are other reasons, as well. First, a great deal of the benefit of CER is downstream: Savings may not be realized until some time has passed. A knee replacement that lasts for 50 years may be preferable to one that lasts 10 years on both clinical and cost-effectiveness bases, but if the cost of replacing the knee after 10 years is almost certain to fall to another insurer, there is no incentive to spend more for the longer lasting knee.

The government, however, generally doesn't lose its patients to other insurers. Once an individual starts on Medicare, he or she is typically in the "plan" for life. That puts the federal government in a great position to benefit from the downstream impacts of more effective care, whether it provides it or mandates that others provide it.

Finally, let's not forget that the federal government has, in simple dollar terms, a larger interest in efficient healthcare than any other entity. The federal government, including CMS, the Department of Defense, and the Department of Veterans Affairs, purchases the majority of all healthcare today, and that will grow as the population ages.[3] Medicaid expansion brought about through the Patient Protection and Affordable Care Act (PPACA) and the subsidies that millions of Americans receive through the insurance exchanges increase the number of people receiving some type of government-supported healthcare.

The concept of CER is not new. In fact, there have been several federal groups engaged in it for several decades. But the primary source of CER has historically been private industry. Producers of drugs and medical devices are required to present evidence of a product's safety and clinical efficacy to the FDA and sometimes will also perform head-to-head trials against a top competitor in an attempt to create the basis for a claim of equivalence or superiority. This head-to-head evidence is extremely useful for comparing treatments, but the scope of the evidence—the range of products for which such head-to-head comparisons are available—is limited. In addition, the risk that comparative research will not produce the desired results and the relatively high cost of producing it, regardless of outcome, limit the circumstances under which industry is willing to conduct it.

Individual researchers at academic institutions occasionally conduct CER meta-analyses, and the UK-based Cochrane Collaboration, a nonprofit organization, has used its network of volunteers to conduct systematic reviews of randomized controlled trials since 1993. The Cochrane Database of Systematic Reviews currently contains approximately 5,000 complete reviews evaluating the effectiveness of various treatments.

Focus of CER

As we stated earlier, CMS needs to reduce costs immediately and dramatically. Consequently, we anticipate it will focus on the highest cost drivers of healthcare (see Table 4.1). Interestingly, this list of priority areas is similar to what is seen in other developed countries (e.g., Australia and the UK).

The CBO has a great deal of influence when it comes to identifying spending priorities. It doesn't make policy (or, strictly speaking, even advocate for specific policies), but its economists and analysts often help to frame options for consideration, and the numbers provided by the CBO are usually accepted by all sides of a debate in the halls of Congress.

The CBO has written a great deal over the last few years on the topic of comparative effectiveness. It is relatively bullish regarding the potential savings to CMS that a properly structured comparative effectiveness program might allow. Former director Peter Orszag has suggested that some $700 billion/year might be saved throughout the entire healthcare system without adversely impacting health outcomes.

Among the implicit recommendations of the CBO are the following:

■ Information about the relative effectiveness of medical products should be matched by incentives for using that information effectively, as those incentives will be required to change practice patterns in ways that will

Table 4.1 Most Expensive Medical Conditions[a] versus Areas of Special Significance to Medicare[b]

Most Expensive Conditions	Areas of Special Significance to Medicare
Heart conditions: $95 billion	Ischemic heart disease
Trauma disorders: $74 billion	N/A
Cancer: $72 billion	Cancer
Mental disorders, including depression: $72 billion	Dementia, including Alzheimer's disease; depression and other mood disorders
Osteoarthritis and other joint diseases: $57 billion	Arthritis and nontraumatic joint disorders
Asthma and chronic obstructive pulmonary disease: $54 billion	Chronic obstructive pulmonary disease
High blood pressure: $47 billion	Stroke, including control of hypertension
Type 2 diabetes: $46 billion	Diabetes mellitus
Back problems: $35 billion	N/A
Normal childbirth: $35 billion	N/A
Disorders of the upper GI: $27 billion	Peptic ulcer/dyspepsia
Pneumonia: $14 billion	Pneumonia

[a] As identified by the Agency for Healthcare Research and Quality, 2004–2008.
[b] As identified by the U.S. Department of Health and Human Services, 2004–2008.

produce substantial savings over the long term. The CBO has also noted that this is likely to require changes to existing legislation.

■ Comparative effectiveness studies should incorporate cost effectiveness, as this would allow them to have a bigger impact on CMS's budget than if they only compared clinical effectiveness.

- Efforts to bolster comparative effectiveness research should be coordinated by a "qualified" organization—in other words, one that is respected and trusted by doctors and other professionals, as this would encourage changes in medical practice.
- Comparative effectiveness research should include all relevant subgroups; failure to do so will result in their not being convincing to healthcare practitioners.
- Research based on meta-analysis and claims data, while less expensive than new head-to-head randomized controlled trials, is less definitive; hence, there will be a need for both kinds of research.
- The practical limits to the number of clinical trials that can be conducted at one time require focus on those studies with the potential to save the system a lot of money.
- Electronic health records should be implemented in such a way as to increase the ease and rapidity of outcomes research.
- Deficit spending for comparative effectiveness research is legitimate, as the full cost of such research is likely to outweigh near-term benefits, but in the long term it can be expected to pay for itself many times over.
- Research should draw heavily upon studies previously conducted by the Cochrane Collaborative and other countries' health services (e.g., the UK's National Institute for Health and Clinical Excellence [NICE]).

The Institute of Medicine (IOM), a widely respected, nonprofit organization chartered to provide authoritative opinions on healthcare issues, also plays a key role in CER and prioritization. The IOM meets the CBO's desired criteria for an organization that would be charged with bolstering comparative effectiveness research and encouraging changes in practice patterns, as it is (a) widely respected by clinicians and others in the healthcare field, and (b) seen as relatively free of bias.

The IOM has indicated its support for increased funding of comparative effectiveness research, stating that $20 billion/ year (a number that it selected because it is 1% of healthcare expenditures) spent on determining what works would clearly improve the ability to get value from healthcare.

The IOM has also cited Kaiser's Archimedes project, a mathematical description of patient health that allows the impact of various interventions to be modeled and assessed with some degree of accuracy, as a way to leverage existing data. The IOM sees it as creating an efficient way to develop comparative information on competing therapies. The adoption of such a model would have significant implications for the structure of the health information technology system. Model-suggested research might eventually come to dominate the comparative effectiveness research priorities.

The IOM explicitly advocates evaluation of the costs *and* benefits of therapies *over the lifetime* of the patient, including the possibility of downstream complications and often ignored benefits like increased productivity.

The PPACA defined yet another broad-based independent group to weigh in and oversee research prioritization as well as discuss the implications of such research. The Patient-Centered Outcomes Research Institute (PCORI) was created as an independent organization whose aim is to "help people make informed healthcare decisions and improve healthcare delivery." With appointed representatives from across industry and academia, its primary goal is to commission research, ostensibly informed by public comment periods reflecting the concerns of patients, caregivers, and the broader healthcare community. Its public face emphasizes *patient engagement* and *transparency* in its deliberations. PCORI is staffed and its efforts fully supported by taxpayer dollars. Its existence speaks to the commitment of the federal government to use research and real-world evidence to guide treatments toward those that *work*. Regardless of the organization's relative effectiveness, it is another statement that CER is here to stay and that choices will be made from among available therapies.

By the end of 2013 PCORI had approved a total of $97.5 million in new funding for 53 CER studies aimed at answering "… questions of most importance to patients and those who care for them."[4] In addition, it approved an additional "… $93.5 million to build and expand 29 individual health data networks." Between 2012 and the end of 2013 PCORI awarded a total of $464.9 million in research support for 279 different projects. Competitive reviews are conducted by patients, caregivers, and scientists who evaluate scientific merit, the level of patient engagement, and methodological rigor. The latter spawned another agency, PCORnet, described as "an ambitious new patient-centered clinical research network to facilitate CER." The network's ostensible goal is to provide patients ("and other healthcare stakeholders") information about the effectiveness of various healthcare options to make better informed decisions about care. It was created in recognition of the fact that enormous amounts of data on the level of patient encounter are collected daily. But the information hasn't been used up to this point, according to PCORnet's creators, due to inadequate opportunities for collaboration. The network (currently 29 separate networks) in turn comprises and funds two distinct arms: clinical data research networks (CDRNs) and patient-powered research networks (PPRNs). The former (N = 11) are based in healthcare delivery systems and the latter (N = 18) attempt to collect health data and "provide a common venue for patients and researchers … interested in moving the research agenda forward for specific medical conditions."[5] Importantly, the PPRN's agenda is to prepare the networks to conduct CER.

As laudable as the mission is, the broad and encompassing range of activity raises serious questions about the tangible benefits likely to accrue from the expenditures. Lack of focus, concentration, and prioritization kill meaningful accomplishment in any field. Research has been funded across multiple federal agencies and private foundations for years without significant improvement. With many competing agendas there is real danger that nothing will be shown for the effort except a lot of activity and engagement. The first 18 months of funding has been devoted to developing the governance structures, including policies and procedures, to accept and prioritize research questions. Once operational, the intent is to fund a wide range of clinical research designs, including observational studies in real-world settings. It is being positioned as a funding source for large-scale CER relying on access to big data.

To this point, PCORI has come under attack from both the Right and the Left.

Dr. Scott Gottlieb, a resident fellow at the conservative-leaning American Enterprise Institute, criticized PCORI for failing to fund what he described as rigorous, comprehensive research comparing the impact of active treatments. His challenge boiled down to PCORI's focus on "trivial" studies focused on "how to study" and supporting "careworn academic projects."[6]

Importantly, the Center for American Progress, a left-leaning group, voiced a similar concern, putting pressure on PCORI to focus its efforts on evident gaps in treatments for common and costly conditions. The group's analysis suggests that 4 years into its 10-year charter, PCORI has devoted less than 40% of its research funding to actual CER.[7] It also noted that the absence of any CER study of medical devices initiated only a few CER studies of drugs and produced only a few analyses of existing studies.

The future of PCORI and potentially of grants coming out of CMS's Center for Medicare and Medicaid Innovation (CMMI) related to cost reduction and value-based payments is likely to include increased scrutiny and potential dismantling of programs in the face of a Republican-dominated Congress. Both PCORI and CMMI have been criticized, albeit for different reasons, and the oversight process will allow for opportunities to better understand and improve existing initiatives. The institute would be well served to focus on the priority areas identified by the independent and highly respected Institute of Medicine.

Other Considerations for Choosing Priorities

There are three criteria we believe are likely to make a particular disease state, medical condition, technology, or treatment protocol a target for CER. These include the total current cost to CMS, the projected rate of increase in total cost to CMS, and political hot-button issues.

There are several segments of the healthcare industry that have raised the ire of people in Congress and the administration. Some vulnerable products, technologies, or practices within these segments will likely be priorities for CER—not primarily for practical reasons, but for political ones. These include:

■ High-priced brand drugs used to treat conditions for which cheaper generic competition exists. Similarly, biologics, with their high cost and limited market size, may also be vulnerable if approval of treatments becomes an exercise in logrolling. The introduction of biosimilars will also challenge the current biologics market. Biosimilars will likely be welcomed by policy makers, even if they don't bring the same discounts to branded biologics as generics brought to small-molecule drugs

■ Products and treatment protocols related to the wound care industry, which has come under Office of Inspector General (OIG) scrutiny over the last few years

■ Products in the spine and orthopedics industry, in which many of the established manufacturers were subject to deferred prosecution agreements, apparently on suspicion of making false claims and offering kickbacks to surgeons for using or endorsing them. Those organizations that enter into such agreements are still subject to corporate integrity agreements that require extensive federal monitoring and financial penalties

The implications of CER for specific sectors of the healthcare industry (i.e., delivery; pharmaceutical, medical device, and diagnostics manufacturers, and payers) are discussed in each of the subsequent chapters.

CER and the Consumer: Does It Really Matter?

At least from a theoretical perspective, the ultimate objective of CER should be to achieve better health outcomes at lower cost. If done right, consumer choices should improve; they and society at large should incur less cost for at least equivalent if not better results.

CER assumes the existence of "evidence": data-based insight derived from scientific research as noted at the beginning of this chapter. As consumers get more engaged in the healthcare choices affecting them, critical questions will need to be addressed—for example, is the evidence credible, is the evidence relevant, and how does the evidence affect me personally?

A study supported by the National Business Group on Health and the California Healthcare Foundation and reported in *Health Affairs* in 2010 found that many consumers are quite skeptical about the validity of "evidence-based healthcare."[8] Whether a function of advertising or carry-over from business sectors, there has been a general belief among major segments of the population that more healthcare services are better than fewer—that newer technologies must be an improvement over older ones.

Given that segments of the population have actually questioned the value of tried and tested vaccines for children, this is an issue that is going to have to be addressed—and quickly.

Clearly, more engagement in research questions of interest to patients and consumers and more actively engaging in treatment decisions with their physicians and other healthcare providers should begin to move the needle on this issue. Most notably, we see a move toward personalized medicine, transparency, and patient-reported outcomes all advancing the push for better, more accessible, and relevant evidence.

In the case of personalized medicine, the fact that "x" drug works better than placebo in 30% of patients who took it is an important piece of information. But the real question is understanding how "x" drug will work for "me"! How will a patient know if he or she is in the 30% of people who will get a good response or the 70% who won't? Lack of specificity in particular applications doesn't help to build confidence in existing evidence.

The movement toward increasing transparency, as noted in earlier chapters, will also create positive pressure for consumer engagement. But we think the real driver of change will be a focus on outcomes (and evidence supporting them) that really matter to consumers.

Clearly, evidence of cost–benefit ratios will matter as consumers shoulder more of the costs of healthcare services. Even more important will be the achievement of specific health-related goals associated with the consumer's unique situation.

Evidence-Based Medicine and the Role of Big Data

Against the general excitement surrounding "big data," it's interesting to note that "evidence-based medicine" was defined in 1996 in the *British Medical Journal* as "... the conscientious, explicit, and judicious use of current best evidence in making decisions about the care of individual patients."[9] In other words, we should take what we know about the evidence derived from *systematic* clinical research and then evaluate how it may or may not apply to a particular individual's situation.

Unfortunately, too often we take the statistical "norms" from big data sets and apply them to individual situations without asking sufficient questions about the relevance to that individual's medical, social, emotional, cognitive, and financial circumstances.

As we become increasingly focused on delivering value across the continuum of care and engaging patients in their own care, understanding what will impact patient behavior and what patients really care about will be critical. Big data alone can't identify every question that needs to be asked; without rigorous analysis, erroneous conclusions can be drawn that may have detrimental effects.

Endnotes

1. Rita E. Numerof. "The Impact of Comparative Effectiveness on the Healthcare Marketplace." Numerof & Associates, Inc. June 2009.
2. Centers for Medicare and Medicaid Services, Office of the Actuary. "National Healthcare Data Expenditures Data." National Health Statistics Group. Last accessed 6/18/2015. https://www.cms.gov/Research-Statistics-Data-and-Systems /Statistics-Trends-and-Reports/NationalHealthExpendData /NationalHealthAccountsHistorical.html.
3. Centers for Medicare and Medicaid Services, Office of the Actuary, National Health Statistics Group; US Department of Commerce, Bureau of Economic Analysis; and US Bureau of the Census.
4. Patient-Centered Outcomes Research Institute. "PCORI Approves $191 million to Support Patient-Centered Comparative Effectiveness Research." December 2013. http://www.pcori.org /content/pcori-approves-191-million-support-patient-centered -comparative-effectiveness-research.
5. National Patient-Centered Clinical Research Network (PCORI). "PCORnet FAQs." http://www.pcornet.org/resource-center/faqs/.
6. Sabriya Rice. "Reform Update: PCORI under Fire as It Prepares to Accept New Proposals." *Modern Healthcare.* August 2014. http://www.modernhealthcare.com/article/20140804/NEWS /308049964/reform-update-pcori-under-fire-as-it-prepares-to -accept-new-proposals.

7. Neera Tanden, Zeke Emanuel, Topher Spiro, Emily Oshima Lee, and Thomas Huelskoetter. "Comparing the Effectiveness of Health Care: Fulfilling the Mission of the Patient-Centered Outcomes Research Institute." Center for American Progress. January 24, 2014. https://www.ameri canprogress.org/issues/healthcare/report/2014/01/24/82775 /comparing-the-effectiveness-of-health-care/.

8. Kristin L. Carman, Maureen Maurer, Jill Mathews Yegian, Pamela Dardess, Jeanne McGee, Mark Evers and Karen O. Marlo. "Evidence That Consumers Are Skeptical about Evidence-Based Health Care." *Health Affairs* 29 (7). 2010. http:// www.chcf.org/publications/2010/06/evidence-that-consumers -are-skeptical-about-evidencebased-health-care.

9. David L. Sackett, William M. C. Rosenberg, J. A. Muir Gray, R. Brian Haynes, and W. Scott Richardson. "Evidence-Based Medicine: What It Is and What It Isn't." *British Medical Journal* 312:71–72. 1996. http://www.bmj.com/content/312/7023/71.full.

Chapter 5

Redesigning Healthcare Delivery: Hospitals Were Never Meant to Be Destinations of Choice

Introduction

Everyone reading this book knows a painful truth: that hospitals were never meant to be destinations of choice. No matter how beautiful they are—no matter the fountains, marble, and glass—they really aren't resorts.

Hospitals are in the sickness business—not the healthcare business. They get paid to diagnose and treat illness, making more money for doing more things to each patient.

We talk about healthcare as a patient-centered enterprise, but that's not really true either. Anyone who's been a patient in most hospitals knows that they are confusing, hard to navigate, and demand an incredible amount of redundant information. Most departments within the hospital have their own information systems and most of those don't speak to each other. Because regulations require the capture of certain information (or maybe because it's needed to ensure that the hospital gets paid), basic information is asked over and over again—not between institutions, mind you, but between departments within the walls of the hospital. Until recently, the appropriateness of clinical intervention and quality hasn't been linked in any way to payment. And if mistakes were made within the system, hospitals made more money by fixing those mistakes (like medication errors, hospital-acquired infections, falls, inappropriate readmissions, etc.). Even now, despite the Centers for Medicare & Medicaid Services' (CMS) intent to deny payment for such *never events,* we're on a path to dilute this nascent connection between payment and outcomes that should have been there from the start.

When financial squeezes have occurred, hospital administrators understandably cut and tightened. However, when you cut corners, run too lean with staff, and deal with sicker and sicker patients in acute care settings, mistakes are much more likely to occur! And we're not suggesting that these errors are made with malicious intent, but rather that the critical focus on accountability for outcomes has been largely absent.

The reality of healthcare is that it's big business. Despite the window dressing, when you get right down to creating change in any industry, it's all about the money: Who pays for what and how. Economic incentives work in a very nuanced way, consciously and subconsciously, and drive decisions. As long as healthcare delivery continues on the path of fee-for-service reimbursement without regard to outcomes, the tendency to do more/make more will remain strong.

CMS has recognized that changes have to be made and has instituted some of these in the way it pays for healthcare. Commercial payers are quickly following suit. But current payment is predominantly done on a piecework basis, and when we're trying to change tiny slices of activity, it's really hard to meaningfully redesign the work.

Even as CMS struggles to reduce the cost of care, individual consumers are increasingly burdened by the combination of higher premiums and cost shifting by employers that leaves them with a larger percentage of that cost to bear. Inevitably these forces are building consumer pressure for a more market-responsive healthcare delivery system and all that implies.

Imagine a future where consumers ask questions about the price and outcomes that healthcare systems deliver—not questions about the cost of one MRI versus another, but rather about *all* the costs for a pregnancy or an orthopedic procedure. Today, costs for these areas are relatively easy to calculate as they have a defined beginning, middle, and end. Yet, very few healthcare systems are prepared to answer such questions. Fewer still are able to include the physician, home care, or rehab components. And for those that can offer a price estimate, even fewer are able to provide transparent data on health outcomes or the patient experience compared to competitors.

Without these data, how can a consumer decide to choose one hospital over another? This is the future of healthcare, and healthcare systems and independent physicians need to get ready for it.

Adapting to the Changing Landscape of Healthcare

The hospital model today stands in the crosswinds of market and nonmarket forces. On the market side, there is the hard reality that a sustainable margin is required for financial viability. On the nonmarket side, there are a host of regulations to comply with, a mission that includes caring for those who can't pay, disproportionate payer bargaining power, and a relative inability to compete on the dimensions of price and quality.

Compounding the problem has been the growing number of freestanding clinics, which are not subject to the same regulations and are able to carve out the most profitable portions of the market for themselves. With newer equipment and lower overhead, they can capture higher margins and can refer the uninsured, the marginally insured with big copays, and those complex cases that pose the biggest medical and financial risks to the hospital.[1]

Hospitals have been left playing *catch-up*. To stay competitive, they've needed to upgrade and expand facilities, compete for a shrinking pool of qualified staff, and implement expensive new technology. The ongoing gap between current income and the requirements for continued competitiveness forced the assumption of debt, further increasing overhead.

Looking ahead, the view is even darker. In the aftermath of recession, banks have tightened their requirements for credit and governments are more wary of guarantees they might previously have given, so capital costs are rising. Worse yet, significant reductions in reimbursement are in process, even as growth in the Medicare population is set to rise to historic levels. Hospitals have previously *cost shifted* to private payers to make up for Medicare's notoriously low rates, but that's sure to meet increasingly stiff resistance. Between new regulations and public fury over a decade of premium increases, private payers will not just resist but also continue to follow CMS lead.

Indeed, major payers have committed significant resources to designing new risk-based and fully capitated products, and they are in various stages of "coaxing" reluctant healthcare delivery organizations and physicians to assume financial risk in the care for people entrusting their well-being to them.

The kinds of cost-cutting tactics that have been typical in the industry for the past few decades won't be adequate going forward. Paired with flat or shrinking margins, this typical situation makes for an unsustainable business model. Something has got to change.

Needed: A Transfusion of Fresh Thinking

For more than a decade, as payers have increasingly squeezed revenues, much of the industry has defined its strategic response as doing what it's always done, but for less. Hospitals aggregated into systems to maximize their leverage with payers and suppliers and "squeeze back" on reimbursement and supplies. Internally, cost-cutting efforts have come and gone, usually with limited long-term impact. The current popularity of Lean and Six Sigma notwithstanding, such efforts have consistently underperformed against expectations. Hobbled by inflated resource requirements, lack of strategic alignment, and implementation that typically fails to make line management accountable, these tactics may capture some savings and process improvement, but offer no guidance toward fixing an outmoded business model.

To get off the "spend and borrow treadmill," hospitals need to redefine the business they are in. For some that means defining themselves, in fact, as a business. While there is no single solution or model that guarantees success, it's clearly time for some out-of-the-box thinking.

Commercial strategy for tomorrow's healthcare requires a shift in thinking from simply cutting costs to actively seeking growth *by doing business differently.* As a first step, hospitals will need to decide what businesses they won't be in, and they'll need to get out of those businesses. It's that first step that improves margins and frees resources for future growth. They also need to think about how to change their cultures to create an environment in which this kind of entrepreneurial activity can flourish. A critical step in this direction is challenging the long-held assumptions that (1) if you practice good medicine, the money will follow, and (2) clinical and financial activity are independent and should remain separate.

Capture All the Value in Consolidation

One opportunity for thinking differently about healthcare delivery lies in more fully realizing the benefits of scale. Most hospital systems have successfully used their aggregated economic power to negotiate better terms with suppliers and payers, but have hardly begun to leverage all of the competitive advantages that scale offers. Outside of healthcare, multidivisional corporate structures look for synergy across operating units by centralizing support functions, integrating sales forces, and specializing manufacturing. Generally, this hasn't happened in healthcare. Systems need to move more decisively to capture operational improvements by specializing within facilities. This will allow more efficient use of assets as volume increases and efficiency efforts become more focused on core processes, and it will help to improve the competitiveness of hospitals with smaller clinics.

The main reason that hospital systems have been slow to capitalize on economies of scale has to do with the culture of healthcare. Most hospitals are local in origin. Whether community based or academic, they have their roots deep in the history of their city or town and have been shaped by the unique influences and personalities that drove them from their beginnings. When such organizations become part of a larger system, resistance to change is profound. Not infrequently, cultural differences between the acquired and the acquirer are wide enough to cause a rupture in the relationship. More often, such differences are just enough to ensure that the standardization of almost any process means dealing with conflict. Unfortunately, in the culture of healthcare—more so than in most other realms of business—conflict is not dealt with well. The net result is that synergies that could be captured are not.

Make Better Use of Service Line Organization

More radically, hospitals and systems need to more effectively integrate individual practice areas and ancillary treatments into a disease-state focus in selective areas. Such integration enables them to capture marketing and expertise synergies, as well as operational efficiencies, as fewer core processes are refined and standardized.

Rethink Your Competitive Strategy

Established healthcare delivery organizations also need a more proactive strategy to counter the "cherry picking" of high-margin patients by free-standing clinics. Historically, the most common "strategy" is to enter into a joint venture reactively, when possible, which simply mitigates the loss. Hospitals need to consider new models of distribution and capital acquisition that will allow them to preempt such competitive activity.

Reconceptualizing delivery models also means considering innovations like walk-in retail clinics staffed by a nurse practitioner with a supervising physician on call for consultation. Entrepreneurial service companies already have broken this ground; forward-thinking corporations have followed suit and hospitals that don't act soon will find themselves shut out.

Retail-based medicine began to appear in 2000 and has grown dramatically since then, driven by frustration with the availability of conventional providers and by higher deductibles and copays, especially for emergency room care. Typically staffed by nurse practitioners and physician assistants, retail clinics in high-traffic areas usually offer quick access and lower costs for treating minor illnesses, as well as health screenings, physicals, and immunizations.

By mid-2014, there were 1,686 retail clinics in the United States, an increase of over 16% year over year. Most clinics are operated by pharmacy chains, grocery chains, and large discount stores like Walmart and Target. Some operate in partnership with hospitals.

Walk-in clinics led the way, providing nonacute diagnostics and treatment for the ills and minor accidents of everyday life. Other specialty areas are emerging as well, like infusion therapy. Walgreens has provided the service for years and now has 1,400 nurses, dietitians, and pharmacists providing infusion therapy. Infusions are administered in patient homes and at ambulatory centers in areas with a capacity to serve 86% of the U.S. population, according to Walgreens officials.

Retail clinics are expanding into chronic disease management, employer-based health services, and telehealth services that bring skilled practitioners to remote areas via electronic technology.

Podiatry and chronic disease management are now turning up in retail settings, and as increasingly sophisticated technology enables many formerly complex procedures to move to an ambulatory setting, it will continue to present new opportunities for growth outside the walls of hospitals.

Build Your Management Infrastructure to Support Change

Hospitals have historically found it difficult to implement new strategy. In part that's a result of their diffuse structure. Departments often function as silos, specialization confers power, and resistance to change is high. Too often, line management is not actively engaged by administration in making the case for and supporting change. As a result, change moves slowly or not at all. Paralleling this issue is an even more fundamental one. The management infrastructure in most hospitals is optimized for performing technical tasks, not for meeting strategic business challenges. Managers themselves are usually promoted on the basis of strong technical skills and the ability to execute efficiently within the existing structure, so they are likely to lack the managerial and financial skills that allow them to drive change through the organization and are often exceptionally resistant to changing the system that worked so well for them.

Effective leaders at all levels of the organization need an understanding of their role that goes beyond technical expertise to encompass things like strategy-directed corporate stewardship and fiscal management. They need to understand where the organization is going and what their role will be in helping it get there. Without redefining the role of management and providing the training and tools to support it, most current managers will never reach that point. Most healthcare organizations need to give a lot more attention to this "management infrastructure."

Creating a management infrastructure that supports change is a critical first step for hospitals to remain competitive. This doesn't simply mean putting appropriate information technology (IT) in place or training managers to get information from it (though both are necessary). It means ensuring that managers know what to do with the information once they have it, that they have the skills to use it effectively, and that they understand what their larger purpose within the organization is so that they can use it to further that purpose. If organizations in the industry are to successfully adapt to the changing healthcare landscape, leadership needs to put these challenges at the top of its list.

Stop the Misuse of IT

The federal government hails an investment in health information technology (HIT)—specifically, electronic medical records (EMRs)—as one of the keystones of healthcare reform. As noted by the Center for American Progress, the effectiveness of this IT utilization will ultimately depend on its alignment with a different payment model.[2]

The healthcare industry has already invested significantly in IT. The irony is that much of the use of IT has been focused on getting paid, rather than on delivering better outcomes. This represents *another unintended cost consequence* of CMS implementation of diagnosis-related groups (DRGs) and a lost opportunity to utilize such technology to achieve better outcomes.

As has been well documented, the current payment system pays for the delivery of services performed, rather than for the quality of healthcare outcomes achieved. It's a payment system that unintentionally punishes providers for achieving efficiencies such as the elimination of avoidable hospital readmissions and unnecessary care. Not surprisingly, hospitals generally haven't pressured the companies that provide health IT solutions for products that support significant improvements in care quality and value. Instead, they've wanted IT solutions to help pick codes for billing purposes and document care for malpractice purposes, rather than for clinical decision support, care path management, and quality performance reporting.

George Halvorson, former CEO of Kaiser Permanente and advocate for change in the healthcare system, also noted the misuse of IT. He has highlighted the irony that such a high-tech, information-dependent profession has relied on data captured and stored on inaccessible and illegible scraps of paper. He has also noted the missed opportunities to utilize IT to better disseminate the flow of new medical knowledge, to better coordinate care, and to capture and track outcomes in support of evidence-based medicine.[3]

Virtually every other industry invests in and utilizes technology to compete by providing better products for lower cost. Because of how we pay for healthcare, however, the industry has historically used IT poorly. It has underinvested in IT because there's been no incentive to improve efficiency or outcomes, leaving the government to mandate and finance the investment. And its primary use of IT has been to manage the administrative nightmare of getting paid, with little discernible impact on improved outcomes or lower cost—the objectives we have now set for healthcare reform.

This critical IT investment program now underway will fail if it embraces technology adoption for the sake of adoption alone. But if this new IT investment is wedded to a strong commitment to provider payment reform and implemented as an accelerator of healthcare delivery innovation, then the investment can help transform U.S. healthcare as we know it.

The $64,000 question is whether it will or if we've already squandered the opportunity. CMS had the opportunity to deliver to the private sector the same IT platform it uses globally to connect the healthcare records of active and retired military wherever they are. While access to timely care has been a serious issue in the VA, access to records has not been. Private sector lobbyists fought against interoperability or a common platform, leaving us with an even more expensive and fragmented system than we had before electronic health records hit the stage. In one large nationally recognized health system, the medical group is on one system but each of five hospitals is on a separate system. Independent physicians with privileges can't access the hospital records. Five years ago they could order up a fax of a patient's scans; today that's not possible unless the physician is at the hospital. A solution is in sight. The multibillion dollar system and largest employer in its state has invested in yet another EHR to replace the current smorgasbord. None of these expenditures has done anything to move us to better care at lower cost, but it has created enormous profits for IT companies and their installers.

To ensure that "meaningful use" standards are met, so as not to get penalized by Medicare, physicians need to move their patients to personal "portals" and electronically submit requests and other information about their care. But it's not enough to submit the information. If patients don't acknowledge receipt, the exchange doesn't count toward meaningful use scores. The additional requirement of patient satisfaction scores on each and every visit adds to the administrative burden and ironically gets in the way of patient care and satisfaction! If you're asked on every visit to rate your satisfaction, at some point it's likely to become a source of irritation. Even if the results were valid, none of this measurement says anything about the quality of patient care—and isn't this supposed to be what's important?

One final cautionary note bears mention. There's often an aura of certitude surrounding electronic records. If it's in the computer, it must be accurate. Right? Or not right? In the same renowned healthcare system mentioned earlier, smart auto-populating content is beginning to show up based on limited information. Imagine that patient X has a diagnosis of congestive heart failure. For the "convenience" of the residents, hospitalists, and other care providers, treatment plans, medications, and typical diagnostic information appear in patient X's individual record. Clinicians are supposed to check the information for accuracy and appropriateness for this particular patient. But suppose her doctor is called to an emergency before she deselects the information that's been recorded? Or suppose in the crush of a busy day it gets overlooked. We think that wrong information entered into the record by well-intended programs is far more dangerous than any omission could be. Patient and provider beware.

Shrinking Reimbursement and Pressure for Transparency Are Reshaping Healthcare Delivery

As time goes on, the healthcare delivery marketplace will be heavily impacted by changing payer and consumer dynamics. Most notably, pressure for transparency in cost and quality along with payment tied to accountability for outcomes will drive efforts to compare treatment protocols and the impact of treatment options within and across facilities. Most fundamentally, those in the industry need to realize that these pressures and research on comparative effectiveness are primarily a means to the end of reducing CMS healthcare expenditures. Given that payments to the providers of healthcare (hospitals, physicians, and nursing homes) account for the lion's share of total expenditures (see Figure 5.1), those same providers are likely to see the largest reduction in revenues.

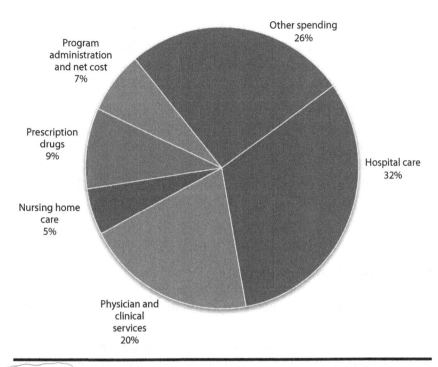

Program
administration
and net cost
7%

Other spending
26%

Prescription
drugs
9%

Nursing home
care
5%

Physician and
clinical
services
20%

Hospital care
32%

Figure 5.1 **Where the nation's health dollar went in calendar year
2013. Other spending includes dental and other professional services,
home health, durable medical products, over-the-counter medicines
and sundries, public health, other personal healthcare, research,
and structures and equipment. (Compiled from CMS, Office of the
Actuary, National Health Statistics Group, National Healthcare
Expenditures Data, December 2014.)**

The two most important impacts of these trends for the
healthcare delivery industry are expected to be the development of predictive care paths and a significant change in quality metrics. Each of these is discussed next.

Development of Predictive Care Paths

As we described in Chapter 4, comparative effectiveness
research is not restricted to research into what products work
best; it also includes research into what *treatment protocols*
work best. Existing protocols will come under scrutiny under

the same general terms as other products and, ultimately, are likely to be subject to mandatory guidelines by payers, including CMS. While deviation may not be "illegal," it may not be reimbursed.

The implication for hospitals is really clear: Take control and define your outcomes or someone else will do it for you.

Providers deriving a large portion of revenues or profits through cardiovascular centers, orthopedics, or bariatric surgery are likely to face the largest, most immediate risks. Spine surgery and even cancer care are beginning to move to the forefront.

Changing Quality Metrics

Traditional quality metrics such as measures of mortality and morbidity are in the process of being supplemented by a combination of process metrics (measuring compliance with "recommended" treatment guidelines) and outcome metrics that integrate patient quality of life into mortality and morbidity metrics. This will take place as part of the shift from a focus on gross clinical effectiveness to a focus on cost effectiveness, because cost effectiveness is nearly universally defined to include quality of life (e.g., the QALY, or quality-adjusted life year). While CMS has emphasized process metrics (i.e., measuring body mass index [BMI], LDL [low-density lipoprotein]/HDL [high-density lipoprotein] cholesterol, HbA1c, etc.) over outcome metrics and clinical impact (i.e., BMI, LDL/HDL or HbA1c "in control" or "within a desired range"), it has spurred organizations to ensure the right activity is in place.

Impact of Comparative Effectiveness Research on Hospital Operations

We expect that fiscal austerity, transparency, and a focus on outcomes will have two main effects on hospitals. The first is the reduction in revenues that comes from fewer and less expensive procedures being performed. This is a direct consequence of CMS need to save money, starting with lower and more restrictive reimbursement, followed by guidelines and treatment protocols. The point of the treatment protocols will be enhanced cost effectiveness, even though the protocols may result in some improvements on the clinical effectiveness side.

The baseline expectation is that attempts will be made to continue to push care down the acuity hierarchy, with the goal of preventing the most expensive procedures. The likely result will be more reliance on objective tests to identify patients who are expected to have a good response to less expensive procedures and therapies—drugs instead of surgery, lifestyle changes instead of drugs, outpatient instead of inpatient treatment, and home care instead of care within a medical facility. Those hospitals that have invested heavily in plant and capital equipment to deliver the most advanced care in service line areas like cardiovascular disease and orthopedics may find their return on these investments significantly reduced relative to their expectations.

The second effect is, at least potentially, the reduced ability to differentiate based on care protocols that are not evidence based. Currently, this is a growing element of the branding efforts of hospitals and hospital systems. In the future, differentiation will come from more effective execution of "standard" protocols, as reflected in new outcome metrics and the presentation of specific economic and clinical value data.

To the extent that new protocols are developed, they'll be subject to much more stringent requirements regarding payment, and it's likely that they'll be developed in partnership with pharmaceutical, medical device, or diagnostics manufacturers who will partially fund the generation of cost-effectiveness evidence for protocols incorporating their products. As an example, a device maker might develop equipment for monitoring the weight of patients with congestive heart failure (in whom rapid weight gain may be a sign of impending trouble) and automatically transmit that information back to a physician. This has the potential to save a trip to the acute care setting. Should the protocol be adopted as the standard of care, the provider and device manufacturer will both benefit. We anticipate the use of these guidelines to pick up immediately. The recent "sustainable growth rate (SGR) fix" has provisions to allow for reimbursement for remote monitoring and telemedicine. The rules governing this will unfold over the next 2 years.

For an industry that currently struggles to avoid never events like leaving surgical instruments inside a patient, the change to process metrics will be especially difficult. Compliance with prescribed care paths will require a new managerial infrastructure that aligns the roles, accountabilities, and incentives of all members of the organization, including physicians, to ensure adequate focus on compliance without losing sight of their strategic accountabilities.

In 2009, in "The Impact of Comparative Effectiveness on the Healthcare Marketplace: A Special Report," we projected the timing for these changes to be 3 years with more ramping up in the following 2 to 2 years. So far this projection has proved to be accurate. Changes to quality metrics have been integrated into CMS larger healthcare reform package in its accountable care organization (ACO) experiments beginning in 2012, with similar initiatives in various stages of development on the commercial side. Comparative effectiveness will inform the selection of quality metrics based on already existing knowledge. Guidance regarding the new quality metrics was issued by the U.S. Department of Health and Human Services (HHS) as part of the health information technology initiative early in 2012 with more rules issued in subsequent years.

Prudent Responses and Defensive Strategies

At this point, we continue to recommend that healthcare delivery organizations pursue four key strategic and defensive responses:

- Insulate against the impact of the shrinking pie.
- Position to benefit from cost savings.
- Anticipate changes to the reimbursement scheme.
- Optimize treatment protocols today.

We discuss each of these in the next sections.

Insulate from the impact of the shrinking pie: The most obvious and probably most prudent way to create this insulation is to begin to diversify sources of revenue away from insurers (including but not limited to CMS) and toward direct payment for service. Examples include the development of walk-in retail clinics (some of which may not take health insurance and offer services for about the cost of a typical copay), the creation of premium services or accommodations within the hospital, and a shift toward providing elective medical services.

The movement will be to shift the locus of care out of the acute care setting to ambulatory care in local clinics, other distributed settings, and, ultimately, the home. Increasing the convenience of care tends to put more control over health decisions in the hands of patients, which increases the likelihood that their unique needs—for the reassurance that diagnostic testing or a clinical opinion provides or for an elective procedure—will be met regardless of the calculated cost effectiveness of these interventions for the population as a whole.

This has given birth to a new business model centered around educated consumers who place a greater premium on quality of care than Medicare is likely to provide and are willing to pay out of pocket (either instead of or in addition to standard reimbursement) to obtain it. In a physician practice, it's called concierge medicine!

Position to benefit from cost savings: If a provider can determine how to restructure work to save cost, it may be able to benefit by allying with manufacturers in the development of treatment approaches (incorporating effective and efficient treatment protocols and new or modified products that make those protocols effective) that will be adopted by payers as the "gold standard" for treatment. Manufacturers are already beginning to see their products come under pressure from an economic value perspective. They would welcome a partner with ideas for using these products, even if in modified form, in ways that maximize their value and hence the likelihood of continued reimbursement. In the last several years, device manufacturers have expanded efforts to engage with healthcare delivery organizations to develop new products that reduce cost and improve outcomes.

The other way in which providers can position themselves to capitalize on cost savings is to preemptively implement the organizational changes that will allow them to outcompete their competition after the changes come. These changes include a more sophisticated, integrated, and effective managerial infrastructure, as well as the implementation of information technology that correctly anticipates the demands of the health information technology initiative.

Government is not (yet) mandating framework and structure for this information technology—just saying that it must be in place. While the government has defined expectations for *meaningful use*, there are no defined incentives to ensure that integration takes place. But there is an opportunity for forward-looking healthcare delivery systems to lead the design of this architecture and create an integrated approach.

Don't underestimate the difficulty of this work, however, or the criticality of getting it right. And be wary of the idea that the right information technology infrastructure will, by itself, break down silos that exist within and across sites of care.

Change is necessary to improve outcomes and reduce the cost of care, but it can only come about when the right human infrastructure is in place, ensuring alignment with strategic goals, coordination across roles, and appropriate accountabilities and incentives. The cultural shifts that must occur within the organization are enormous.

Anticipate changes to the reimbursement scheme: To the extent that providers can anticipate what disease states will be most heavily and quickly impacted, and are able to diversify away from those areas (or avoid additional investment in them), they will reduce the risks associated with these areas. Even today, delaying the purchase of capital equipment associated with the projected priority areas (and acute care areas more broadly) is prudent. Reevaluation of the risks and likely return on such equipment is needed.

It is clear, however, that the service line centers of excellence that many hospitals have made a strategic priority show an uncanny level of overlap with the priority areas for cost reduction identified previously. Cardiovascular disease, cancer, diabetes, and osteoarthritis are all likely to be subject to intense pressure through the reimbursement system over the next several years.

This will tend to reduce the return on investment for these areas, and the challenge will be to replace the lost revenue by broadening the focus within the targeted disease states. This may mean that the capital, equipment, and personnel brought on board in the expectation of a large influx in acute care will instead be redeployed from the acute setting to ambulatory and lifestyle interventions and possibly long-term care.

The other major change likely to happen is the creation of incentives for maintaining wellness outside the hospital setting. Reimbursement for wellness programs will be based on the incorporation of *prevention* into healthcare standards.

Optimize treatment protocols today: The need to control costs means that DRG reimbursement levels will become increasingly stingy, even while quality metrics become

increasingly broad. In response, providers will have to perform their own form of cost–benefit analysis. This will mean
evaluating new technologies in the context of care within the
hospital; adding them only if they improve outcomes, decrease
cost, or both; and eliminating those that no longer add to the
cost effectiveness of care. All acquisitions of capital equipment
and even the addition of tests to be run on existing equipment will be evaluated in the context of economic and clinical
value. The challenge will be to identify and develop standardized practices supported by a base of evidence drawn from
within the institution incorporating medical society guidelines
as appropriate.

The use of an optimized set of diagnostic tests to guide
physicians in choosing the most cost-effective course of treatment for patients is an area especially ripe for improvement.
Hospitals have already started to demand that manufacturers provide evidence of the economic and clinical value of
diagnostic tests, how they should be used, how much they
will cost, what costs can be eliminated, and what the benefits
will be. The extent of these demands for evidence will, and
should, increase.

Accountable Care Is Needed; ACOs Are Not

The Patient Protection and Affordable Care Act (PPACA) of
2010 created a new, federally financed mechanism for healthcare delivery via Medicare: the accountable care organization
(ACO). The ACO concept has been raised to prominence by
its promotion in the legislation as an answer to the problems
with the U.S. healthcare system. Proponents of the concept
have pressed forward for ACO implementation. Based on
decades of direct experience working with healthcare stakeholders, our position in 2010 and still 5 years later is that
ACOs are not the magic solution that their creators envisioned
them to be.

As we noted in the ACO policy paper we wrote for the Heritage Foundation,[4] ACOs are merely the latest in a long history of health policy "silver bullets." Since the 1970s, Congress and successive administrations have promoted a number of mechanisms to control rising healthcare costs, including the introduction of Medicare hospital payment formulas based on fixed payments for hospital services (payments for DRGs), health maintenance organizations (HMOs), and preferred provider organizations (PPOs). Yet costs have continued to rise despite these efforts. At the same time, concerns about fragmentation of care and diminished quality have increased significantly.

ACOs have been promoted as a new mechanism for addressing the shortcomings of previous reforms.[5] Congress, apparently unmindful of legislating an untested model in a field as complex as healthcare, included provisions in the PPACA to establish accountable care organizations.[6] Only loosely defined by the original legislation, ACOs consist of groups of physicians and other providers that work together to manage and coordinate care for Medicare fee-for-service beneficiaries and to meet certain quality-performance standards. Through *shared savings programs*, ACOs receive a portion of the shared savings if they sufficiently reduce costs and simultaneously improve quality.

Curiously, under the statute, the Secretary of HHS was charged with developing a method to assign Medicare beneficiaries to ACOs.[7] Because the statute was unclear about the resolution of many vital issues, the crucial details are supplied and refined by federal regulators—as has been the case for so many other provisions of this complex and still controversial health law. When the initial set of rules came out in April 2011, the more than 500 pages of Byzantine guidance were met by so much negativity by "model" ACOs that CMS backed off and modified its requirements.

Pioneer ACOs, the original crop of organizations signing up for two-sided risk, have been challenged to get the numbers to work. As of this writing, 13 of the original 32 have dropped out of the program. Even leading ACO supporters like Dartmouth-Hitchcock continue to challenge the timeliness and accuracy of the very numbers on which decisions are made regarding payment or penalty—to say nothing about the administrative burden to execute the program by the health system(s) and the federal government. It is the rare exception that finds ACOs delivering financial results. And the irony is that they are still fundamentally fee-for-service payment structures. Among the Medicare ACOs initiated in 2012, less than half lowered costs and only 25% slowed health spending enough to earn bonus payments in years 1 and 2.

At the time of this writing new rules are still emerging. The initial flaws we saw in the original legislation persist, and we expect these experiments to waste taxpayer dollars. Rather than improving health outcomes and lowering cost, we expect ACOs as envisioned by CMS to make things worse.

Laudable Goals

The stated goal of an ACO is laudable: to reduce costs and improve quality of care through cooperation and coordination among providers. While a number of potential models were proposed before the PPACA was passed, the legislation incorporated a model that didn't exist in practice. Each of the proposed models, including the one incorporated in PPACA, had a unique set of drawbacks, limitations, and difficulties. Creating a new organizational structure to remedy problems inherent in the existing system creates complications and risks. These complications, we envisioned, would likely result in the same or similar types of unintended consequences as earlier efforts—namely, consolidation and increased costs without improvements in quality.

It is unlikely under any circumstances that an untested organizational structure would be the most effective way to create accountability for care. In theory, the ACO program "promotes accountability for a patient population and coordinates items and services ... and encourages investment in infrastructure and redesigned care processes for high-quality and efficient service delivery."[6] However, as we predicted in 2010, the result has been a concentration of power—not in the most efficient and highest-quality healthcare organizations, but rather in the largest simply because they control large segments of the market. Since the law was passed, we've seen dramatic consolidation across the country as physicians—primary care and even specialties once fiercely independent such as cardiovascular and orthopedic surgeons—join the "safe haven" of employment by hospitals. But physicians aren't the only ones seeking safe haven.

Meanwhile, health systems are snapping up other systems, hospitals, physician practices and providers; targeting the financially strong; and further reducing competition. They are consolidating at an accelerating pace in an attempt to leverage scale to gain efficiencies and greater purchasing power. Of the roughly 5,000 hospitals in the country, approximately 41% were independent as of 2010, but merger and acquisition (M&A) activity has increased every year since then. The industry averaged 91 consolidations annually from 2010 to 2012, compared to an average of 55 in the 5 preceding years, and only approximately 12% of hospitals have a strategy to maintain complete independence.

And the fact is that they don't even need to own all ACO components. Boeing does not own all the manufacturers of its aircraft components, and automobile manufacturers don't own all the suppliers who contribute components for their cars. In healthcare, collaborative agreements would do just fine.

Instead, competition goes down, prices go up, and quality stands still. A study of 12 million claims in New Hampshire between 2007 and 2011 associated greater market concentration with higher charges and payments.[8] Another study, involving California hospitals between 2000 and 2010, found that competition results in higher quality and improved clinical outcomes.[9] In Massachusetts, the controversial merger of

Partners HealthCare and its Harvard-affiliated hospitals with the Hallmark Health System was challenged in that it would increase costs and likely not improve quality according to the Massachusetts Health Policy Commission.[10]

Already impacting local market prices, consolidation will soon make its higher prices felt nationally. That's because there's more to come.

The Healthcare Financial Management Association (HFMA) recently found more than 80% of senior financial executives reporting they had entered into an acquisition or affiliation arrangement or were actively considering or open to the idea.[11] More than 50% said they were open to acquiring or being acquired by another hospital system, citing economies of scale, cost reductions, and improved or sustained competitive position. Only 12% said they were interested in an ACO agreement that doesn't involve an acquisition.

The Federal Trade Commission (FTC) and the states with their own hospital competition laws are watching this acquisition activity closely. And, where laws may not be sufficient, political pressure may apply a brake (for example, with the Partners HealthCare controversy). However, these speed bumps are unlikely to stop consolidation.

At the end of the day, whether a healthcare system owns all of the pieces or creates strategic partnerships with service level agreements that have teeth, *all* systems will need to efficiently and effectively integrate the pieces into a coherent whole. Given the historically siloed and fragmented nature of healthcare delivery organizations—even within the same physical facility—this represents a very tall order. The magnitude of effective merger–acquisition integration should not be underestimated. And it's a problem that "ownership" will never address.

Any Provider Can Provide More Accountable Care

Nothing is keeping (or ever has kept) any provider from creating more accountable care. Whether or not an ACO structure is an effective means to achieve this end is irrelevant. Rather than focusing on restructuring, organizations should really be thinking about how to ensure that there is basic accountability across the system.

Let's take the example of aseptic technique and the basic act of *handwashing*, a perennial compliance problem for many healthcare delivery organizations across the country. In a nutshell, hospitals have been challenged to enforce the expectation that healthcare providers, including physicians, wash their hands between patient encounters. Failure to comply with the practice is associated with the spread of hospital-acquired infections (HAIs) and astronomical costs: tens of thousands of deaths per year. In 1999, the Institute of Medicine reported approximately 98,000 deaths annually from medical errors in the United States;[12] the *New England Journal of Medicine* reported that 25% of hospitalized patients are harmed by medical error.[13] The lack of public outrage regarding this is pretty remarkable.

Let's put this in proper perspective. In the 2010 Toyota brake recall, 37 people allegedly lost their lives due to negligence, and the *congressional* outrage was deafening. More recently, executives from GM and Takada were brought before Congress to testify about faulty ignition switches and air bags.

There hasn't been a corresponding outcry regarding healthcare safety issues despite the numbers. Ironically, PPACA provides for financial incentives to help hospitals reduce medication errors, HAIs, and so on. In industries subject to market forces, such tolerance wouldn't occur.

In high-tech, for instance, stringent procedures are expected and followed in making microchips. Everyone understands the costs to the business if the sterile field isn't maintained in designated *clean rooms*. In healthcare it hasn't worked the same way. Administrators express fatigue at trying to get physicians and other staff to comply with the basic rules, often putting responsibility for policy adherence on patients and visitors! This is clearly a failure of accountability—a failure of leadership to articulate a clear set of expectations and then consistently enforce a basic set of rules with consequences for nonadherence.

So, beyond basic individual accountability for legitimate procedural compliance, with or without an ACO, here's what it takes to provide accountable care more broadly:

1. **Establish key process metrics (e.g., costs by procedure, patient flow cycle time):** Use these data in real time to manage cost variability and to identify opportunities to improve efficiency.

2. **Establish meaningful quality and outcome metrics (e.g., patient cycle time to achieve key behavioral milestones such as "x" pounds lost in "y" time):** Use these data to manage variability as well as to improve quality and outcomes. Make performance matter.

3. **Develop predictive care paths that reflect evidence-based medicine:** Mapping out your process for delivering care is essential to ensuring collaboration and accountability, managing variability, and improving clinical practice across your organization. But it can't look like the efforts of yesteryear with minute provider prescriptive activity. Effective predictive care paths that reflect the continuum of care (vs. narrow episodes) are patient centered and reflect clinical decision making, thus allowing patients to better understand what's likely to happen *and* enabling physicians to do what's required for a specific patient. While achieving behavioral change can be difficult, incorporating evidence-based practice will support the objective of achieving better outcomes at lower cost. Additionally, external research can serve as a benchmark for your organization's improvement efforts.

4. **Develop competencies and incentives that drive increased accountability:** Engage in process redesign that really redesigns care across the continuum and change management that enables clinicians to be more

effective in monitoring, evaluating, and improving outcomes while controlling costs. Establish performance expectations and incentive structures to ensure greater ownership.

5. **Take steps to facilitate provider coordination:** Your organization should be a vehicle for effective, efficient, and transparent provider collaboration. Developing the IT and system integration capabilities to implement a uniform electronic health record (EHR) system that will allow providers to communicate with each other more seamlessly is key. However, it has to include tools that enable real-time feedback, reflect clinical decision making, and facilitate trend analysis across the continuum of care on a patient-specific and group basis.

These steps are not easy to operationalize. They require an integrated effort and shared accountability between administrative and clinical leaders. They also require organizations to set cost and quality goals that go hand in hand; they cannot be segregated and addressed independently. All decisions in the care model have to be in the dual context of the economic *and* clinical value that would result. Accountable care is about improving this dual value proposition.

What Are You Waiting For?

As we've suggested, there isn't anything holding health systems back. There is, though, a rare market opportunity to seize the initiative and deliver more accountable care. Improving accountability will differentiate organizations in an increasingly competitive market in which cost and quality outcomes are growing more critical to success.

How well each of these interventions works depends in part on the development of a new underlying payment mechanism—in other words, transparent, predictive, and inclusive at-risk provider accountability for comprehensive care ss the continuum, whether it's called population health, bundled pricing, or anything else. We explore that next.

Questions for Delivery Organizations

- ■ What is our organization's core strategy?
  - − Have we determined which businesses we will be in and those in which we won't?
- ■ Do our incentives and performance measures drive the desired behaviors?
  - − Are they aligned with organizational goals?
- ■ How effective is our IT system at providing real-time, usable data to individual providers?
  - − Are we able to track and measure meaningful outcomes?
- ■ Do we have key process metrics in place?
  - − Are we able to use the information real-time?
- ■ Do our care paths reflect the continuum of care?
  - − Do we have appropriate evidence to support their use?

Endnotes

1. Michael N. Abrams and Mark Morgan. "Adapting to the Changing Landscape of Healthcare." *H&HN Online*. April 2007.
2. Todd Park and Peter Basch. "A Historic Opportunity: Wedding Health Information Technology to Care Delivery Innovation and Provider Payment Reform." Center for American Progress. May 2009. https://www.americanprogress.org/wp-content /uploads/issues/2009/05/pdf/health_it.pdf.
3. George C. Halvorson. *Health Care Reform Now! A Prescription for Change*. San Francisco: Jossey-Bass. January 2007.
4. Rita E. Numerof. "Why Accountable Care Organizations Won't Deliver Better Health Care—And Market Innovation Will." The Heritage Foundation. April 2011. http://www.heritage.org /research/reports/2011/04/why-accountable-care-organizations -wont-deliver-better-health-care-and-market-innovation-will.

5. Elliott S. Fisher, Douglas O. Staiger, Julie P. W. Bynum, and Daniel J. Gottlieb. "Creating Accountable Care Organizations: The Extended Hospital Medical Staff." Health Affairs 26 (1): w44–w46. 2007. http://content.healthaffairs.org/cgi/reprint/26/1/w44.

6. One Hundred Eleventh Congress of the United States of America. "Medicare Shared Savings Program." Patient Protection and Affordable Care Act, H. R. 3590, Sec. 3022. January 2010.

7. Grace-Marie Turner, James C. Capretta, Thomas P. Miller, and Robert E. Moffit. *Why Obamacare Is Wrong for America.* New York: Harper Collins, p. 63. 2011. The US Department of Health and Human Services issued proposed rules for ACOs in the press release, "Affordable Care Act to Improve Quality of Care for People with Medicare" in March 2011.

8. Ha T. Tu and Johanna Lauer. "Impact of Health Care Price Transparency on Price Variation: The New Hampshire Experience." Center for Studying Health System Change, Issue brief no. 128. November 2009. http://www.hschange.com/CONTENT/1095/.

9. Matthew S. Lewis and Kevin E. Pflum. "Competition and Quality Choice in Hospital Markets." November 2014. http://www.kevinpflum.com/wp-content/uploads/quality_competition.pdf.

10. Commonwealth of Massachusetts Health Policy Commission. "Review of Partners HealthCare System's Proposed Acquisition of Hallmark Health Corporation: Preliminary Report." July 2014. http://www.mass.gov/anf/budget-taxes-and-procurement/oversight-agencies/health-policy-commission/20140702-phs-hallmark-preliminary-report.pdf.

11. Healthcare Financial Management Association. "Acquisition and Affiliation Strategies." HFMA's Value Project: Phase 3. June 2014. https://www.hfma.org/WorkArea/DownloadAsset.aspx?id=23451.

12. Janet M. Corrigan, Molla S. Donaldson, Linda T. Kohn, Tracy Mckay, and Kelly C. Pike. "To Err Is Human: Building a Safer Health System." Institute of Medicine. November 1999. https://www.iom.edu/~/media/Files/Report%20Files/1999/To-Err-is-Human/To%20Err%20is%20Human%201999%20%20report%20brief.pdf.

13. Christopher P. Landrigan, Gareth J. Parry, Catherine B. Bones, Andrew D. Hackbarth, Donald A. Goldmann, and Paul J. Sharek. "Temporal Trends in Rates of Patient Harm Resulting from Medical Care." *New England Journal of Medicine.* 363:2124–2134. 2010. http://www.nejm.org/doi/full/10.1056 /NEJMsa1004404?viewType=Print.

Chapter 6

The Next Chapter in Healthcare Delivery

At-Risk Contracting: The Next Step in Improving Quality and Reducing Cost

Although the main focus of reform legislation has been on improving access through regulation of healthcare insurance, its implications for the healthcare delivery industry are profound and will require truly innovative change. We have discussed throughout the book that fee-for-service payment is now being openly challenged—not because fee for service is problematic in and of itself, but rather because it has been *unconnected to outcomes and has driven up utilization*. The Patient Protection and Affordable Care Act (PPACA) authorized ongoing experimentation on alternative payment mechanisms that could profoundly alter market dynamics for healthcare delivery. Commercial insurers are in pursuit of similar objectives. This issue will not go away. Delivery organizations must choose to dramatically challenge key assumptions about the care they deliver or risk their financial viability.

As we argued in Chapter 5, most hospitals have learned to manage financially with the discounted fee-for-service model that's been in place, but that will soon be history. At this point, hospitals face a payer mix in which government's share is increasing, while its reimbursement rate continues to shrink. To make matters worse, private payers—no longer free to ride the cost curve up—will be following government's lead more than ever. With nowhere to turn to recover its losses on government reimbursement, the sector needs to develop new ways to manage costs and to make good on demands for increased quality. And it needs to be prepared to assume risk for the care it delivers in an increasingly transparent manner.

The answer is at-risk or *value-based payment* or, specifically, *bundled payment*[1] and capitation for a given population. Traditional approaches to cost management are clearly not up to the job and, anyway, providers may not have a choice because bundled payment or some form of capitation may become a competitive requirement. For most institutions, the decision to provide services in this way requires a paradigm change.

Bundled payment is a stepping stone to population health and is likely to be retained as a component in a broader population health context for cost-intensive acute care episodes. Whether the payment is for a narrow, acute episode with or without associated rehab or other postacute services or is more broadly defined to include the entire continuum of care for a therapeutic area (e.g., congestive heart failure [CHF]) or, even more broadly as in all the care for a defined set of people (i.e., "population health"), there are key principles and core competencies that will need to be mastered.

Why Will At-Risk Payment Models Do Any Better?

Promising to deliver a standardized set of services for a fixed price with specific quality guarantees will finally force care providers to align their efforts to contain underlying cost drivers. Taking action on such issues as overutilization, technology choices, and inadequate coordination across the care continuum can drive meaningful change in cost and quality, but only if providers are uniformly focused on these outcomes, without the distortions caused by the current fee-for-service approach. A concurrent focus on development of a differentiated clinical value case will ensure a balanced approach that doesn't forgo quality and safety for the sake of economic efficiency. Such efforts require major paradigm shifts in thinking at the top as well as new competencies and focus within the management infrastructure. Developing that infrastructure will require organizations to challenge historic norms and fundamental business assumptions, ultimately leading to the creation of a new business model.

Today, payment flows predominantly to acute care hospitals and their attached facilities (e.g., ERs, hospital-based ambulatory programs, even hospital-owned physician offices). On a proportionate basis, relatively less has flowed to prevention and postacute care as depicted in Figure 6.1.

Payment is site specific and driven by current procedural terminology code with diagnoses used to maximize reimbursement.

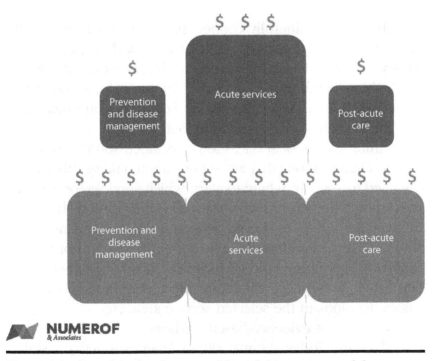

Figure 6.1   Transitioning from an old model to a new model.

? How to get $ for preventative over time ?
→ Point is get paid flat fee all, but to measure impact?

While coordination within sites of care has been notoriously poor, it is even worse *between* sites of care. The "new" model we advocate enables "lump-sum" payment on either a broad episodic bundled or capitated basis. In this model money is available to treat patients wherever it makes the most sense and is tied to performance outcomes. Removing differential payment by site gives providers the freedom to bring the right care to the right patient at the right time at the right location.

Imagine a future in which you e-mail questions to your physician about maintaining your blood pressure or diabetes. Your doctor is reimbursed under a primary care management agreement that takes into account outcomes for his panel. Gone are the days of "this office is closed and this phone does not take messages."

What It Will Take to Deliver Value Tomorrow

Any effort to meaningfully connect payment to outcomes will need to start with a defined set of services with a specified quality outcome delivered at a predictable, transparent price across the continuum of care. This is the basis for going at risk and is the *foundation for population health and bundled pricing.* The elements are described in Figure 6.2.

Defining the set of services to be included sounds easy. It's not. Organizations that are serious about taking this journey need to sort out where to start: which services (or service lines) should be chosen, what the end points for the "bundle" are, whether the focus should be inpatient or outpatient or both (across the continuum), whether employed and/or independent physicians should be included, whether predictive care paths are in place, whether evidence-based medicine guides decisions in the selected service area, etc.

The impact of evidence-based medicine will be crucial going forward. Today, the majority of Americans actually still believe we have the best healthcare in the world. This belief

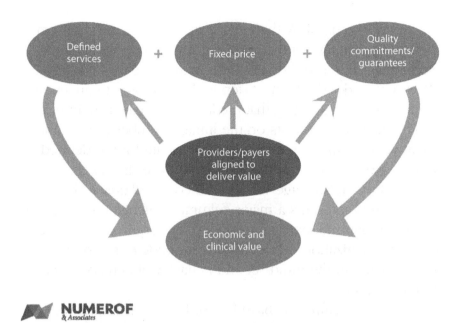

NUMEROF
& Associates

* **Figure 6.2   What it will take to deliver value *tomorrow*.**

is held despite the reality that life expectancy in this country is in the bottom third of the world, just behind Chile and
Costa Rica. And, as we outlined in Chapter 3, patient/consumer
attitude toward and usage of the healthcare system is a factor
in driving excessive cost and inappropriate usage of services.
According to one leading physician CEO, "the majority of
Americans ... don't understand that one-third of what we do
to them is unsupported and often harmful!" His concern is that
if we "flipped the switch" and every physician started practicing evidence-based medicine tomorrow, we'd have a revolu-
tion. Patients in this country do drive demand for excess drugs,
testing, devices, etc. Having to undergo watchful waiting when
they're expecting a script isn't always received well. Clearly,
managing patient/consumer expectations in this mix will be an
essential element in the "next chapter in healthcare delivery."

Once the service set is defined, *then* the costs can be
evaluated and the process to arrive at a fixed price can begin.
Understanding historic costs and reimbursement associated with

the services is critical. With the right analytic tools and platform there is no requirement that all of the data rest on the same electronic health record (EHR). Gaps in available data can also be effectively modeled. The next step in the process is to understand future revenues, assuming that predictive care paths are in place.

The next element rests on the limited number of relevant quality commitments/guarantees appropriate for the defined service. How to arrive at this is explored later in the chapter.

The ability to manage variation in cost *and* quality is key to success and represents a major cultural challenge for almost all delivery organizations. Failure to develop required disciplines will put organizations at risk. The magnitude of the problem is rooted in the mind-set and behavior of clinicians and administrators.

Historically, clinicians have focused on clinical questions at an individual patient level; they haven't been concerned with cost. It was deemed irrelevant to their decision making. Not surprisingly, most computerized physician order entry systems were designed without the capability to provide information about the cost of drugs, tests, etc.

In a similar vein, finance staff kept out of the clinical realm and were largely concerned about gross costs having to do with supplies, full-time equivalents (FTEs), overhead, technology and equipment, etc. Staff in most finance departments haven't been concerned about costs at the unit or patient level, and they haven't had the focus to understand costs across the continuum.

What finance and clinical staff look at is half the problem. The other half is the level of analysis that each considers and the experience that each brings to the task.

Physicians evaluate journal articles and make decisions based on their expertise because historically there wasn't a database. Medical education still largely functions as though this were still true. Most clinicians—unless they are researchers, too—don't pose questions to a database. Aggregate analysis has been left to journal study and meta-analysis.

So, in most organizations finance looks at everything financial, in the aggregate, and clinicians look at clinical anecdotes. Neither tends to pose questions to a database. Each tends not to have any questions that need to be answered with aggregate data analysis. No warehouse or EHR will fix this fundamental problem. Healthcare systems today typically have more data than they know what to do with. It's not about "more data"; it's about better, more precise information that's key to managing variation in cost/quality. This in turn is key to add. This is the future of healthcare. Sadly, managing variation in cost and quality is no one's job; questions about the average cost per case per doctor aren't often asked. And there's another problem: If a patient is in the hospital for a week and six different doctors order different things, to whom does the patient belong?

Finally, the economic and clinical value of the "product" must be defined in competitive terms. We take this up at the end of the chapter.

So How Do We Get There?

Healthcare executives who want to prepare for population health and bundled pricing models, regardless of how narrowly or broadly they define them, will need to take these five steps:

1. *Examine their current economic and clinical value proposition:* Healthcare delivery organizations will need to identify their own strengths and gaps. This will help identify where to start, what services are already delivering good outcomes, and where practices can be improved.
2. *Identify cost drivers in key services:* Clinical, technical, and process elements all factor into the total cost of healthcare. Providers will need to create the infrastructure to address inefficiencies and distinguish necessary from unnecessary variability.

3. *Develop predictive care paths:* Predictive care paths should capture key decision points that have an impact on costs and outcomes and should include differentiators that set the delivery organization apart. They should be patient centric—better yet, consumer centric—and map care from the consumer's perspective across the episode. These will need to be implemented across the continuum of care to help track variability in cost and quality.

4. *Collaborate with payers:* In order to move reimbursement away from episodic care, providers implementing bundled pricing will need to collaborate with payers. By examining the economic and clinical value of the services included in the bundle and systematically capturing key differentiators, providers will be able to make a strong value case for the care they deliver.

5. *Continuously monitor and update bundled services:* This includes both internal monitoring for compliance and external review, to ensure that their organizations stay current with ongoing research. This will help guarantee that treatment protocols continue to deliver better care at lower cost.

Healthcare executives *must* prepare now for new payment models, because adapting will not be easy or quick. They will have to implement integrated, systemic changes to remain viable. Times of transition can be extremely challenging, but also extraordinarily rewarding for those who seize the opportunities.

Cost transparency will push healthcare systems to transition from fee-for-service reimbursement to value-based payment. Key to success is knowing how to navigate this. Facing a lot of uncertainty about the future, hospital leaders are asking the right question: "How do I succeed in today's fee-for-service system, while preparing for but not getting too far ahead of value-based payment?" The question has become more pressing since the Centers for Medicare & Medicaid Services (CMS) and leading payers and providers announced ambitious value-based payment goals. The new goals clearly increase the pressure on hospitals to change, but leave uncertainties about when and how to transition, especially at a granular level.

Fortunately, the steps we outlined will help improve performance now, even in a fee-for-service environment, while preparing executives to assume risk in value-based payment models. As we described, these steps focus on understanding underlying cost structures, managing variation in cost and quality, and delivering predictable, transparent outcomes. Unfortunately, as we've discussed, the business model of healthcare has not valued these elements, so for most healthcare executives this is foreign territory. They understandably don't want to get ahead of themselves, and many of them don't score high on a risk-taking scale.

Hospital administrators are by nature risk averse. In the 1990s, many healthcare executives lost their jobs after taking on risk and failing to provide long-term solutions. So, it should come as no surprise that much of the healthcare world is still functioning on volume and is hesitant to transition to value-based care.

When it comes to making this transition, there is a notion among healthcare executives that they're having to run the rapids with each foot in a different canoe. This idea is ubiquitous, dangerous, and, in many respects, self-defeating. It seems to rationalize failure to take meaningful action. If executives believe that success in a fee-for-service environment associated with transparency is fundamentally at odds with a risk-based approach and, ultimately, capitation, the canoe image may have resonance. However, we don't believe this to be the case.

In just about every other industry, transparency is an easy concept. A consumer knows what he or she is purchasing, the implied guarantee that's offered with that purchase, and the mode of recourse if satisfaction isn't achieved. That's been difficult to come by in healthcare delivery, which is so removed from a true market-based model. It's time for providers to offer a more transparent approach to business with increased accountability and efficiency.

St. Elsewhere: A Case Study in Bundled Pricing

To illustrate the steps for creating a bundled price, let's examine the experience of a specialty national hospital that we'll call *St. Elsewhere.*

St. Elsewhere competes by attracting patients across the United States who have a local community care provider option. From its inception, St. Elsewhere offered something different: a more integrated and comprehensive care approach that it believed improved patient outcomes and that patients experienced as centered on them.

To succeed in this effort and capture market share, the hospital needed to create a compelling argument for both the *cost and value* of its unique approach. This required:

Establishing predictive care paths: St. Elsewhere needed to ensure that treatment protocols reflecting the practice of its unique course of treatment would be followed in a consistent fashion. Reducing practice variability and understanding the causes of it are essential to any attempt at bundled payment.

Creating an economic and clinical value model: St. Elsewhere also needed to define the key economic and clinical components of value to patients and payers that were realized with its unique care approach. This model guided the development of the evidence needed to demonstrate better health outcomes and commensurate value for its price. More importantly, the model served as a basis for setting a higher bar in the industry, redefining the quality metrics that would be used as a comparator between institutions.

Creating a resource utilization model: St. Elsewhere needed to identify the key drivers of treatment cost and variability. This required an understanding of the organizational infrastructure (e.g., data and people resources, management tools for understanding variability, mechanisms for managing variability) necessary to implement fiscally safe new pricing. The resulting model enabled setting a transparent, fixed price for the total course of treatment. Setting this price required certainty that it would cover predictable costs and provide an adequate margin, without building in a safety factor that would make the bundled price cost prohibitive.

Taking a Proactive Approach to a Market in Transition

In a market demanding better outcomes at lower cost, St. Elsewhere is now poised to respond to this demand and to accelerate growth at healthy margins. As healthcare costs have spiraled out of control and the daily headlines shout out the latest quality snafus, it was inevitable that demand for better care at lower cost would escalate. St. Elsewhere anticipated and prepared to meet this inevitable demand, investing in the models and infrastructure to develop a better care approach and to prove it. As a result, where other hospitals see a gathering storm of reduced reimbursements and shrinking margins, St. Elsewhere sees an opportunity to grow share and preserve margin.

Competing with a Bundled Price

Defining a care path and corresponding price doesn't necessarily result in growth or improved margins.[2] The care that's offered has to be differentiated, delivering more value as defined by the healthcare consumer.

The market share winners in this environment will be those providers who can define and deliver on better health outcome metrics, and these need to go beyond traditional mortality and morbidity measures. Managing health to avoid expensive inpatient care is one of the most obvious consumer objectives.

Competing with a bundled price also requires considerable transparency of information responsive to the needs of a more engaged, value-conscious consumer. The customer of the future wants comparable evidence of health outcomes delivered for a set total price. As in any other market, the winning supplier will have the best answer to the question, "What am I getting for my money?"

Can we answer as an org?

Building the Value Narrative for Consumers, Employers, and Insurers[3]

Customer expectations of healthcare providers are clearly increasing. The national debate about skyrocketing costs, concerns about quality, and lack of transparency have placed healthcare delivery in the crosshairs. This is reinforced by the fact that consumers are shouldering more responsibility for the cost of insurance and treatment. Employees insured under group plans are paying a larger share of premiums, and are migrating to high-deductible plans that trade lower premiums for more exposure to care expenditures. With 30% of covered employees enrolled in such plans,[4] sensitivity to price and other value elements is growing. These consumers are demanding more from providers—either directly or through their employers and insurers.

Providers need to be aware of these emerging market requirements and build their competitive capability to meet these needs. Those providers that can demonstrate that they deliver greater value—in terms of both cost and quality—will be able to differentiate themselves and generate sustainable competitive advantage in a challenging marketplace.

Some providers may feel that they have insulated themselves from the demands of the marketplace through the consolidation noted earlier in Chapter 5, either as part of accountable care organization (ACO) formation or outright merger. As this trend continues, the large, fully integrated hospital systems may feel that, as the only player in town, they have a stronger negotiating position with insurers and that patients have no choice but to come to them.

While this may be true for certain services such as emergency room care, it is also true that, for most treatments, many patients and employers are willing to consider traveling for their care if they can get better value. Many providers have created a brand for themselves that extends the geographic catchment area nationally and even internationally: Consider the Cleveland Clinic, Mayo Clinic, M. D. Anderson, Sloan-Kettering, and others. Large employers have negotiated directly with these hospitals for specialized care for their workers across the country.

Who (Else) Is Making the Transition?

Even in more traditional healthcare provider settings, hospitals have begun to compete in new ways. An increasing number of hospitals are redefining competition to include employer procedural carve-outs and even going directly to consumers. These hospitals are, in effect, leveraging their brands, quality, and cost effectiveness to create preferred relationships with national employers in specific treatment areas. For example, Lowe's and Boeing have entered into agreements with Cleveland Clinic for fully covered cardiac surgery. Lowe's recently expanded its plan to include chronic pain management and spinal surgery. PepsiCo has a similar arrangement with Johns Hopkins Hospital that covers employees' cardiac or complex joint surgeries. Recently, Walmart announced that employees covered under the company's health insurance will now be able to receive, at no cost, heart and spine surgeries at one of six health systems identified as "centers of excellence" for each service.

Cleveland Clinic has similar programs for employees of Kohl's, Rich Products, and Alliance Oil. Other companies have or are developing similar arrangements with other hospitals. This trend is not limited to a small number of high-profile hospitals. Other health systems are also working to establish similar relationships with companies and payers. Grocery store chain Kroger Co. has agreements with 19 hospitals for specific services, and medical benefits companies have brokered similar arrangements between employers and at least several dozen hospitals across the country.

These developments have important implications for executives and board members who are responsible for ensuring the continued viability of their healthcare systems. Looking to the future and ensuring the identification of risks and opportunities is part of that fiduciary responsibility. Demands for value already are having significant impacts and changing market dynamics. Providers that can demonstrate their value in terms of high-quality care and patient outcomes are now competing for patients on a national basis. The nature of competition is being redefined at an accelerating rate. Many provincial healthcare systems will pay a price for ignoring these new market rules.

Not only are these providers competing nationally in new markets, but they're also using new payment models to do so—namely, bundled rates or fixed payment amounts. Hospitals can ensure a stream of business from these arrangements based on their demonstrated quality. Employers see a number of benefits, including a fixed price, overall cost savings, and better care for employees. Patients benefit by receiving care from providers with demonstrated quality of care and fewer complications. These providers save both employers and patients from the costs of additional procedures or complications.

Payers, increasingly under pressure to reduce costs, are aggressively renegotiating reimbursement contracts with providers. They have claims data on hospitals and their competitors on their side. Without compelling evidence and data, hospitals will be negotiating from a position of weakness.

How Should Hospitals and Health Systems Change?

Many healthcare systems remain successful despite the massive changes the field is beginning to experience. As a result, leaders are often reluctant to take bold steps to prepare for a new environment. But as the previous sections should demonstrate, this "wait and see" tactic is extraordinarily risky. Healthcare delivery organizations that are slow to meet demands for "better care at lower cost" by shifting from a volume to value model will be left behind. The transition is neither quick nor painless, and those who wait too long to "start their engines" may run out of road. At some point payers will drop or skip over providers that cannot demonstrate value and quality. Changing incentives to close the looming value gap between market expectations and what their organizations deliver is a critical job for healthcare leaders who want to ensure continued financial viability.

Going forward, healthcare leadership must ensure that their organizations have a market-based, patient-centered approach that provides demonstrated value to stakeholders. As we noted in Chapter 2, in every other industry, advancing technology has generally resulted in lower costs and improved products and services. It has not worked that way in healthcare.

Without a true market-based approach to healthcare delivery, it will not be possible to address cost and quality issues in a meaningful way. And, as the previous section illustrates, there are healthcare systems today that can demonstrate their value to key stakeholders, most notably large employers, and compete for patients in new ways on a national basis. Transparency, increased accountability, and a consumer-centered model for healthcare are quickly becoming the basis for achieving the goal of better health outcomes at lower cost.

To compete in a market-based, patient-centered model, providers must invest in the infrastructure necessary to demonstrate better care. Providers need to be able to offer care that is differentiated, delivering more value as defined by the healthcare consumer. As we suggested earlier in the chapter, a starting point is "bundled payments" and expanding the set of services to include larger and larger "bundles" across the continuum of care—perhaps starting with acute episodes and rapidly moving to chronic care management and "population health" on a per member per month (PMPM) basis tied to outcomes.

Indeed, Cleveland Clinic, Mayo Clinic, and other health systems are providing value to stakeholders by using a bundled price, which is not necessarily the least expensive, for services in certain areas. These providers can define and deliver on better health outcome metrics. We expect more innovative leaders, large and small—physician groups and health systems—to accelerate the move in this direction.

How Is Value Defined?

Through extensive research, providers need to understand how each group of stakeholders defines value. While there is a common desire for better outcomes at lower cost, the emphasis placed on each element of the value story will vary by segment and market. Providers need to identify the components that resonate most with their target audience and support their story with data. Payers are under increasing cost pressures themselves; in the absence of outcomes data, they will assume that all providers are equal and drive reimbursements to the lowest price possible.

As one frustrated healthcare executive recently said to us, "The payers just expect us to take a 30% haircut and won't even guarantee a volume increase to offset the loss … that's NO way to run a hospital." We think this is a telling comment about the business model in healthcare and the inability of many to see that the future isn't about running a hospital!

Likewise, consumers (employers and patients) want to see outcomes data—on issues like length of stay, recovery time, and complication rates—to help them select their providers.

As healthcare cost inflation causes them to bear more of the cost of their own healthcare, consumers will examine the comparative value provided by a delivery organization, just as they do for most major purchases. This will be crucial on the marketing front. This value story will enable stakeholders to select one facility over another. Also, with the growth of transparency, a value story will be required to justify price differentials between providers. And more transparency is coming. If hospitals don't proactively tell their value story, others will define it for them.

The recent decision by CMS to make public the rates charged by participating hospitals clearly indicates that, from a public policy perspective, competition is regarded as a tool to be used to restrain price growth.

Aside from such mandated transparency, other sources are springing up to help consumers evaluate comparative cost and quality for the care they need. The Leapfrog Group and *Consumer Reports* are both compiling and publishing quality data on hospitals across the country. At the state level, a website called AZ Hospital Compare allows consumers to compare more than 100 hospitals around Arizona. In addition to reporting outcomes, the site lists what each hospital bills for each of several hundred different medical procedures and it spells out what each hospital reports the procedure actually costs it. Any institution that does not provide such economic and clinical value data—some of which are now mandated by law—risks being omitted from consideration and thus losing out on potential patients. Past reputation will be insufficient unless decision makers can see *data* to support their claims.[5]

The Future of Rural Hospitals: Are They Still Viable?

This chapter wouldn't be complete if we failed to address some of the challenges facing small rural institutions. They, like their urban counterparts, face the same regulatory pressures and competitive issues. However, unlike the larger institutions, with few exceptions these organizations don't have the volume and financial reserves to manage through difficult times. Some have been absorbed by larger national systems (e.g., CHI, CHS, Ascension) but for many, even those that are now owned by a corporate parent, they face an uncertain future squeezed by the forces depicted in Figure 6.3.

Communities and the patients served by rural hospitals have taken great pride in these institutions. As medicine has advanced they have been challenged to make investments needed to keep up with the latest technology and sophisticated, highly trained staff. Assuming they could make the investments, the question is whether they see enough volume to sustain skills and ensure optimal outcomes. Add the ability of emerging technology to deliver care remotely and there's even more pressure on these institutions.

In the wake of transparency and emerging competition from retail players, what does the future hold? Clearly, each situation needs to be evaluated on its own merits. That said, we predict that retail entities can and will chip away at the larger segments of this market, leaving rural hospitals with the challenge of identifying what they can do well cost effectively. It will mean even rethinking their ability to manage trauma, potentially treating patients in sophisticated mobile vans and air-lifting them to the nearest tertiary facility.

For those rural markets that are large enough, retail entities may chip away at common and routine care. The complex and nonroutine will be left to the hospital, much like ambulatory surgery centers have "creamed" the market over the

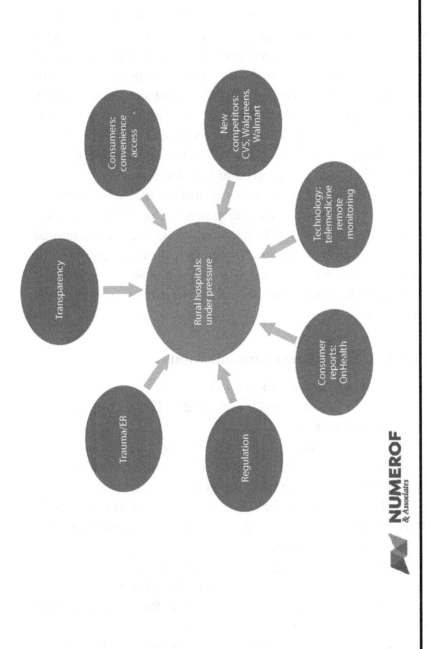

Figure 6.3   Intersection of rural hospitals and retail medicine.

last 10–15 years. As these retail centers deliver an acceptable experience at the patient level that wins and maintains loyalty at a reasonable price, even rural centers won't be immune, just because they have a geographic niche. It's just a matter of time. Commercial entities will start with the low-hanging fruit in denser metropolitan areas. As they develop these new health-care businesses they will look to other places to deploy capital.

Rural hospitals are well plugged into the local communities they serve. Their auxiliaries, volunteers, and patients take great pride in these institutions. They wouldn't be the low-hanging fruit. That said, Walmart intruded into local markets and won the day with pricing, convenience, and choice. Will Walmart, CVS, Walgreens, or another entity win the day with pricing, convenience, choice, and better quality? As these commercial entities learn more about the businesses they've chosen to be in and as technology advances, making it easier to operate cost effectively, rural hospitals will be that much more at risk of market erosion.

 Questions for Delivery Organizations

- ■ What is our organization's value story?
  - – Does it resonate with consumers? Employers? Payers? Our employees?
- ■ What data do we have to support our value story?
  - – How are we differentiated from our competition?
- ■ Are we thinking about a merger?
  - – If so, is there a plan in place to ensure that it works?
- ■ Is our system ready to create a bundle or other form of risk-based relationship?
  - – How well defined are the services?
  - – What's the price and what's included in it?
  - – What are we willing to commit to for a certain price? For a certain premium?
  - – Are we engaging with the right person at the payer organization (or employer) to move this idea forward?

Endnotes

1. Eric Abrams. "Bundled Pricing: Strategies for Success." *Becker's Hospital Review.* November 2011. http://www.beckershospital review.com/hospital-management-administration/bundled -pricing-strategies-for-success.html.
2. Rita E. Numerof and Bill Ott. "The Case for Bundled Payments." *H&HN Online.* July 2010.
3. Rita E. Numerof and Christopher de Wolff. "Building the Value Narrative for Employers and Insurers." *H&HN Online.* October 2013.
4. Rita Pyrillis. "High-Deductible Health Plans Gaining Employer Support." *Workforce.* March 2013. http://www .workforce.com/article/20130322/NEWS02/130329983/high -deductible-health-plans-gaining-employer-support.
5. Arizona Department of Health Services. "2011 AZ Hospital Compare." http://pub.azdhs.gov/hospital-discharge-stats /2011/index.html.

Chapter 7

A Brave New World for Payers

Introduction

As we've been arguing, the United States has reached the point where key constituent groups have significant economic and financial concerns—providers and physicians about their revenues, and payers and patients about the affordability of care. At the heart of any discussion about healthcare reform is an increasingly clear mandate to provide *better care at lower cost.* Health policy shifts are placing increased accountability and cost pressures on providers to improve patient safety, quality of care, and consistency of care delivered, and payers and consumers alike are increasing their demands for improved economic and clinical value.

After years of steadily building pressure from escalating patient care and subsequent healthcare insurance premium costs, the U.S. healthcare system has reached a tipping point. With the passage of the Patient Protection and Affordable Care Act of 2010 (PPACA) and the Healthcare and Education Reconciliation Act of 2010 (HCERA), the country has irrevocably acknowledged that change must occur, and quickly, to head off financial insolvency. While the legislation left no healthcare stakeholder untouched, the most profound interventions were reserved for insurers.

Let's face it: insurers are the one segment of the healthcare industry that everyone has loved to hate. Employers blame insurers for the rising costs of healthcare; physicians and hospitals blame insurers for their declining reimbursement rates, consumers blame insurers for lack of sufficient coverage, and many decry inadequate services as well as opaque rules and payment terms; and policy makers think insurers make too much money.

The legislation was intended to disrupt this status quo, and it has certainly done so. It forced insurance companies to reassess their business models, identify new market opportunities, and take action or suffer financial consequences. New regulatory requirements imposed constraints on investment, and by standardizing benefit profiles, accelerated the trend toward commoditization of products. By the same token, the legislation has created opportunities, especially for those able to recognize them and translate their implications into action in a timely way.

Adapting to the Changing Landscape of Healthcare Insurance

Clearly, the healthcare insurance business model today stands in the crosswinds of market and nonmarket forces.[1] On the market side, there is now a daunting challenge to remain competitive in order to sustain, much less increase, market share and margin. The constantly escalating costs of healthcare, increasingly passed on to consumers by their employers and health insurers, have pushed consumers to the brink, as noted in Chapter 3 (see Figure 3.1). Employers are seeking ways to reduce costs by reducing coverage options, increasing copays and deductibles, and moving to narrow networks, thereby limiting the choices their employees have for insurance.

On the nonmarket side, PPACA took up the cause of those who had fallen through the cracks of America's private healthcare insurance system. From a beachhead of Medicare and Medicaid, the legislation established a path to mandate insurance coverage for all Americans, without the constraint of having to remain financially viable at the end of the day.

As we laid out in Chapter 2, although the national debate over healthcare reform is far from over, there are some fundamental things about which most people agree—the need to achieve better care outcomes at lower cost, and the need to change what gets paid for and how. Increasing demand for value, new competitors, and increasingly intrusive government intervention all make for an unsustainable private insurance business model. Clearly, something has to change.

The operating environment for insurers has been characterized by conflicting pressures and new demands, as depicted in Figure 7.1. Insurers have faced conflicting

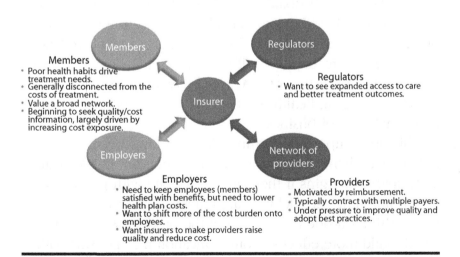

Members
- Poor health habits drive treatment needs.
- Generally disconnected from the costs of treatment.
- Value a broad network.
- Beginning to seek quality/cost information, largely driven by increasing cost exposure.

Regulators
- Want to see expanded access to care and better treatment outcomes.

Employers
- Need to keep employees (members) satisfied with benefits, but need to lower health plan costs.
- Want to shift more of the cost burden onto employees.
- Want insurers to make providers raise quality and reduce cost.

Providers
- Motivated by reimbursement.
- Typically contract with multiple payers.
- Under pressure to improve quality and adopt best practices.

Figure 7.1 The conflicting pressures for insurers. (Adapted from *Healthcare at a Turning Point: A Roadmap for Change,* Rita E. Numerof and Michael N. Abrams, CRC Press, Boca Raton, FL, 2013.)

demands from customers (employers and members) and network providers: members and employers want insurers to help deliver higher-quality health outcomes at lower cost, but also want insurers to maintain the broadest possible networks; providers want higher reimbursement for medical treatments, but employers and members want lower costs and broad networks. These conflicting demands can result in reduced leverage for insurers, in other words, pushing providers too hard to make improvements in cost and quality may result in their leaving the network, reducing its attractiveness.

The disconnect between the decision makers (patients and providers) and the source for payment (insurers and employers) is forcing insurers to intervene as never before to slow the trend of rising treatment costs. Mandates emanating from PPACA, such as medical loss ratios (MLRs), the essential healthcare benefits (EHB) package, insurance exchanges, and accountable care organizations (ACOs) further complicate the ability of insurers to respond to these conflicting pressures, introducing additional risk and uncertainty. Nontraditional organizations like hospitals and IT companies are moving into the space long held by commercial insurers. Some major IT providers and others are developing models to "manage" the cost of healthcare, support self-insured programs, and develop third-party administrator (TPA) capability. Conversely, insurers are purchasing healthcare delivery organizations, blurring traditional lines of business.

This opens up an opportunity for insurers who want to differentiate themselves competitively to build network loyalty and superior margins if they can collaborate with providers in developing new care delivery approaches. This requires that payers think outside the box about the products/services provided, build more effective communication mechanisms with providers, and leverage technology and data assets to deliver outcomes of mutual interest.

Needed Here, Too: A Transfusion of Fresh Thinking

As the financial dynamics of the market have become increasingly challenging, much of the healthcare insurance industry has defined its strategic response as doing what it's always done, but for less. Insurers have gotten tougher in negotiations with providers and employers in order to pay for less. And repeated internal cost-cutting efforts have come and gone, usually with limited long-term impact and often contributing to an increasingly cynical and jaded workforce (with a predictable negative effect on customer service).

To get off this cost-cutting spiral—which isn't much help in winning and keeping customers—healthcare insurers need to redefine the business they are in. While there is no single solution or model that guarantees success, it's clearly time for some new ideas.

Rethinking the *Customer*

Most people get their healthcare insurance from their employer. This model started when employers could attract and retain employees with a benefit of fully paid health insurance, which at the time cost less than competing for employees based on compensation alone. This model worked well for insurers, who could focus on the employer as *the customer* and differentiate their insurance offerings based on service rather than price. The model also worked well for employers, who could tie employees into attractive benefit packages. What this model never did was to focus on or satisfy the varied needs of the healthcare consumer/employee.

Now employers would love to get out of the insurance benefits business. Every calendar year is another exercise in explaining to financially stressed employees why they have to pay a larger share of more expensive insurance. And when these employers meet with insurance companies the focus of negotiations is on price, rather than value-added service. The result is that health insurance has suddenly become mostly a commoditized business; it is increasingly difficult to sustain, much less improve margins.

Those employers staying in the healthcare benefits game are demanding more value for the dollars they spend and are actively seeking new options to provide them that value. Some large, self-insured employers have signed up directly with "centers of excellence" and integrated delivery networks as noted in Chapter 6, choosing to define their own provider networks and gain greater control over their healthcare spending. Others are working with new entities trying to obviate the need for the traditional insurer model. This clearly creates new sources of competition for payers, and it's a statement of dissatisfaction with the current model.

Companies in other consumer product industries have become very innovative in selling to their "real" customers directly, eliminating traditional *pseudocustomer* distribution channels when they no longer add value. If employers were to exit as mediators of individual coverage, payers could wind up understanding their customer needs better, tailoring products to those needs, and capturing a high share of distinct subsets of customers who will pay for their brand and stay loyal to it. Rethinking the *customer* would be an equally suitable place to start for healthcare insurers as they define a more viable business model.

Employers and consumers are reacting to the rising costs of health plans that have followed or exceeded medical cost inflation. Employees now shoulder a larger portion of the costs of their care in the form of higher premiums, copays, and deductibles, and this is driving a consumer orientation trend in the market. Patients, as consumers, increasingly want to purchase healthcare services much like they make other purchasing decisions, by evaluating cost and quality in pursuit of value. Because of this, consumers are seeking more transparency about care services, options, and value. As demands for transparency grow, demonstrating quality in terms that matter to consumers will become a factor for choosing not just providers, but also payers. And, insurers will need to improve their image with consumers, building trust and improving accessibility.

New policies and regulations such as health insurance exchanges have also accelerated the move to greater transparency, putting more pressure on payers to demonstrate sustainable differentiation. The jury is still out with regard to both public and private exchanges. Administrative fees tend to be higher than those for nonexchange products in some markets, and the claim that they will stabilize healthcare costs is yet to be proven. According to government data, the average premium paid by those signing up through the federal Healthcare. gov site was $101 per month for 2015 after taking into account subsidies. This reflects a 23% increase over the year before.[2] The increase reflects two important changes: Subsidies went down, and premiums went up by 5%. This trend is projected to continue into 2016, in part as a reflection of PPACA insurance bailout programs phasing out and a projected increase in insurance costs. Both trends translate into higher premiums and more burden for consumers.

Rethinking *Products*

Earlier in this book we discussed two significant elements that have converged to fuel the drive for healthcare reform. One element is the yearly, sometimes double-digit increase in premium costs. The other element is the macro statistical picture indicating that Americans (or their employers or government) pay more for healthcare than consumers in other countries do, but aren't necessarily receiving better care by any outcome measure currently in use. A key underlying assumption derived from these statistics is that a significant number of healthcare services being provided—and paid for—is either unnecessary or ineffective. As we noted in Chapter 2, many industry leaders estimate that 30%–40% of costs are due to services not needed, upcoding, medical errors, and process issues. Even new preventive screenings covered by PPACA have added to the proliferation of unneeded services as "positive" findings often result in expensive, potentially harmful follow-up procedures.[3]

As consumers continue to feel firsthand the increasing burden of their healthcare costs, they are beginning to act more and more like customers, demanding value for their money and proof of that value. Providers and insurers have to engineer the right products to remain competitive in this market. Leading companies are starting to collaborate to develop and implement plans for evidence-based medicine and disease management programs that are less costly and more effective over a consumer's lifetime.

One of the most critical success factors for such programs will be the proper alignment of payment with results, providing incentives for the right provider *and* consumer behaviors in order to achieve measurably better health outcomes.

These new types of products will also challenge healthcare insurers to change how they measure success. There is general agreement that integrated care over a continuum will result in better outcomes at lower cost. This isn't possible without long-term customer retention and metrics based on total cost versus episodic costs. Insurers will need to learn how to measure and quantify the lifetime value of a customer and make decisions accordingly.

Implications for Healthcare Insurers

Leading insurers must commit to *bending the trend*—in other words, slowing the growth in treatment costs, working to reduce healthcare expenditures, and improving health and care outcomes *across the continuum of care.* In a nutshell, it's about creating value. Insurers can directly slow the growth in treatment costs by denying reimbursement for clearly unnecessary care such as medical errors, adverse events, or fraud and waste. The Centers for Medicare & Medicaid Services (CMS) has paved the way to make this normatively acceptable by introducing never events and penalties for readmissions as described in Chapter 5. Since insurers typically lack direct leverage, they have to find new ways to influence behaviors and choices on the part of employers, their members, and providers.

Payers have the power to influence the behavior of policy holders and network providers. They can influence, but not control, the choices made by employers and members by offering lower-cost alternatives, highlighting star performers in their network, and rewarding members for accepting accountability for their health. They can also influence providers to adopt higher-quality care processes and other methods that result in lower treatment costs and better outcomes across the continuum of care, essentially demonstrating greater value (like a more time-intensive and therefore "time-expensive" primary care visit) that may actually result in better care and less overall expense because of fewer unnecessary tests and better coordination of care. This would include paying for the time to actually coordinate care, educate patients, and have phone consults for routine questions.

If insurers are serious about driving change in healthcare delivery they *need to take a leadership role in creating a new basis for payment.* Reduced treatment costs mean reduced revenue for providers and lower premiums for insurers. Beyond clearly unnecessary care, other reductions in medical treatment costs translate to lower revenues for physicians and hospitals. This challenge to their business models has to be addressed in some way to overcome resistance to change. But the challenge is not the insurer's alone. All market factors point to lower reimbursement rates and more restrictive access.[4]

If medical treatment costs drop significantly, under PPACA rules today, insurers would have to lower health plan premiums to stay in compliance with MLR minimums. A reduction in the volume of claims may or may not mean any savings in administrative costs for a given insurer. One opportunity rests in dramatically improved efficiency through new payment approaches that address *outcomes* rather than volume and specific codes for given procedures.

The trend is toward further commoditization of health plans, *so insurers must leverage their networks as a source of differentiation.* A key challenge for any commercial payer is whether it can turn its network into a competitive differentiator with qualities beyond breadth—such as overall efficiency or higher quality of care. Those payers that can engage in closer collaboration with providers will build network loyalty, minimizing disruption for its employer customers and their employees and reducing internal costs related to network churn.

Identifying and developing relationships with organizations that can help them accelerate the goal of improved outcomes and lower cost has become a focus for payers. Although most have been reticent in the past to push providers to change their models for care delivery, PPACA has given them some cover to create innovative new risk-based models with selected provider partners. How these relationships are structured is critical to ensuring alignment and movement toward common goals.

In early 2015 CMS announced[5] its plan to shift half of its non-managed-care spending (approximately $362 billion) into risk-based contracts (e.g., episode-based bundled payments and ACOs) that have financial reward and penalties based on cost control and improved quality, by 2018. Despite legitimate concerns about the quality measures in use and the extent to which improved outcomes *and* cost will really be the focus, the move points to a real shift in the business of healthcare. CMS's commitment was followed by similar pledges from major payers, including UnitedHealthcare, Aetna, and Anthem, to increase the use of cost and quality incentives. At the same time, the Health Care Transformation Task Force was created, representing a wide range of industry stakeholders, and chaired by the CEO of a not-for-profit health system operating in approximately 20 states.[6] While it's not the first such group, it has publicly committed to shifting 75% of its members' business to risk-based contracts with incentives for improved health outcomes, quality, and cost management by 2020.

What Payers Can Do

In light of all the recent healthcare changes, many insurers have developed a range of initiatives to develop more strategic relationships with hospital systems and independent physician practices. The goal of these initiatives is to generate better health outcomes at lower cost. One of the problems is that most insurers have attempted to do this incrementally within the existing business model. This approach, while it makes sense on one level—because it's a continuation of what's been done—is guaranteed not to work because it's a continuation of the current business model.

To really create better health outcomes at lower cost, the approach has to address the continuum of care over a broader time horizon than what has been previously considered. Yet, if we introduce change but we don't address the underlying causes of inefficiency, duplication, and error, we won't solve the problem!

Let's take the case of a healthcare delivery client that's trying to negotiate a bundled price with payers and employers on a direct basis. The client is interested in, willing, and able to create a predictive price and assume risk. It has defined comprehensively what will be included with deliverables and metrics on the back end. Employers—who care about their employees—are very excited and open to this model. But if the next conversation is with a benefits person on the employer side, then they find themselves back in the old model because the benefits person doesn't know what to do with this "exception."

To move to a different model, there has to be a bridge from the executive who's interested in introducing a new model to the people who operationally execute agreements with providers. The same dynamic occurs between providers and insurers. At the strategy level, executives are interested in new payment models: defining and paying for care differently. However, where claims get adjudicated, the systems are already set up and people are incented to perform in the old model and can't or won't process exceptions.

So what are insurers doing as we move to bundled payments? Some insurers define bundled payments and risk sharing with providers as a roll-up of all the current procedural terminology (CPT) codes that are used today with a total reduced cost, essentially putting the risk back on the provider—an approach unlikely to get much traction on the provider side. On the other hand, insurers are understandably wary and would be ill advised to create a blank check and hand it over to a provider. Insurers have been concerned with the practice of upcoding and unnecessary utilization that has lined providers' pockets for years.

So, what's the solution here? Clearly, any solution requires the development of partnerships with selected providers who are able to bring innovation and accountability for outcomes and who are also willing to accept payment outside the typical adjudication system. To create the necessary infrastructure, insurers will need to step out of their silos and the usual method of doing business. They'll need to think through and identify exceptions and then define how they'll address them, probably doing "work-arounds" in order to prove the concept before any system redesign.

Develop Partnerships with Providers

During the course of our work with insurers, we've run into some common themes as insurers structure strategic initiatives and operationalize systems to support them. While many of the initiatives in recent years have been designed to encourage providers to make desired changes in business processes and care delivery (primarily to drive down costs), many insurers have failed to adequately engage providers in the change process. Doing so requires an understanding of what providers value and then finding ways to make those elements part of the deal. Since success is so dependent on the ability of network providers to change the way they deliver care, insurers will need to provide more structure for providers in order to ensure positive outcomes.

Historically, insurers have not been successful in driving change through providers, so doing "what we've always done" is not a solution! If providers agree to adopt performance-based contracts and fail, they are likely to demand a return to annual escalators. Insurers need to review their network strategies to ensure that they are driving the *right* outcomes and addressing the needs of *all* stakeholders impacted.

Three critical strategies will be required to deliver value *tomorrow*:

- Enter into joint agreements in which payers/providers both have skin in the game ... as a starting point.
- Collaborate to develop innovative new products that will resonate in the market.
- Ensure that pricing and clinical data are tied to outcomes that *matter to consumers*—with an economic and clinical value story.

These strategies rely on risk agreements that pay differently from the traditional model. If payers don't embrace an approach like this, others are busily planning to fill the void for at least some portion of healthcare services.

Segment Providers

Insurers need to recognize that any initiatives they undertake will only add value if they are implemented successfully, and at the end of the day, generate better health outcomes at lower cost. Targeting or segmenting network providers to identify those that are most likely to be successful with a given initiative and then concentrating resources on that group will be critical to forward progress. In turn, successful implementation will help to sell other providers on the approach while generating positive clinical and financial outcomes. As noted earlier, insurers are at risk if providers don't implement change initiatives well, and if quality isn't improved, costs won't be lowered.

Insurers need to move away from broadly offering initiatives to the entire range of providers. Instead, they need to segment or qualify providers based on their ability to implement cost and quality improvements effectively and then only promote initiatives to those with the highest potential to succeed.

Those that have demonstrated the ability to manage variation in cost and quality across the continuum in specific therapeutic areas are likely to have built needed disciplines, at least to some degree. If you add to this a robust physician governance structure, strong patient satisfaction, and some demonstrated commitment to effective management of care transitions, payers will have a strong basis for partner collaboration.

Payer-driven initiatives should be realistic in scope, bearing in mind the support needs and limited change management capabilities of most healthcare organizations. Specific safety initiatives or 30-day readmissions, which already have CMS sanctions attached to them, would be obvious candidates. Better to succeed with more modest goals than to have the provider fail to meet its objectives in a more ambitious context.

Focus Partnerships on the Prevention of Never Events

Historically, CMS has been weak at enforcing policies around never events. But the country's largest payer is recognizing that this is an area of significant cost savings. After all, in what other industry do we pay companies to fix problems that shouldn't have occurred in the first place? Private insurers also have a lot to gain if never events are reduced and are in a great position to support hospitals in their efforts to comply with the new rules. Once never events are reduced significantly, insurers would be in a great position to enforce strict denial-of-claims rules with reduced risk of losing providers from their networks. They could also take a very public stance on not reimbursing for never events.

Require and Pay for Predictive Care Paths

While some health conditions are clearly too complex and variable to map a treatment path, this is not true for all conditions. Leading healthcare providers such as Geisinger Health System, Gundersen Health System, Mayo Clinic, Cleveland Clinic, and Sutter Health have already done considerable research establishing predictive care paths. This is an example of evidence-based medicine at work. It is now generally understood that the amount and types of care required for some conditions can be anticipated. Therefore, a total cost for treatment can be established that eliminates the administrative cost burden of coding, invoicing, adjudicating, and paying separately for each component.[7-12] In the area of cancer care, Cancer Treatment Centers of America has taken the lead in providing a comprehensive, integrated diagnostic evaluation and treatment plan for the four major types of cancer (i.e., breast, colorectal, prostate, and lung) for a fixed fee and in 5 days or less. They are poised to provide treatment for selected cancers on a fully transparent, bundled price basis.

Predictive care paths, and the outcomes they achieve, are the true "product" of hospitals and physicians, rather than each procedural detail. Considering the goals of healthcare reform, this implies that, like manufacturers, investments in research and development (R&D) (e.g., new approaches to care delivery) will need to become part of the new business model. Differential pricing is then based on the quality of outcomes produced. As such, these "products" can be audited for quality just as products of pharmaceutical and medical device manufacturers are audited. This addresses one of the biggest disconnects of fee-for-service and capitation[13] payment methods: *They do nothing to ensure quality of care.* Care paths as a tangible product of evidence-based medicine also promise a better standard of care than the Joint Commission on the Accreditation of Healthcare Organizations (JCAHO), which continues to accredit hospitals that other sources say are unsafe. Innovations in healthcare delivery should lower costs and improve outcomes, as is true in other industries.

With a fixed total price for an evidence-based course of treatment associated with outcomes, there is no incentive to provide additional, unnecessary care. Significant administrative efficiency can also be achieved, moving away from the cost-accounting minutiae of the current system, which consume provider time and encourage upcoding abuse.

For "products," there must also be transparency of both the price and the quality of the care path products being offered. Responsible buyers need this information if we expect them to be accountable for the cost consequences of their decisions. This is true of CMS, private insurance, or consumer buyers. Transparency of price and quality is already evident and established in elective healthcare markets such as cosmetic dermatology and corrective vision surgery. There's no reason why such practices can't successfully be extended to the broader range of high-volume treatments.

Change the Basis for Paying Primary Care Physicians

At the same time we are recognizing the importance of primary care in prevention and managing health to avoid more costly care, we are facing a critical shortage of primary care physicians. The reason for this is how we pay these physicians today. Their average compensation is so much less than subspecialists who perform procedures that are more richly compensated that we have eliminated any incentive to practice primary care. This is now widely recognized as one of the most important issues payment reform must address.[7,9,14-16]

Primary care takes time with a patient—to ask questions and diagnose the root cause behind symptoms, to study diagnostic tests and patient history, to educate patients and guide them in managing their own health, and to coordinate their care when subspecialists need to be involved. As such, *the important unit of value for primary care physicians is time.*

We can establish a dollar value for an hour of a primary care physician's time, and we can adjust this regionally based on cost-of-living data. This eliminates the incentive to minimize time with patients in order to see as many patients as possible, which is what these physicians need to do today to sustain an income. This value must also be set at a level that eliminates the disincentive to choose primary care practice. The 5%–10% pay increases outlined in the PPACA legislation don't come close to adequately addressing the current compensation disparity between primary care and subspecialty practice.

Insurers, including CMS, can periodically audit physician practices, focusing on outlier time charges. If there is a trend of such outlier practice, without any supporting rationale, insurers can choose to dismiss such physicians from their networks. In addition, patients can fill out *standard-of-care report cards,* which would verify that the care that should be delivered was in fact delivered—in effect measuring how well a physician used his or her time with the patient.

Just as we defined a predictive care path as a product, so too is primary care management. Changing the unit of value to time doesn't remove the requirement for *price and value transparency* of primary physician care. For example, there *will* be primary care physicians who achieve better results over a continuum in helping their patients manage diabetes or obesity. Buyers—consumers or insurers—can only make responsible choices when the price and value are known. Concierge primary care has already established the precedent for a known product (ready access to the physician) and a corresponding price.

Today, physicians are in an insurer's network because they have agreed to accept that payer's discounted schedule of charges. The physician then determines how to play the coding game to get more money. We're suffering from the consequences of this payment approach. Our proposal for tomorrow provides for fair, time-based compensation to physicians and kicks them out of the network if audits and patient standard-of-care report cards indicate that they are "working the system."

Appropriate valuing of primary care and rebalancing compensation accordingly is a two-edged sword. Just as we are substantially underpaying for primary care, we are correspondingly overcompensating surgeons and subspecialists. Our redesign of financing mechanisms must address compensation imbalance *from both directions.* To be direct, this strategy calls for the relative reduction of subspecialist compensation as primary care compensation would increase.

Over time, the natural law of supply and demand will result in more primary care physicians and fewer subspecialists. As we've suggested, removing the income disincentive to choose the practice of primary care will change the ratio of primary care to subspecialists. This, and the impact of better primary care in avoiding surgery and specialist work and, thus reducing demand, will also result in reducing the number of subspecialists.

Increase Consumer Engagement and Personal Responsibility, Reducing Abuse of the System by Consumers

We are currently paying avoidable healthcare costs due to two types of abuse by consumers. One is not managing their own health, and the other is not buying any type of insurance coverage even if they are able to afford it. PPACA modified the second problem to some extent by imposing penalties for not carrying "qualified" health insurance. New opportunities, incentives, and extensive consumer engagement strategies have proliferated in the last couple of years. The extent to which these strategies will actually work in changing health habits is yet to be seen.

A necessary part of this strategy is the need to accept the reality that some people will always take advantage of the system. Regardless, significantly reducing the number of abusers represents tremendous cost savings and collectively better health.

Reduce Fraud and Abuse by Providers

Private insurers on average do a reasonable job of verifying claims, monitoring trends, and taking action to identify and address fraud. Their for-profit, bottom-line orientation drives them to perform this work, a responsibility of any organization buying products or services.

CMS doesn't currently operate at this same standard, a point argued clearly in a series of essays by industry experts in *Stop Paying the Crooks*.[17] Merrill and Meredith Matthews note the irony that the Medicare program is held up by some as the model for healthcare in this country.[18] In 2008, Senator Charles Grassley pegged Medicare fraud, waste, and abuse at approximately $60 billion annually out of an annual budget of $460 billion—essentially 13%.[18] To put this all in perspective, Bernard Madoff ran a Ponzi scheme bilking customers out of some $50 billion, which appropriately set off a firestorm across the country. Madoff's transgressions were a one-time event; Medicare's losses to fraud, waste, and abuse are annual. Fraud can be immediately and substantively reduced by CMS adopting private insurers' best practices in this area. In fact, the former Secretary of the U.S. Department of Health and Human Services (HHS), Kathleen Sebelius, noted that fraud prevention efforts netted the government $4.1 billion in 2011 alone.

Are You Ready for Disruptive Innovation?

Private health insurance stands on the precipice of an uncertain future. After decades of financial success, it's difficult for many in the industry to think about meaningfully changing the current model. Yet no business model continues to deliver results into perpetuity. When market realities change, so must the model, and market realities have definitely changed.

Now, even the biggest employers are facing unprecedented cost pressures. Where they once valued premium-priced medical management tools and services, their insurer selection has quickly devolved to shopping on price. As a result, margins are eroding, and once secure customer relationships can no longer be counted on in the next sales forecast.

As we noted earlier, on the nonmarket side, many in government are intent on driving healthcare reform through increased government intervention to control insurance costs. This comes on top of the fact that over half of insured Americans get their insurance from the government (Medicaid and Medicare).

Many healthcare insurers have felt vulnerable—rightfully so. But they have successfully adapted to the new rules that PPACA imposed, with many posting continued share price gains. Subsidies offered to payers in the form of risk will shortly go away. Conducting business as usual won't cut it in a future of ongoing radical change. Recognizing the need for a fundamentally new business model is a necessary first step to change. Developing such a model is the more difficult challenge that lies ahead.

Underlying the obvious perils facing private healthcare insurers are some potentially potent opportunities to make disruptive changes and seize substantial market share. Leaders throughout the industry need to be proactive in initiating business model innovation and guiding its effective implementation. Throughout the industry, new winners—and losers—will emerge based on their ability to design and deliver superior economic and health outcome value. Are you ready for that contest?

Questions for Payers

- ■ What have we done to change our business model to enable alternative payment models?
  - – Are the models we've developed really different? Or are they a continuum of the old model?
- ■ Are we focused on identifying the right partners and collaborating with them to identify solutions that will deliver greater economic and clinical value?
- ■ Have we established mutual risk relationships with providers?
  - – If so, how well are they working?
    - • What are the barriers preventing successful implementation?
    - • Are we able to provide them with timely information that is helpful to their efforts?
    - • Does our broader organization understand the vision and direction in which we are headed?
  - – If no, what's holding us back?
- ■ Are the new products we're building of interest to consumers?
  - – Are these based on cost? Quality? Both? Something else?

- How good a job are we doing at driving better outcomes?
  - Do these outcomes even matter to consumers?
- Are our internal systems making the necessary changes to ensure that we can operate differently and provide providers with real-time data that will enhance their performance?

Endnotes

1. Rita E. Numerof and Bill Ott. "Adapting to the Changing Landscape of Healthcare Insurance." October 2009. http://nai-consulting .com/adapting-to-the-changing-landscape-of-healthcare-insurance/.
2. John Merline. "ObamaCare Premiums Jumped 23% This Year— After Subsidies." *Investor's Business Daily.* March 2015. http:// news.investors.com/blogs-capital-hill/031715-743926-obama -premiums-climbed-23-percent-on-average.htm.
3. Jenny Gold. "Prevention for Profit: Questions Raised about Some Health Screenings." *Kaiser Health News.* October 2013. http://kaiserhealthnews.org/news/medical-screenings/.
4. Rita E. Numerof. "Healthcare Reform: Strategy, Myths and Solutions." *Medical Progress Today.* November 2009. http:// www.medicalprogresstoday.com/spotlight/spotlight_indarchive .php?id=1830.
5. Melanie Evans and Bob Herman. "Where Healthcare Is Now on March to Value-Based Pay." *Modern Health care.* January 2015. http:// www.modernhealthcare.com/article/20150128/NEWS/301289952 /where-healthcare-is-now-on-march-to-value-based-pay.
6. John Wilkerson. "Gilfillan-Led Private Sector Coalition Recommends ACO Policy Changes." InsideHealthPolicy. February 2015. https://healthpolicynewsstand.com/topic /spotlight-on-acos.
7. Lola Butcher. "Bundled Payments: Brilliant Idea or Boondoggle?" *Physician Executive* 35 (4): 6–8, 10. 2009. http://net.acpe.org /MembersOnly/pejournal/2009/JulyAugust/Butcher.pdf.
8. Francois de Brantes, Meredith B. Rosenthal, and Michael Painter. "Building a Bridge from Fragmentation to Accountability: The Prometheus Payment." *New England Journal of Medicine* 361 (11): 1033–1036. 2009. http://content .nejm.org/cgi/content/full/NEJMp0906121.

9. Tom Doerr, Randy Bak, Frank Ingari, and Debra Gribble. "The Collaborative Payer Model: New Hope for Medicare and Primary Care." *ESSENCE Healthcare.* November 2008. http://www.essencecorp.com/pdf/ExecutiveSummary_CPM.pdf.

10. Harold D. Miller. "From Volume to Value: Better Ways to Pay for Health Care." *Health Affairs.* September 2009. http://content.healthaffairs.org/cgi/content/abstract/28/5/1418.

11. Arnold Milstein. "Medical Homes—And Medical 'Home Runs'?" *Health Affairs.* September 2008. http://healthaffairs.org/blog/2008/09/10/medical-homes-and-medical-home-runs/.

12. Anne Underwood. "A New Way to Pay Physicians." Interview with Dr. John C. Lewin. *New York Times* online. Prescriptions: Making Sense of the Health Care Debate Blog. September 2009. http://prescriptions.blogs.nytimes.com/2009/09/23/a-new-way-to-pay-physicians/.

13. Capitation is a payment method that pays a fixed fee to serve a patient population. When this method was established in the 1980s, there was no measurement or requirement for quality of care. As such, the incentive was for providers to maximize profit by minimizing the health services they provided.

14. American Board of Medical Specialties, Member Boards. "Specialty and Subspecialty Certificates." http://www.abms.org/member-boards/specialty-subspecialty-certificates/.

15. Blue Cross Blue Shield Association. "BCBSA Recommendations for Expanding Primary Care Access." September 2009.

16. Thomas Bodenheimer, Robert A. Berenson, and Paul Rudolf. "The Primary Care–Specialty Income Gap: Why It Matters." *Annals of Internal Medicine* 146 (4): 301–306. 2007. http://www.annals.org/cgi/content/abstract/146/4/301.

17. James R. Frogue et al. *Stop Paying the Crooks.* Center for Health Transformation. Chittagong, Bangladesh: CHT Press. 2009.

18. Merrill Matthews and Meredith R. Matthews. *Medicare Fraud: What the Government Can Learn from the Private Sector.* Center for Health Transformation. Chittagong, Bangladesh: CHT Press. 2009.

Chapter 8

Big Pharma: How to Regain Success

Introduction

Successful companies, even entire industries, have a life cycle. All of them eventually reach the point where their business model approaches the end of its life cycle and is no longer viable. Companies that recognize the shift early on, assuming they conceptualize and execute a successor model effectively, become leaders as the next stage emerges. Sometimes the transitions are incremental and gradual; more often, they involve discontinuity and dislocation. Outlines of the transition are always clear in retrospect, and most of our wisdom about such transitions comes from retrospective analysis. But what's the appropriate advice for companies in the middle of a transition—when the old model still appears to have life and the new model is underdeveloped and unproven?

The global pharmaceutical industry faces this situation today. It's well known that pharma has been going through tough times. It's now fashionable among politicians, pundits, and journalists to criticize all the ways in which the industry's pursuit of profit conflicts with the healthcare needs of patients.

The industry has had to bear greater scrutiny and skepticism from all its stakeholders than it has known for decades. The tangible impact has taken the form of patient lawsuits, governmental investigations, increasingly aggressive efforts of third-party payers to influence pricing and utilization of branded drugs, a more cautious approach to clinical evidence and new drug approval on the part of regulators, and new constraints on sales and marketing practices.

Given the rapid progress of medical science and the huge swaths of unmet medical needs that remain, the opportunity for innovation is undiminished. Big pharma is still the natural champion for bringing safe and cost-effective therapies to the market on a global scale, and it continues to possess enormous competitive advantages in that role. At the end of the day, no one else can muster the critical competencies on the necessary scale to bring new medical therapies to market on a consistent basis.

To some extent, the industry has been unfairly maligned. It's a more convenient target of criticism than current dysfunctional systems for delivering and paying for medical care. It's also the victim of limited understanding of the realities of medical science and healthcare economics among the general population—the inherent trade-offs involved between innovation and short-term cost, between short-term cost of preventive care and long-term cost of acute and long-term care, and among the various combinations of efficacy and safety that all treatments (or nontreatments) involve.

On the basis of these underlying strengths, one could argue that the current problems are temporary and that the industry's primary imperative is to become more effective at public diplomacy. In our view, this conclusion is the wrong one for the industry to make. Healthcare delivery models are undergoing a sea change. Rising costs will force us to change the way in which we look at healthcare. Over time, we will embrace the concept of a continuum of care that emphasizes prevention and more active engagement of consumers in their own treatment, not unlike the model being adopted in the treatment of diabetes.

Unfortunately, the pathway to get there will almost certainly involve more short-sighted and heavy-handed attempts to control costs. It's imperative for major pharmaceutical companies to become active participants in shaping public policy and the public's attitudes toward it. At the same time, there are very real problems with the current pharma business model. Leaders of pharma companies should seize this opportunity to conduct a fundamental self-examination and begin laying the foundation for their future.

Sovaldi: Spotlight on Pharmaceutical Value

Recent headlines surrounding Sovaldi, the expensive treatment for Hepatitis C and its even more expensive counterpart, Harvoni, spotlight what's to come. The two drugs, manufactured by Gilead, have received harsh criticism from all fronts: the Senate Finance Committee, physicians, pharmacy benefit managers (PBMs), the media, and consumers.

At $84,000 for a 12-week treatment period ($1,000 per pill), Steve Miller, Express Scripts' chief medical officer (CMO), has gone on record publicly challenging Sovaldi's price and reportedly advocating for doctors to limit or delay treatment, if appropriate, until competitor products come online.[1] Subsequently, AbbVie cut an exclusive deal with Express Scripts for its product; CVS agreed to carry Sovaldi but only at a deep discount.

In the summer of 2014, two members of the U.S. Senate Finance Committee, including its then chair, Ron Wyden, issued a letter to Gilead demanding justification for the drug's high price and challenging the manufacturer's methodology for arriving at it especially given the typically low-income patient population affected by hep C.[2] The resulting burden on Medicare and Medicaid was highlighted as excessive, a point noted by many others as well, including an earlier challenge by the House Energy and Commerce Committee and various states erecting Medicaid coverage hurdles.[3]

Ironically, the original developer of Sovaldi, Pharmasset, had planned to sell the drug for a fraction of the controversial market price, a mere $36,000 per round of treatment. This, of course, was prior to Gilead's acquisition of the company in early 2012.[1] Not surprisingly, it's a pattern we see repeated across the industry. Gilead's response to the charges of price gouging are rooted in its analysis of the relative value of the drug compared to other therapies and serious comorbidities.

Importantly, a CVS study suggested that approximately 8% of patients taking the drug discontinued the treatment regimen prematurely, raising questions about adherence and ultimately the drug's effectiveness outside a controlled clinical trial.[4]

Not surprisingly, Sovaldi has also been challenged on price outside the United States, notwithstanding its clinical efficacy. In the UK, NICE (National Institute for Health and Care Excellence) initially approved Sovaldi for use by the National Health Service (NHS), but NHS subsequently ruled that the drug was just too expensive and the system couldn't afford it.[5] Over a dozen European countries joined together in pressing Gilead for deep discounts, noting that the high cost of treatment put the entire health system at risk.[6]

While Sovaldi has been in the spotlight, it's actually not the most expensive drug on the market; it's 19th out of the top 20.[7]

The U.S. market has historically borne the cost of discovery, development, approval, and ultimately commercialization. However, the pharmaceutical industry cannot assume that the United States will continue to shoulder the financial burden as it has in the past, no matter how well the drugs work. The future will most definitely require risk-based contracts focused on real economic and clinical value for defined products and populations. Pressure will continue to come from the Centers for Medicare & Medicaid Services (CMS) and also from delivery organizations, increasingly at-risk for the total cost of care.

Vulnerabilities of the Current Model

The dominant business model for the pharmaceutical industry today has been the blockbuster model.[8] In its simplest terms, the blockbuster model is about

- Focusing development investments on drugs that address large patient populations and appeal to a broad prescriber base
- Achieving high penetration of those markets through aggressive and expensive promotional activities to physicians and patients
- Expanding market boundaries by pursuing new indications and broadening the prescriber base beyond the initially targeted specialists

The remarkable success of some blockbuster products has reinforced each of these elements. At the same time, the inherent costs and risks of the model have encouraged company mergers on a mammoth scale and reinforced the barriers to entry into this elite club of global companies. All elements of the model continue to operate, but under increasing strain, due to some fundamental vulnerabilities.

The first vulnerability reflects the model's dependence on mass markets. The larger the target audience is, the greater is the likelihood that some segment of it will respond negatively to the product in question. Legal liability and societal backlash are likewise proportional to market size. In response to recent recalls of major products, the reaction of key stakeholders has been to emphasize safety as an overriding concern. The perception that big pharma has not been sufficiently sensitive to this issue has hurt the industry's reputation, and it also translates into an escalating regulatory burden on the industry.

The second vulnerability surrounds significant costs in an increasingly cost-conscious market. The model is very expensive and requires three major cost drivers that continue to trend higher: discovery or acquisition of promising compounds, development through human trials, and marketing of approved drugs. Historically, companies have been able to recoup their investments and generate an attractive return by pricing their products based on efficacy and safety, with only limited attention to the prices for competitive therapies or no therapy.

These escalating costs, passed through to payers, are in direct conflict with a growing urgency in the United States and elsewhere in the developed world to control the accelerating cost of healthcare. Payers have some powerful tools at their disposal in this conflict. The greatest of these is the accumulation of existing therapies that are off patent or approaching patent expiration. As it has become easier to bring generic drugs to market, their overwhelming cost advantages have provided powerful incentives to payers and pharmacists to promote substitution. Even within the world of branded pharmaceuticals, the proliferation of compounds with similar properties makes it easier for payers to force greater price competition by granting preferential formulary status to selected brands. In a sense, the very advantage of many blockbuster products—that they address broad markets—has been turned against them.

The third vulnerability of the model is that it depends on mass messaging. In the past era of limited price sensitivity, competition was based on companies' ability to convey messages about features and benefits to physicians and patients. In this game, reach and frequency were the critical metrics. As companies have increased the frequency of their messaging, the market has become saturated with physician detailing and direct-to-customer (DTC) advertising. Beyond providing basic familiarity, the messages themselves tend to be low value added to their audiences. Not surprisingly, there is growing resistance—to the point of backlash—to this approach to marketing.

The traditional product-driven model often fails to take into account broader market needs or issues. For example, the traditional approach fails to ask a number of questions critical in today's market, such as

- Is there evidence that the product is better than what is currently on the market?
- Will payers and physicians be interested without evidence of superior clinical outcomes even at the same price?
- Will providers buy the product (at a premium) if it is only as good as current products?
- What evidence of improved outcomes or lower treatment costs will payers want in order to accept the product?

Market-Driven Business Model

Inherent limitations of the current business model will lead to the emergence of a fundamentally new approach for the industry that addresses the needs and interests of all critical stakeholders. This market-driven model rests on the assumption that successful companies of the future will determine what therapeutic areas they will "own," which in turn will drive investments. Unlike the current approach, which is really *product* centric, the new model will be *patient* centric and take a *continuum of care versus episodic care* approach. What this will mean is a core focus on prevention, diagnosis, and treatment of the range of conditions within a therapeutic area, taking into account the needs of specific markets around the globe.

At the same time, companies increasingly must be able to demonstrate the economic and clinical value of their products. This paradigm shift requires that marketing strategies focus on the market needs (pull), instead of promoting a particular product (push). The market-driven model can be characterized by its focus on delivering real value to stakeholders, strategic marketing, and innovation. The market is a good indicator of when market forces are working. Take a look at

Avastin®—even before the Food and Drug Administration (FDA) removed its indication for breast cancer, the market had responded to postapproval studies, as indicated by the fact that use of the drug for treating metastatic breast cancer had plummeted as more data about its limitations became available.

Ensuring Stakeholder Value

The central imperative of the new model is delivering real value to *all* stakeholders—payers, regulators, physicians, providers, and patients—and understanding whose voice matters in terms of relative weight is of critical importance.

Globally, the power of payers is growing as product acceptance and purchase decision making moves further and further from the physician. Payers and hospitals are clamping down on healthcare costs by saying no to new products, line extensions, and of course, price increases. Reacting to the prospect of exponentially increasing liabilities, payers of all types are demanding hard comparative clinical and economic data to justify any change with bottom-line impact. Historically, market access was considered a reimbursement issue that was given attention late in the product development process. Yet, as pressure on payers and providers to reduce costs and increase quality grows, pharmaceutical manufacturers must understand who the stakeholders are—patients, providers, and payers—and build relevant data to demonstrate their value to each one. Consequently, manufacturers must think about market access considerations much earlier in the product development process.

This represents a significant change for many companies. Those tasked with marketing products are beginning to recognize the internal challenges they face in gaining acceptance for market access considerations—specifically, the need for comparative effectiveness research and the identification of new ways of obtaining appropriate evidence. They are increasingly seeking help translating these messages internally and implementing sustainable changes within their companies.

The FDA and other regulators also remain a critical constituency. Companies need to find ways to accelerate time to market while reducing clinical trial costs and attaining optimal claims. Clinical and regulatory affairs groups will need to hone their capabilities for early and effective engagement of regulators to influence regulatory thinking, avoid surprises, and develop well-defined clinical strategies to ensure that the right studies are conducted in the right order to minimize delays and rework.

The FDA has created new regulatory programs in an attempt to expedite the approval process in order to get much-needed drugs more quickly to patients requiring them. One of these, the Breakthrough Therapy designation—has had a successful start, since its creation in 2012.[9] Enacted to provide another mechanism to accelerate the path of critical therapeutics to market, the statute has exceeded expectations. In its first year, the regulatory agency granted the designation a total of 31 times, compared to initial estimates that only three or four drugs per year would earn the title and the advantages that follow.

With this accelerated pathway and increased communication with regulators in place, a designee could potentially gain approval nearly 3 years faster than a product without the designation. The majority of the initial designees have been oncology drugs, with others treating severe conditions for which early intervention can extend lives, such as cystic fibrosis and hepatitis C.

Even with these expedited programs, manufacturers will still need to ensure that the right evidence is being collected to gain approval in the accelerated time frame.

Payers have clearly emerged in recent years as the newest powerful constituency. Pharmaceutical companies need to engage with government, employers, and insurers to understand their needs, deliver solutions that address those needs, and frame the discussion over healthcare economics more advantageously. To accomplish this, several significant changes to the current process will be required. First, healthcare economics considerations need to move to the front end of the product development and investment prioritization cycle. Second, clinical trials need to be structured to demonstrate compelling clinical and economic value in comparison with available alternatives; and finally, the engagement of payer organizations needs to be managed as a complex selling process.

Perhaps most importantly, companies need to change their go-to-market models—redefining the value delivered to physicians, providers, and patients—while lowering costs. While the numbers have declined since their peak, there is still heavy reliance on physician detailing. This practice is inconsistent with cost constraints and the need for more tailored and responsive dialogue. The role of personal promotion to physicians hasn't disappeared, but it requires greater sophistication, clinical knowledge, and business acumen than typical sales reps possess today. Current technology will also play a role in getting information out to key constituents. Companies will need to define new approaches and develop new competencies to deliver value in ways that are cost effective, convenient, and tailored to meet individual needs. In addition, opportunities to develop relationships with patients/consumers need to be part of the equation as well.

For the pharmaceutical industry, focus on patients has historically translated to direct-to-consumer advertising, strongly encouraging patients to talk with their doctors about "x" product. The new world of "patient centricity" means changing the way in which manufacturers engage with patients, acknowledging them as legitimate healthcare decision makers, essentially "patients as partners."[10]

This means identifying the types of evidence (e.g., patient-reported outcomes) that will best resonate with patients and incorporating patient perspective in trial design. Just as manufacturers must leverage comparative effectiveness research (CER) and real-world evidence (RWE) to gain favorable positioning with payers, they need to collect and demonstrate information that matters to patients in a way that makes patients listen.

This is where patients become important partners. Patients play a dual role as both the end users of clinical research *and* the research subjects helping to produce the data. Therefore, including a patient-centric perspective in early product research and development becomes critical to generating the data that will ultimately tell the patient-centric value story. Treating patients as partners will ensure a positive patient experience during the clinical trials, as well as producing outcomes that matter.

Strategic Marketing and New Commercial Capabilities

One of the insidious characteristics of the blockbuster model is that it is inherently product driven. Insiders at even the largest global pharmaceutical companies can name the blockbuster products that drive business strategy for the company. Because product revenues are so central to the companies' success, they also tend to be sales-driven cultures. All pharmaceutical companies invest in marketing capabilities, but these groups typically have too tactical a focus. In practice, marketing operates largely as a sales support organization.

In the market-driven model, strategic marketing drives all other activities, and sales are repositioned as just one arm of the marketing mix. The central premise (and promise) of the model is that better understanding of, and responsiveness to, the needs of all stakeholders will enable companies to better identify and define unmet medical needs, determine therapeutic focus to drive disciplined portfolio investment decisions, deliver appropriate new therapies and ancillary services, and capture sufficient value for their products. This promise can only be realized if companies invest in the capabilities of strategic marketing. Truly strategic marketing involves segmentation of markets based on characteristics that correlate with distinctive needs. It also requires a level of insight that goes well beyond the standard specialty- and decile-driven approaches in common use today.

As we've argued throughout the book, payers, employers, and patients are demanding greater transparency and evidence of value: better health outcomes at lower cost.[11,12] Delivery organizations are responding in three ways. First, they are consolidating across the care continuum at an accelerating pace to leverage scale, gain efficiencies, and obtain greater purchasing power.

Second, hospitals and systems are experimenting with various forms of at-risk payment, such as accountable care organizations, patient-centered medical homes, bundled pricing, and population health management. A common element shared by these approaches is that they give providers a stake in the cost of care provided, rewarding them if they deliver at less than agreed-upon costs, and (ultimately) punishing them for higher costs. The pace at which hospitals have adopted at-risk models varies. Some organizations have moved quickly to enter into shared savings arrangements, while others are much more conservative, adopting a "wait and see" philosophy.

Third, they are changing how they decide which products to use. Decisions are increasingly evidence based and driven by a product's economic and clinical value to various stakeholders. This increased focus on value has coincided with a decrease in the influence of individual physicians in the decision-making process. Administrators and C-suite executives are implementing cost management techniques and moving toward standardization. They are intently looking to their suppliers to provide greater evidence of products' economic and clinical value.

Innovation Stewardship

Innovation remains the lifeblood of major pharmaceutical companies. Pharmaceutical innovation is inherently high risk, expensive, part science, part art. But these attributes are magnified in the blockbuster model, which focuses on indications and molecules that have the revenue potential to sustain the commercial infrastructure of the company.

In the new model, companies will use marketing insights to determine therapeutic focus and drive disciplined portfolio investment decisions that reflect a more holistic view of product life cycle value and the continuum of care. Once companies move to a market model with a more efficient and effective commercial arm, they can focus more resources on research and development (R&D) in those therapeutic areas that strategic marketing has determined to represent the greatest opportunities for the company.

Along with this greater flexibility and focus, in a more cost-conscious environment, companies also need to extract more value from their innovation activities. In their management of both early- and late-stage pipelines, they need to take a seamless, market-driven approach to selecting therapeutic targets. They also need to apply more flexible risk management and value-capture strategies, including greater use of out-licensing and co-development, to derive the greatest expected value from the pipeline. Service wraps that support portfolio products and help to position the company as the "owner" of the therapeutic area are also an important part of this picture.[13] In their management of products toward the end of their life cycles, companies need to become more aggressive at pursuing exit strategies in order to focus resources on what big pharma does best—bringing novel therapies to market.

But they also need to think differently about their clinical research—the design and conduct of trials and the role of real-world evidence—especially as we look ahead to the possibility of real advances in personalized medicine and the role of theranostics.

As a demonstration of how important these areas will be in the future, the National Institutes for Health's (NIH) Precision Medicine Initiative was announced in January 2015 as a way to funnel federal research funding into personalized therapies, starting with cancer treatments and moving to the whole range of health and disease.[14] Dr. Francis Collins, director of the NIH, hopes that the initiative "will encourage and support the next generation of scientists to develop creative new approaches for detecting, measuring, and analyzing a wide range of biomedical information—including molecular, genomic, cellular, clinical, behavioral, physiological, and environmental parameters."[15] With or without official participation in projects sponsored by this initiative, we agree that the next generation of innovation in pharma will come from these new endeavors.

Some manufacturers are already beginning to develop the research infrastructure needed for a robust personalized medicine research platform. Pfizer and Genentech have both publicly announced partnerships with Google-backed consumer genomics company 23andMe to study inflammatory bowel disease (IBD) and Parkinson's disease, respectively.[16] These early partnerships provide drug developers access to genomic information as well as information on risk factors and family histories collected through patient surveys for thousands of individuals. Recognizing the potential innovative power of these genomic and other personal detail databases, 23andMe has recently gone one step further toward developing personalized medicine, announcing that it intends to develop and launch its own drugs.[17] While the success of this venture is yet to be determined, we're likely to see new sources of competition in the drug manufacturing world as the race toward personalized medicine speeds up.

Pressures on Innovation

Today, pharmaceutical and medical device manufacturers rely on patents to protect their innovations as they compete in commercial markets. In most cases, innovators have 17 years from the date of patent issuance to recoup their investment. But having a patent isn't the same as having a product. First you need FDA approval if you plan to sell products in the United States.

That's when the real work begins. Experts estimate that it costs more than $1 billion and takes 10 years to bring a new drug to market. There are lots of patents sitting on the shelf, never to see the commercial light of day. Molecules may not perform the way scientists expected in the earliest stages of discovery; side effects may prove to be problematic, thus stopping development in the middle of clinical trials. And getting the biggest U.S. insurer, CMS, to agree to reimburse the product is a further hurdle that must be crossed.

Given the substantial time and financial commitments required to bring a new drug to market, congressional and public pressure to further reduce the length of patent protection represents a major challenge for the U.S. medical products industry. What most people don't realize is that this very pressure puts at risk one of our few remaining industrial jewels. The argument put forth in support of more limited protection is the opportunity to bring generics to market faster and at a significantly lower cost than branded pharmaceuticals.

That generics come at a cheaper price shouldn't be a surprise to anyone. Generic manufacturers don't have to invest in risky R&D, don't bear the brunt of regulatory approval, and don't have the same commercialization costs to bear. But the focus on bringing generics out faster to lower overall healthcare costs misses one critical point. Pharmaceuticals, while highly visible, represent only about 10% of the cost of healthcare in the United States. And they enable greater productivity on the part of people taking them for the most part! If we're serious about lowering healthcare costs, then we need to look elsewhere.

Role of Comparative Effectiveness in the Pharmaceutical Industry

Earlier we discussed the impact of recent healthcare legislation on the overall industry. One component, CER, has had a major impact on the pharmaceutical and medical device industries. CER represents a significant shift for the industry and promises to radically alter the level of government involvement in the way in which healthcare products and services are developed; it is seen by CMS as *the* solution to healthcare cost containment.[18]

As we discussed in Chapter 4, CER is not restricted to research into what products work best; it also includes research into what *treatment protocols* work best. What this means is a fundamental restructuring of priorities within large segments of the industry, away from incremental improvements (i.e., formula modification, extended release) and toward improvements that are of interest to payers, patients, and providers. As noted earlier, there are as likely to be demands to reduce cost as there are for *quality improvements*. This will put significant pressure on pharmaceutical manufacturers to produce products that demonstrate *substantial* improvements in outcomes.

Given that pharmaceuticals are a very visible portion of those expenditures, they are likely to continue to be among the primary targets of CER as highlighted in our earlier discussion of Sovaldi. Primarily, we expect that this will take the form of comparisons between drugs, classes of drugs, and even noninterventional approaches (e.g., watchful waiting). Branded pharmaceuticals are still the targets of choice for political purposes, but biologics may be close behind, especially given their often extremely high costs. These pressures will come in the form of treatment guidelines, focus on cost effectiveness, and the end of the placebo-controlled trial. In addition, the development of companion targeted diagnostics that identify appropriate patients and reduce side effects will become increasingly important.

Treatment Guidelines

Looking down the road a few years, there will almost certainly be relatively stringent guidelines for the treatment of the most expensive medical conditions, including what drugs to prescribe and under what circumstances.

Because of the objection of the American Medical Association (AMA) and other powerful lobbies to the outright restriction of physician prerogatives in choosing a treatment, there are likely to be exceptions to these guidelines. But given the march of physicians to employment models, coupled with downward reimbursement pressure on healthcare systems and their need to reduce costs significantly, standardized clinical protocols based on available evidence will surely characterize the landscape of the future.

In the long term, we expect that compliance will be strong, especially as retail providers (e.g., Walmart and Walgreens) enter the primary care delivery space. What's more, once these specific treatment patterns become the standard, they will be by (a) most private insurers (some of whom are actively buying delivery organizations), and (b) physicians themselves as the default standard of treatment. This will create a high degree of conformity. *Those drugs not baked into protocols and treatment guidelines will have a tough time surviving!*

Conditions most likely to be targeted include:

1. *Cancer.* Research priorities in this area are likely to revolve around the relative effectiveness of various drug and radiation regimens, and attempts to segment the clinical population to prescribe the most effective drugs based on diagnostic and genetic testing. This has the potential to evolve into a strict set of segmentation criteria that

allows more precise, data-based prescribing and narrower indications for in-market drugs.

2. *Cardiovascular conditions, including stroke, ischemic heart disease, congestive heart failure, atherosclerosis, and hypertension.* Finding the most cost-effective preventives and treatments will be a priority. The cost effectiveness of drugs versus angioplasty and stenting will be evaluated, as will the effectiveness of branded versus generic drugs.

3. *Type 2 diabetes prevention and treatment.* Expect comparison of weight loss interventions like exercise and bariatric surgery versus drugs and combination therapies that include drugs, as well as evaluation of various predictive screening regimens and alternative points of intervention during the progression of the disease. Expect this research to focus heavily on the potential for differential effectiveness across specific subpopulations.

4. *Obesity.* Expect comparison of weight-loss interventions, including reevaluation of the safety and benefits of older drugs for weight loss, as well as the relative advantages of drugs versus bariatric surgery.

5. *Neurological disorders, including Alzheimer's and other forms of senile dementia.* The cost effectiveness of current drugs for treating Alzheimer's disease and Parkinson's disease will be called into question, as will classes of drugs that are, cumulatively, very expensive (e.g., antidepressants).

6. *Arthritis and joint problems.* Especially given recent findings that some procedures (e.g., lavage and debridement) are ineffective in most cases and the high cost and frequency of joint replacement, evaluating whether nonsurgical approaches are effective will be a high priority.

7. *Respiratory illness.* Pneumonia will make the list, and we think it is likely to be combined with influenza as part of a respiratory illness priority area. Treatment protocols and prevention of nosocomial infections are likely to be focus areas.

8. *Chronic obstructive pulmonary disorder.* This condition will make the list, and research will focus on the relative effectiveness and cost of various treatment protocols.

9. *HIV and AIDS.* These conditions are likely to make the list of priorities, not so much because there is controversy regarding the relative clinical or cost effectiveness of current treatment regimens, but rather because it would be politically imprudent not to name them to a list of federal research priorities.

Companies gaining a large portion of their revenues or profits from drugs used in *priority areas,* such as in the treatment of cardiovascular disease, cancer, and mental health (especially Alzheimer's disease and depression), are most at risk. We should note, however, that they also stand to gain the most should their products be the ultimate "winners"—that is, if their products are selected by CMS as the first-line treatment for people suffering from these conditions.

Focus on Cost Effectiveness

The focus on cost effectiveness reflected in the funding of CER places an increased burden on pharmaceutical companies to preemptively evaluate the likely value of their products. Economic and clinical value considerations will have to be an integral part of R&D and clinical trials work as noted earlier.

In that context, it's imperative that major pharmaceutical companies focus on creating products of real marginal value to patients, providers, and payers. In many cases, this requires rethinking the approach to discovery and development in ways that increase the probability and frequency of successful new drugs. As with any change in approach, ensuring adoption will also require modifying the organizational context—the roles, accountabilities, compliance practices, and incentives—to ensure compliance with the new approach.

End of the Placebo-Only Controlled Trial

Placebo-only controlled trials will no longer be acceptable to CMS and other payers around the globe unless there are no other treatments available for a given condition, because the data they create are nearly worthless for comparative effectiveness purposes. For cost-effectiveness evaluation, the ideal has been a direct head-to-head trial against whatever drug would be supplanted by the new one (e.g., against the current first-line treatment if the new drug is projected to become the new first-line treatment; against the current second-line treatment if it's projected to become the new second-line treatment). This greatly increases the risk of bringing a new compound to market, because a "lost" comparison may exclude the drug from the market or relegate it to very marginal status. Drugs currently in phase I or II are likely to be subject to increasingly more stringent requirements as well as global pressures for pre-defined comparators.

Evidence, Value, and the Emerging Role of Risk-Sharing and Reference Pricing[19]

Imagine purchasing a new car or appliance only to learn that it doesn't work as advertised and there's nothing you can do about it. In most realms of commerce, if a product fails to deliver what's been promised, consumers are financially covered through refunds and warranties. Yet consumers and other stakeholders have not been protected from ineffective medical care.

As pressure mounts from payers and consumers seeking value—better outcomes—for their healthcare spending, manufacturers also need to articulate a differentiated cost–benefit story. The use of real-world data as a way to establish a product's value continues to gain traction as manufacturers explore alternatives to conventional pricing and reimbursement practices (e.g., rebates).

Tightening budgets have prompted national health authorities in European markets to increasingly "hedge" their reimbursement decisions with risk-sharing agreements (RSAs), pricing controls, or negotiated price cuts to control costs. Risk-sharing, value-based pricing, and performance-based agreements are all terms that describe arrangements between payers and other key stakeholders that link payment to performance. Such strategies have been implemented, albeit sparingly, since the 1990s, and while they may not be universally applicable, they are gaining momentum in certain markets and may play a useful role in enhancing economic efficiency.

In the United States, private and public payers have recently begun to transition to value-based contracts with hospitals. Most notably, CMS hospital value-based purchasing program, enacted into law in 2010, created an incentive system that rewards "exceptional" performance based on defined metrics and penalizes hospitals' "ineffective" care and associated cost. Drug (and medical device) manufacturers should be asking themselves, "What does our organization stand to gain—or to lose—through these contractual arrangements?"

Risk sharing based on product performance can serve as an effective approach in certain circumstances, but it's not a model that applies to all situations, and it certainly does not guarantee success. While approximately 179 performance-based schemes have been publicly identified as of 2014,[20] their success has been inconsistent, largely attributed to poor conceptualization and design. Clearly, from a payer's perspective, RSAs help protect against paying for innovations that do not return value to patients. However, the short-term and long-term advantages of entering into RSAs for manufacturers may not be as clear. Unless there's a true upside to the agreement it's really a euphemism for cost concessions.

Unfortunately, the decision to explore contractual RSAs with payers may not always be theirs to make. For instance, manufacturers may be forced into these arrangements to secure reimbursement for products characterized by weak value propositions or ambiguous outcomes data, especially if the alternative is reference pricing or noncoverage. In fact, most outcome-based schemes, at least in markets outside the United States, have originated in response to negative recommendations for market access based on lack of cost-effectiveness (e.g., Johnson & Johnson's Velcade in the UK).

Manufacturers who are confident in their product and the value it creates may proactively seek out RSA opportunities to achieve a premium price or to create a market barrier for existing and future competitors. Key to success is the strength and relevance of outcomes data, and the real value that the product delivers.

In short, insurers are no longer willing to pay for products that lack a convincing value story without some form of "guarantee." This will force manufacturers to rethink their commercial models and market access strategies.

Impact of Comparative Data and Value-Based Payment on Pharmaceutical Operations

The most glaring impact of defined treatment guidelines and cost effectiveness will be the immediate obsolescence of the standard *frequency and coverage,* detailing-based sales model. With a set of guidelines in place that specifies what drugs will be prescribed for whom (under penalty of nonreimbursement for their patients and possibly for themselves), the ability to change physician behavior through education efforts (and hence the return on sales efforts) will be greatly reduced.

This doesn't necessarily mean that detailing will be completely dead, but it will be limited to specific providers that have shown willingness to buck the reimbursement-led paradigm either by laboriously justifying exceptions or by catering to patients who are willing to pay out of pocket for premium drugs. Nevertheless, the optimal size of the sales force will continue to be drastically reduced. Efforts to move in this direction have increased recently, and we expect that the trend will continue.

The need to take economic and clinical value considerations into account early in the process will require a redefinition of the role of research scientists, as well as the development of new competencies among these scientists and their managers. Health economics groups are likely to become integrated into marketing, because the need to *build* the economic and clinical value case and the need to *explain* it to multiple constituencies will become increasingly intertwined.

This redefined marketing group will also need to be closely integrated with R&D and clinical research, so that the expected cost effectiveness of a potential product, relative to existing treatments and those in development, can be assessed on an ongoing basis. What many in the industry *still* fail to appreciate is that going forward, demonstration of cost-effective superior outcomes will be table stakes for reimbursement. Competition from generics will accelerate, and, with the introduction of biosimilars over the next several years, the biologics sector— historically immune from such competition—will experience significant pain, just like traditional pharmaceutical companies.

Changing behavior to be consistent with this approach will require a new kind of organizational infrastructure—one that clearly defines the roles of various parties to be consistent with the new organizational reality, ensures that those roles are adopted, and creates seamless collaboration across functional areas. The problem is not as simple as creating the new plan for collaborative research or presenting R&D with a new prioritization scheme. It also requires creating the infrastructure to ensure accountability and develop new competencies. The need to correctly define the positioning of a new product within treatment guidelines prior to conducting clinical trials will require deeper up-front analysis of the potential risks and benefits of various evidence generation strategies. It also suggests that a *rolling blockbuster* model may be appropriate. This is discussed in more detail in the next section, "Prudent Responses and Defensive Strategies." The difficulty and time required to accomplish this should not be underestimated.

The increased focus on cost effectiveness began several years ago, but the trend toward using it as a criterion for reimbursement will accelerate over the next few years. Drugs that are in R&D today are very likely to be launched into a market that explicitly issues guidelines on the basis of cost effectiveness. Consideration of economic and clinical value must be integrated into the entire product development and commercialization process, and this will not happen overnight.

Commercial models must be focused on value delivery. This means organizational alignment on value delivery and dramatically enhanced capabilities for engaging with customers. Pharmaceutical companies need to align their R&D, medical affairs, market access, and commercial teams to function effectively in the evolving healthcare environment, ensuring that evidence is generated early enough to support a compelling value proposition and optimal reimbursement on market entry, rather than as a postmarket afterthought.

A further hurdle exists beyond reimbursement. The commercial model must also address the challenges of getting the product adopted in the marketplace. Just because an insurer or PBM is willing to pay for a product doesn't guarantee that a provider will be willing to include it in its formulary or on a more restrictive care path. The commercial organization must be designed to communicate the value of the product to all stakeholders in terms that resonate with clinical and business objectives.

No longer are reps primarily interacting with physicians and presenting features and benefits. Increasingly, they need to engage in value-added conversations with executive decision makers to identify needs, develop responsive product and nonproduct solutions, and articulate compelling value propositions. Moreover, they will need to represent and be able to deploy the full capabilities of their company. Customers increasingly want to discuss the entire portfolio of products and services offered by the manufacturer. This sophisticated selling approach will also rely on contributions from a wider team, rather than individual sales people alone.

To be successful in this new model, companies need to create new infrastructure: accountabilities, roles, structures, processes, and incentives. It will mean new metrics and new capacity to define and realize account potential consistently from an account through territory to franchise levels.

Stronger business acumen, and analytic, diagnostic, and influence skills are needed to meet the growing challenge of complex accounts and improved sales performance.

There is no quick fix to prepare the commercial organization for "Healthcare 2.0." Companies must base their transformation on rigorous analysis that objectively compares current capabilities against the emerging needs and demands of their customer set. A comprehensive approach that addresses gaps in structure, tools, skills, and behavior will be needed to compete successfully in the evolving healthcare environment (Figure 8.1).

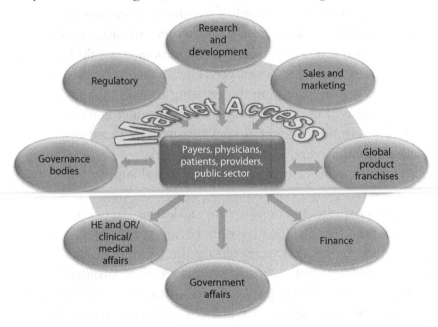

Figure 8.1 **The diverse capabilities, strategic and tactical, that reside across multiple organizational units must be coordinated to gain market access. (From Kim E. White and Christopher de Wolff, "Expanding Your Market Access Capability," Numerof & Associates, Inc. Published as "Obamacare Is Changing Market Access." *MD+DI* online. August 2013.)**

Prudent Responses and Defensive Strategies

Several years ago we recommended that pharmaceutical companies would be wise to pursue three key defensive responses: develop service wraps, diversify revenue streams away from payers, and adopt a rolling blockbuster approach. We stand by these recommendations.

Develop Service Wraps

There are opportunities for pharmaceutical companies to increase the value of their offerings by bundling them with well-designed services. Use of a drug within a well-defined treatment protocol may enhance its value relative to other treatment options. To the extent that a specific service wrap becomes part of the standard of treatment, it creates an advantage, difficult for competitors to overcome. In order to successfully displace a wrapped service, a competitor would have not only to demonstrate superior cost effectiveness, but also to sort out whether executing the existing protocol (or an alternative protocol) in conjunction with its product is more cost effective than the product alone. This may be more trouble and risk than a competitor is willing to take.

Of course, the only way to create initial support for the service wrap/drug combination is to demonstrate the same boost to cost effectiveness, so the added resistance to competition isn't free. It does have its benefits, however. A drug's patent may be several years old by the time it's ready to come to market, but a service wrap/treatment protocol that accompanies it will be protected from the time it's finalized. Just as surgical protocols are subject to intellectual property (IP) protection (allowing surgeons to collect licensing fees for the use of the protocol), service wraps that maximize the effectiveness of a pharmaceutical intervention are, too. This creates an extended revenue opportunity for the manufacturer.

It also means that hospital systems are more likely to be willing partners in the work of developing a protocol. They're also looking for ways to ensure that their "products" (their own treatment practices, especially those that are differentiated in some way from competitors) are recommended in the treatment guidelines and would be very happy to share in licensing revenues for the treatment protocol. With the growth of disease management companies, opportunities for strategic partnerships abound. Here, too, success will depend on the relative robustness of the economic and clinical evidence.

Diversify Revenue Streams Away from Payers

Effectively, this means refocusing development efforts on drugs that fall outside the reimbursement system—in other words, lifestyle or premium drugs that consumers will pay for entirely out of pocket. Entry into the lightly regulated (and almost entirely unreimbursed) nutritional market, where a pharmaceutical manufacturer's brand name can serve as assurance of the potency and purity of products, may also be a viable option.

It may also be possible to follow this path with customized medicine (e.g., using biomarkers to determine what treatment is most effective and appropriate). People may be willing to pay out of pocket for a drug that is clearly indicated as appropriate specifically for them, even if insurers aren't willing to pay because the economic and clinical value evidence isn't sufficiently compelling from a payer perspective. In the same vein, pharmaceutical manufacturers may want to enter the market for diagnostic tests that identify those who are likely to benefit specifically from their drugs.

Even when these drugs pass economic and clinical criteria, they may still be controversial, as was the case when the NHS fast-tracked approval for Herceptin®, and several NHS primary care trusts protested, saying they would have to cut other treatments to pay for it. The risk posed by this kind of dispute can be avoided to the extent that consumers come to accept the idea of individual payment for individualized treatment.

Adopt a Rolling Blockbuster Approach

The *rolling blockbuster* approach segments the market for a drug much more minutely than has historically been the case, creating a large number of target populations in which the drug's cost effectiveness can be assessed.[21] This reduces the risk inherent in clinical trials, because the binary outcome (reimbursed/not reimbursed) applies only for the small segment under consideration. For the population as a whole, it's the sum of those binary outcomes, which is a much more predictable outcome.

A second advantage of the approach is that it may make the drug a smaller target in the eyes of the cost-effectiveness hawks, as they would have to demonstrate its inferiority in a large number of diverse populations, each of which carries a relatively small price tag. The return for replacing the product with a more cost-effective one would be reduced.

The clear takeaway is that innovative companies that demonstrate the value of their products in this environment will flourish. Successful players will work to incorporate the needs of all stakeholders (payers, consumers/patients, physicians) into the product development process and generate new medicines that meet unmet needs and provide real value.

Those new products, by definition, won't face generic competition (at least not for a while) and will command top-tier prices.

The near-term pain comes from shifting from an old paradigm to the new paradigm. The old business rules, focused on blockbuster products approved through large one-size-fits-all clinical trials, need to change, both at the FDA and in industry.

Some patients benefit more from specific products than others, some patients don't benefit at all, and some are even seriously harmed. Usually this last group is such a small number that in randomized clinical trials, it's considered noise. Given the enormous size of the patient groups treated, the net benefits of blockbuster drugs far outweighed their costs.

But recent and ongoing waves of blockbuster drug patent expirations are offering insurers cheap and very effective products. Rare side effects trumpeted in the media (like those for Vioxx®) have eroded regulators' willingness to approve drugs for primary care indications without prohibitively large and expensive clinical trials.

The blockbuster model that made billions for industry is putting itself out of business.

Instead of thinking big, innovators need to think small. If you shrink the denominator to just the segment of the market that genuinely benefits, then the value proposition for those small groups of targeted patients goes way up.

This approach builds on small niches of patients. *Niche busters*, like Gleevec®, offer incredible outcomes to patients and profits to innovators. Taking a personalized medicine approach will allow companies to move from a *product-driven* model to one that is truly *market driven*. Ironically, this model begins to resemble orphan drug development, which may, indeed, represent a shift in the R&D paradigm for the future.

The benefits of shifting focus to orphan drugs are many, including a streamlined approval process, patent extension and exclusivity, tax credits, and smaller clinical trials because of a narrow indication. Instead of looking at the population as everybody (let's say everybody with high cholesterol), you start looking at people with high cholesterol *and* a particular genetic profile. By targeting smaller, specific populations for disease management, companies get their product to market more quickly and can reduce spending *without sacrificing innovation*.

The change in focus does come with its own set of challenges. As competition moves into the smaller spaces, everyone will be looking for an opportunity to get an *orphan drug designation* (ODD). This will likely lead to additional scrutiny and will intensify the need to demonstrate the economic and clinical value of your product as it applies to a particular population before approval. Shifting the R&D focus will require new capabilities across the entire business to meet these demands. In addition, consideration will need to be given to the pricing implications of a drug across multiple indications.

Despite some new challenges, the rewards can outweigh the risks. The overall cost of developing orphan drugs is typically less than that of other drugs. The paradigm shift even reaches beyond *just* R&D, since the smaller population doesn't require large marketing or promotional campaigns. Ultimately, the segmented approach enables drug companies to see competitive returns on investment, while increasing the value to the targeted market.

Interest in a new R&D paradigm is increasing, offering opportunity for the long term. Today's orphan drug could even become tomorrow's rolling blockbuster, a point not lost by Allergan in its support of the controversial drug, Botox®.

Real-World Example

In the late 1960s and early 1970s, Dr. Alan Scott, an ophthalmologist in San Francisco, investigated treatments for his patients who had crossed eyes (strabismus) and uncontrollable blinking (blepharospasm). He found one particular compound to be pretty successful at managing both these conditions and built a company, Oculinum, Inc., entirely around his new drug.[22]

Approved in 1984 as an orphan drug for uncontrolled blinking, neck pain, and muscle spasms, Oculinum® treatment typically lasts about 4 to 6 months. As its use only relieved the chronic conditions temporarily, patients needed to come back to see the doctor two to three times a year, sometimes more, over a long period of time.

Around the same time that Dr. Scott's company received approval for Oculinum, Canadian ophthalmologist Jean

Carruthers was treating her patients in Vancouver with the same drug. Over time, her staff noticed that her patients were looking healthier, more vibrant, and even *younger* every time they came back for a treatment. This amazing phenomenon led Dr. Carruthers and her husband, Dr. Alistair Carruthers (a dermatologist) to begin experimenting on themselves.

In 1989, Oculinum received broader approval. Then in 1991, Allergan bought the company for $9 million and decided to rename it. Shortly thereafter, the Drs. Carruthers published their study on the effect of treatment of *frown lines* with Allergan's new drug—you guessed it—*Botox*.

In 2002, the FDA approved Botox for treatment of frown lines. In 2010, Botox gained approval for the treatment of chronic migraines. There are five million doses administered annually in North America, which translate into $1.5 *billion* in sales. Allergan has now applied for patents for around 90 different uses.

Although controversial, Botox epitomizes how an orphan drug once designated for a particular condition might progressively receive approval for several other indications. While past performance is no certain indication of future results, the Botox story provides a great example of the potential for orphan drugs to become the blockbuster of the future.

Looking Ahead

Many pharmaceutical companies have implemented changes in their commercial and R&D processes and capabilities. Most haven't gone far enough. Sustainable leadership in this market requires a radically different development engine and a radically different commercial model. The key requirement is to build a scientific foundation for highly differentiated and sustainable franchises around selected disease states.

While excellent science must be a given, it is not enough by itself. Pharmaceutical companies will also need to master the critical building blocks we outlined throughout the chapter. Those that do will be the leaders in the new healthcare marketplace.

Questions for Pharmaceutical Manufacturers

- What do we know about how payers look at products in therapeutic areas of interest to us? What about consumers?
- Are economic and clinical value considerations and evidence requirements taken into account during product development, or only just before commercialization?
- What kind of evidence do we have to demonstrate the economic and clinical value of our products? How strong is it?
  - Have we given thought to the economic endpoints we can include in RCTs? Will these resonate with payers? Providers?
  - Have we built in comparators besides placebo to our drug trials? Will these resonate with payers? Providers?
  - What kinds of endpoints are of most interest to consumers? Have we included these in our study design?
- Do our development and licensing and acquisition (L&A) efforts take the broader market context into account, particularly the need to substantially restrain cost growth and improve outcomes?
  - Have we given thought to how we'll communicate these messages to payers? Providers? Consumers? Investors?
- Have we adapted our commercial model to meet the needs of the evolving provider landscape?

Endnotes

1. Tracy Staton. "Express Scripts Assembling Anti-Sovaldi Coalition to Shut Out Gilead Hep C Drug." *FiercePharma.* April 2014. http://www.fiercepharma.com/story/express-scripts -assembling-anti-sovaldi-coalition-shut-out-gilead-hep-c-dru /2014-04-08.

2. Zacks Equity Research. "Hefty Price Tag of Gilead's Sovaldi Questioned Again." July 2014. http://www.zacks.com/stock/news/139903/hefty-price-tag-of-gileads-sovaldi-questioned-again.

3. Bruce Japsen. "As Pricey Hepatitis Pill Harvoni Joins Sovaldi, States Erect Medicaid Hurdles." *Forbes.* October 2014. http://www.forbes.com/sites/brucejapsen/2014/10/10/as-hepatitis-pill-harvoni-joins-sovaldi-states-erect-medicaid-hurdles/.

4. Jaimy Lee. "8% of Patients Stop Taking Sovaldi, CVS Study Finds." *Modern Healthcare.* September 2014. http://www.modernhealthcare.com/article/20140917/NEWS/309179963.

5. Tracy Staton. "Sovaldi May Be Cost-Effective, But the U.K. Can't Afford It, Documents Say." *FiercePharma.* October 2014. http://www.fiercepharma.com/story/sovaldi-may-be-cost-effective-uk-cant-afford-it-documents-say/2014-10-07.

6. Eric Palmer. "France Health Minister Says EU Will Fight Price of Gilead's Sovaldi: She Says the 14 Countries Will Share Information as They Negotiate with Gilead." *FiercePharma.* July 2014. http://www.fiercepharma.com/story/france-health-minister-says-eu-will-fight-price-gileads-sovaldi/2014-07-11.

7. Eric Palmer. "The Top 10 Most Expensive Drugs of 2013." *FiercePharma.* October 2014. http://www.fiercepharma.com/offer/gc_expensive_drugs?sourceform=Organic-GC-Expensive_Drugs-FiercePharma.

8. Rita E. Numerof, Michael N. Abrams, and Jack Nightingale. "Big Pharma: How to Regain Success." *Scrip Magazine.* 156:15–17. 2006.

9. Rita E. Numerof. "The Breakthrough Designation Program: Four Factors for Long Term Success." *eyeforpharma.* November 2013. http://social.eyeforpharma.com/column/breakthrough-designation-program-four-factors-long-term-success.

10. Rita E. Numerof. "Patients as Partners? The Role for 'Patient Centricity' in the New Healthcare Landscape." *eyeforpharma.* October 2014. http://social.eyeforpharma.com/commercial/patients-partners-role-patient-centricity-new-healthcare-landscape.

11. Rita E. Numerof. "Is Your Commercial Operation Ready for Healthcare 2.0?" *eyeforpharma.* November 2014. http://social.eyeforpharma.com/column/your-commercial-operation-ready-healthcare-20.

12. Michael N. Abrams and Rita E. Numerof. "New Commercial Models for the New Hospital Customer." *MD&DI.* November 2014. http://www.mddionline.com/article/new-commercial-models-new-hospital-customer.

13. Christopher de Wolff. "Capturing Value from Value-Added Services." *PM360*. October 2014. http://www.pm360online.com /capturing-the-value-from-value-added-services/.

14. National Institutes of Health (NIH). "Precision Medicine Initiative." U.S. Department of Health and Human Services. January 2015. http://www.nih.gov/precisionmedicine/.

15. Francis S. Collins and Harold Varmus. "A New Initiative on Precision Medicine." *New England Journal of Medicine*. March 2015. http://www.nejm.org/doi/full/10.1056/NEJMp1500523.

16. Matthew Herper. "Surprise! With $60 Million Genentech Deal, 23andMe Has a Business Plan." *Forbes.* January 2015. http:// www.forbes.com/sites/matthewherper/2015/01/06/surprise-with -60-million-genentech-deal-23andme-has-a-business-plan/.

17. Matthew Herper. "In Big Shift, 23andMe Will Invent Drugs Using Customer Data." *Forbes.* March 2015. http://www.forbes .com/sites/matthewherper/2015/03/12/23andme-enters-the-drug -business-just-as-apple-changes-it/.

18. Rita E. Numerof. "The Impact of Comparative Effectiveness on the Healthcare Marketplace." Numerof & Associates, Inc. June 2009.

19. Adapted from Rita E. Numerof and Christopher de Wolff. "Key Considerations for Entering Into Risk Sharing." *eyeforpharma.* December 2013. http://social.eyeforpharma.com/column/key -considerations-entering-risk-sharing.

20. Pharmaceutical Outcomes Research and Policy Program. "Performance Based Risk Sharing Database (PBRS)." University of Washington, School of Pharmacy. May 2013.

21. Jean-Pierre Garnier. "Rebuilding the R&D Engine in Big Pharma." *Harvard Business Review,* 86 (5): 68ff. 2008.

22. Rita E. Numerof. "Today's Orphan Drug Could Be Tomorrow's Blockbuster." *Medical Progress Today* blog. November 2011. http://www.medicalprogresstoday.com/2011/11/todays-orphan -drug-could-be-tomorrows-blockbuster.php.

Chapter 9

A New Day Is Dawning for Medical Device and Diagnostics Manufacturers

Getting Products to Market when Value Is the Focus[1]

The medical device and diagnostics industry isn't as much fun as it used to be. Products are aging and increasingly more difficult to differentiate. Market success has attracted more competitors, many from outside the United States. Changing regulatory requirements in the United States and across the globe have resulted in increasing costs and time to develop new products. What's more, regulatory agencies around the world are requiring postmarket data about the long-term safety and efficacy of products, especially when they are used by broader patient populations in real-world settings.

Concerns about the safety of medical devices took center stage in the United States in 2011. Recalls and lawsuits in headlines led to public scrutiny from the public, directed at both manufacturers and the Food and Drug Administration (FDA).

Congressional pressure at the time focused on giving the FDA the authority to *require* companies to submit postmarket data as a *condition for continued approval* of moderate-risk medical devices under the fast-track process and would have allowed the FDA to rescind approval if this condition was not met. While the FDA *already* had broad authority to require postapproval studies, bills working their way through Congress underscored the growing sentiment that medical device manufacturers and the FDA ought to *increase* activities aimed at ensuring product safety. Even in 2010, the Institute of Medicine (IOM) also called for an integrated pre- and postmarket regulatory framework aimed at improving device and diagnostic safety. The FDA clearly heard this advice. Review times for products have increased with even blood glucose monitors getting more scrutiny recently due to concerns over accuracy and safety.

Unlike other recommendations in the report—for example, the recommendation to scrap the 510(k) approval process altogether, requirements for more postmarket safety surveillance were considered relatively uncontroversial by the device industry and even the FDA.

The reality is that *much* more will be required of manufacturers to comply with emerging postmarket safety surveillance rules *and* to bring products to market. Increasingly, clinical data will be *required* for 510(k) clearance where historically such data were only needed in support of investigational device exemption (IDE) and premarket approval (PMA) submissions.

As regulators enact more stringent requirements for medical device safety, reviewing passively acquired complaints through call centers is no longer sufficient. Companies have begun to adopt a more comprehensive approach to ensuring medical device safety throughout the product life cycle. This means more proactive planning for postmarket safety surveillance based on product characteristics (e.g., product novelty, consequences of product failure, device complexity) identified in early product development. But the real challenge will be bringing products to market going forward.

Over the past several years, the medical device industry has been rocked by product recalls, Department of Justice investigations into improper marketing practices, and incidents that highlight potential conflicts of interest with physicians. Product safety concerns are especially predominant, given FDA reports that from 2005 through 2009 over 3,500 medical devices were recalled for potential safety problems. There was a 97% increase in recalls of medical devices between fiscal 2003 and 2012. In 2012 alone, there were 1,190 recalls in a single year.[2] In the first seven months of 2009, more than 1,000 recall notices were sent out, of which over 100 were designated as *class 1*, involving a defect serious enough to create a "reasonable probability of adverse health consequences or death." To address concerns about device safety and the medical device approval process, the FDA's Center for Devices and Radiological Health (CDRH) conducted an internal review and commissioned the IOM to review the 510(k) process in 2011.

Perhaps in anticipation of the IOM's report, the FDA took a number of steps to address concerns related to the 510(k) process. CDRH's plan,[3] released in August 2010, specified 25 specific actions to be taken in order to overhaul the 510(k) process, including issuing draft guidance and proposed regulations. The FDA's plan leaves the current regulatory framework intact, with substantial revisions and an increased emphasis on the scientific evaluation of medical devices in the hope of avoiding future recalls by approving only innovative, safe products.

The IOM released its independent review in July 2011. It concluded that the 510(k) process is not a reliable premarket screen of safety and effectiveness and recommended that the FDA would be better served by eliminating the 510(k) process altogether, rather than expending any additional resources attempting to improve it. It recommended replacing the current system with an integrated premarket and postmarket regulatory framework to ensure the safety and effectiveness of future devices.

As the FDA's actions demonstrate, even without the IOM's critical findings and recommendations, device companies must expect additional, significant changes to the 510(k) process and postmarket safety requirements. When viewed in the broader context of healthcare reform, comparative effectiveness research, and other current challenges, changes to the 510(k) process have serious implications for device companies.

While the FDA has rejected the IOM's recommendation to replace the 510(k) process, it apparently anticipated this criticism. Within a month of the release of the IOM's report, the FDA issued a number of guidance documents concerning 510(k) modifications, design of medical device clinical studies, postmarket surveillance studies and requirements, and new methods of monitoring clinical trials.[4–8]

So, not surprisingly, in the fall of 2013 the FDA formally took steps to create a national medical device postmarket surveillance system.[9] A multistakeholder governance board was tasked with establishing a sustainable surveillance system including practices, policies, procedures, detail methods, etc. The rules laid out the establishment of a unique device identification (UDI) system, in which each device is labelled appropriately and tracked in electronic health records (EHRs). The rules also called for a publicly accessible global UDI database, aimed at providing detailed and nonconfidential information about these devices to the public and linked to claims and specific care delivery sites. At about the same time (summer 2013), a Medical Device Registry Task Force was established. The intent was to determine the relationship between specific devices and improved quality, patient safety, and reimbursement. Registries were also established to support premarket approval and clearance.[10] Finally, the FDA action plan laid out approaches to improve and "modernize" adverse event reporting and analysis through 2013 and 2014. The objective of these efforts was straightforward: Provide longitudinal insight to ensure more timely and comprehensive assessments of device risk-benefit profiles.[11] Compliance for class III devices was required by September 2014, class II by September 2015, and class I by September 2016.[12]

The very real issue of safety concerns and the weakness of the current 510(k) approval process are clearly illustrated in the problem of power morcellators. These devices are used by gynecologists to grind up tissue internally and remove it using minimally invasive procedures. The result is that women undergoing hysterectomy can have the procedure with minimal scarring and less blood loss. While it sounds good from a cosmetic and healing perspective, there are a few major complications. Many women who undergo the procedure have uterine fibroids which could be cancerous in as many as 1 out of 350 cases.[13] When cancerous growths are ground up inside the abdominal cavity, there's a risk of spreading the disease elsewhere in the body.

Patient activist Amy Reed, who experienced such harm, attempted to have the devices banned. At the end of 2014, the only action the FDA had taken was to force a prominent warning associated with the use of the devices. One large healthcare system, HCA, did ban the devices from operating rooms both in the United States and the UK.[13]

At the heart of this problem is the use of outmoded regulatory reviews associated with 510(k) clearance and the level of rigor and diligence by the FDA in assessing products coming up for approval. While Class III products (like implantable defibrillators and heart valves) require bench and animal data as well as clinical trials *before* being cleared for market (i.e., "premarket approval"), Class II devices, like the morcellator, pacemakers, and hip and knee implants, do not. These devices come under the "510(k) clearance" rule which only requires premarket notification. This allows manufacturers to get new products onto the market by merely showing that they are "substantially equivalent" to predicate devices. The problem with the morcellator is that the first one didn't appear until the 1990s, 20 years after the predicate device was approved! The study that allowed FDA clearance for the morcellator addressed efficacy (the rate of tissue removal and associated blood loss), but not medium or long-term safety.

The limited action taken by the FDA on morcellator safety is troubling. There is still widespread concern that the 510(k) process, introduced four decades ago and actually meant to be temporary, is deeply flawed. We expect it will continue to be the subject of much scrutiny and that postmarket safety surveillance activity will create a path to greater transparency in both cost and quality of medical devices.

Implications for the Industry

While it's impossible to eliminate risks associated with medical devices, it is clear that the FDA will require more effort, both premarket and postmarket, from device makers to improve safety. There's clearly tension between getting a product to market quickly versus obtaining additional data to ensure safety, a point we address in more detail in Chapter 10.

Given the FDA's ongoing plans to address the 510(k) process, device companies should expect it to be more demanding in reviewing submissions. In addition, companies will need to expand their view of device development and approval to include planning for postmarket safety requirements. While the FDA has rejected the IOM's proposed elimination of the 510(k) process as a practical matter, there was much less disagreement with the IOM's recommendations to improve postmarket surveillance capabilities. The new requirements described earlier point to just how ready the FDA is to act. As companies respond to demands for clinical evidence to obtain clearance, they need to plan for increased postmarket safety requirements as well. For purposes of postmarket safety surveillance, companies need to examine whether preclinical, clinical, and product development insights about devices are used sufficiently in developing robust postmarket surveillance strategies.

There are a number of implications beyond postmarket requirements for the industry as well. Companies should expect longer 510(k) reviews, as the FDA focuses on its internal processes, safety, and additional oversight. To a certain extent, however, companies should be able to anticipate issues. If a device is invasive or is based on new technology, heightened scrutiny and/or demands for clinical data should be expected. Companies should recognize, in light of the CDRH and IOM reviews, that if there is something new in a device, it will be more difficult to compare it to a predicate, and it's increasingly likely that the FDA will require clinical data. As a result, companies probably should expect higher research and development costs and longer product development cycles.

Commercial Challenges

The commercial front isn't immune; advertising and selling costs are also skyrocketing. But the really bad news is just starting to emerge.

Across the world, payers are clamping down on healthcare costs by saying no to new products, line extensions, and price increases. Reacting to the prospect of exponentially increasing liabilities, payers of all types are demanding hard clinical and health economic data to justify any change with bottom-line impact. We've advised our clients for a number of years that, going forward, they should expect that growth will depend on very focused strategies and fairly sophisticated product market segmentation—country-by-country, payer-by-payer, and patient-by-patient decisions to pursue a treatment or not, or to choose a newer, more expensive treatment versus an older, less-expensive one.

In addition, as of January 1, 2013, medical device and diagnostic manufacturers have faced a 2.3% excise tax. This tax applied to nonretail hospital and physician supplies as well as leases for devices; eyeglasses, contact lenses, hearing aids, and so on are exempt. There are also greater reporting standards designed to increase transparency around payments to physicians (for each event > $10 or > $100 annually) and payments to teaching hospitals.

Fraud and abuse have been the subject of greater focus through new rules regarding compliance program integrity. Penalties have increased for individuals and companies, so the criticality of more robust risk assessments, better accountability, and new approaches to fair market value (FMV) governing relationships with physicians have become essential, and market claims have needed stronger data to support them. Specifically to this point Medicare began reducing its payment for imaging in 2012, concerned about overutilization and its associated costs. The trend has continued with commercial payers following suit.

What's less known by many in the industry is how comparative effectiveness and real-world evidence will impact these changes. As we outlined in Chapter 4, new evidence requirements represent a significant shift for the entire industry and promise to radically alter the level of government and payer involvement in the way healthcare products and services are developed, delivered, and paid for. CMS, for example, has viewed comparative effectiveness as a major solution to healthcare cost containment.

The medical device industry may be the sector *most strongly impacted* by the rise of comparative effectiveness as a force in the U.S. healthcare marketplace, and the diagnostics industry may be the one *best positioned* to take advantage of the shift toward a cost-effectiveness orientation. Let's look at how this is likely to play out.

Evidence Requirements:
The Threat for Medical Devices

There will be a fundamental restructuring of priorities within large segments of the medical device industry, away from incremental improvements that are mostly of interest to surgeons, and toward improvements that are of interest to payers and delivery stakeholders across the continuum of care.[14] This will put *significant* pressure on device manufacturers to produce products that require fewer ancillary resources (e.g., fewer surgeon hours, less postoperative recovery). Competition from drugs, other devices, and even noninterventional approaches (e.g., watchful waiting) will increase.

The most important implications for medical device manufacturers are expected to be:

■ The end of the "last version plus 5%" business model
■ Increased pressure to "rightsize" device functionality
■ Increased competition with drugs
■ Restricted qualification for devices

End of the "Last Version plus 5%" Business Model

The historic operating model for much of the device industry has been to develop a new, incrementally improved version of a device and seek incrementally increased reimbursement for it. In the last several years, this model has been under pressure exacerbated by the global recession. It's likely to come to a screeching halt within the next few years.

There are two primary reasons for its impending demise. First, it effectively reflected a gentlemen's agreement between payers and device manufacturers: Keep pushing the frontiers, and we'll keep paying. Often, the improvements were primarily of interest to surgeons, who were in a position to pressure the other stakeholders to make the improved device available.

Many industry insiders believe that these improvements had relatively little incremental value and certainly didn't justify significant increases in reimbursement.

Today there is greater scrutiny of the relative value of the product, and many companies have found their products not fetching the increased reimbursement they expected. This will be more common in the years to come. Hospitals, under increasing cost pressure themselves, are also unlikely to try to keep up in the new technology acquisition race unless there is a clear economic and clinical value argument to be made. And, as specialists leave private practice to become employees of healthcare systems, their incentives are increasingly aligned with healthcare executives. The industry faces continued consolidation pressure as these executives work to standardize on a more limited number of products and manufacturers.

As incremental improvements give way to more substantial ones, companies that rely on 510(k) equivalence for the majority of their products will find themselves needing to enhance their capability to conduct clinical research in support of PMAs. Even those that look to contract with clinical research organizations to oversee this research will still need the capabilities that allow them to adequately oversee and monitor the work.[15]

Second, a system that issues guidelines based on research into the cost effectiveness of a treatment regime is not designed to keep up with the newest innovations in treatment. Incorporating a new product into the guidelines means either considering it equivalent to what already exists (which implies that it can't cost any more than the prior technology if it is to be cost effective) or evaluating the evidence to determine the circumstances under which the new product is more cost effective than the old. This takes time, which increases the delay to be expected between incremental increases in reimbursement.

As the extent to which devices compete with drugs increases, the need to develop devices with potential pharmaceutical competition in mind does too. An immediate assessment of the exposure of specific classes of devices that are heavily weighted in the portfolio to drug competition (which is beyond the scope of this book) should be undertaken immediately.

Increased Pressure to "Rightsize" Functionality

Ongoing and significant pressure to rightsize the therapeutic value of a product for a particular patient population will emerge. CMS will become increasingly unwilling to pay for *excess functionality*—features that most patients won't use or that are deemed to be beyond what is "necessary." This has two impacts. First, it will create markets for older products, extending their life cycles in spite of the introduction of more sophisticated versions, as long as the functionality of the older model is sufficient for selected patient segments.

It will also mean that the willingness of CMS to increase reimbursement for the newest product extension will depend heavily on the case for marginal economic and clinical value that can be made for the new model. And while there will still be a place for improved functionality at higher cost, the primary emphasis at first will be on defining segments that can get nearly equivalent benefits from less-expensive products. New product development during this phase is less likely to be focused on questions like, "Does a ceramic bearing work better than a metallic one?" than "Will this old design still work if we replace the metal with cheaper injection-molded plastic?"

Pressure to produce products that meet, but do not exceed, functionality needs will require that device companies proactively segment the market based on functional requirements globally and within specific regional markets. Product development itself will take on a new aspect in which cost consciousness is given as much weight as technical capability. This will represent a significant cultural change challenge.

Rightsizing of functionality is likely to be among the first objectives of comparative effectiveness. We expect the demand for more functional, less expensive devices that began in late 2010 to pick up momentum, growing rapidly for the foreseeable future.

As the locus of decision making moves from the individual doctor to the C-suite, and doctors are increasingly incented to deliver better outcomes at lower cost, manufacturers will be under more pressure to design simpler products that are easier to use and less expensive. Questions that address the impact of new technology on outcomes will need to have answers. Deciding which product is best for a given subset of patients will also impact design, expected market share, and, ultimately, revenues. The best materials, design, and flexibility might be optimal for the ex-Olympic ski racer who needs knee surgery at the age of 41. But, is the "30-year knee" design really the best choice for the 68-year-old woman whose goal is to play on the floor with her grandkids?

Increased Competition with Drugs

As the drive to more closely link coverage determinations with demonstrated cost effectiveness gets underway, medical devices will be in more direct competition with drugs. Drug therapies are, in many cases, significantly less expensive than surgical ones, and even if they are less clinically effective, they may, therefore, be more cost effective. In addition, if CMS, like other payers, can replace costly surgeries with drugs for specific classes of patients on the basis of cost, benefit, or risk, this would be an attractive option.

Classes of devices that are especially likely to be subjected to renewed efforts to compare outcomes include stents and angioplasty devices, implantable stimulation devices for pain relief and Parkinson's disease, continuous blood glucose monitors and insulin pumps, and devices used in bariatric surgery, joint replacements, and spinal surgery.

The expectation that these classes of devices will come under increased scrutiny does not mean that they will necessarily lose out to drug therapies—some may become the new standard of care. Others, however, may be restricted to very specific populations. Still others may be demoted behind competitors' products as a second-line treatment on the basis of cost or performance.

Restricted Qualification for Devices

As cost effectiveness becomes a critical factor for determining coverage and reimbursement, certain populations that once were candidates for devices may lose their eligibility. This has happened in the United Kingdom, where, in 2005, the Suffolk Primary Care Trust (part of the National Health Service [NHS]) started to deny orthopedic implants to obese patients and smokers. This practice has spread to include other regions of the country, as well as other procedures (such as in vitro fertilization [IVF]).

In the United States, restrictions are most clearly evident in trends reflecting the establishment of "centers of excellence" by large self-insured employers. Walmart, for example, has established such centers for cardiac and spinal surgeries. The initial centers included Cleveland Clinic, Virginia Mason, Mayo Clinic, Scott and White, Geisinger, and Mercy. One of the primary intents has been to lower the incidence of unneeded surgeries and, if one is medically indicated, to ensure optimal outcomes and cost.

Self-insured employers (e.g., PepsiCo, Boeing, Kroger, Walmart, Lowe's) have negotiated specific bundled payments over the last several years. We expect this to continue. With the increasing focus on transparency and a trend toward consumerism, pressure on outcomes and cost will force manufacturers to reevaluate core fundamentals of their business models—on both the product development and commercialization sides of the equation.

With consumers having increased skin-in-the-game as noted in earlier chapters, they are more and more mindful of cost and outcomes, with information sources such as *On Health,* a *Consumer Reports* publication that provides answers to such questions as where to get surgery for hip/knee replacement or spine surgery for lower back pain. The publication addresses whether or not the surgery is likely to work, how to choose a facility, how to pick the right doctor, etc. It also has specific outcome and safety data on 4,500 hospitals around the country.

Healthcare Delivery Pressures: Additional Threats for Medical Devices

Enormous challenges will also emerge as manufacturers are confronted by healthcare delivery organizations struggling to respond to the changing environment. These changes include:

■ Growth in medical tourism
■ Use of reference pricing
■ Transition to value-based payment
■ Emergence of risk-sharing agreements

Indeed, in 2015 device manufacturers, like their pharmaceutical and biotech counterparts, began to search for ways to "add value" and ensure that their products remain on the approved and used product list.[16]

Growth in Medical Tourism

Add to this the blossoming trend in medical tourism. It used to be that medical tourism was essentially a flow of patients to the United States from other markets. While this does continue, especially for complex situations (think transplants), there is an outflow trend that's picking up speed. Increasingly, U.S. consumers are shopping options in India, other parts of Southeast Asia and the Caribbean. With U.S.-trained medical teams and costs a fraction of what they might be at home, the package can be very appealing. Knee surgery in the United States averages $16,000; in India it's $4,500. Open heart surgery (CABG) typically runs $50,000 in the United States and $4,400 in India.

Imagine that your insurance company offers to spring for all expenses paid for you and a significant other—including a week of recovery/rehab on the back end—no copay, no deductible, no travel expense. It gets even more appealing when it's the dead of winter and you live in Boston, Chicago, or some other snow-covered city! It looks even more attractive as these same delivery organizations set up facilities in the Caribbean.

Growth of Risk-Sharing Agreements

Under pressure, delivery organizations will look to medical device manufacturers to dramatically reduce cost. Care protocols, quality metrics, and the trend toward population health discussed in Chapter 5 will intensify this pressure.

In response, manufacturers will need to consider entering into risk-sharing agreements. Those that have a compelling value story can do so willingly; those that don't will be forced to make significant price concessions. Irrespective of whether manufacturers enter performance-based agreements willingly or at the demand of payers and providers, they need to have data demonstrating a product's value, or risk commoditization.

It is likely that cardiac devices along with orthopedic implants (hips and knees) will be the primary focus of new risk-sharing agreements between device manufacturers and providers, driven out of concern for lower reimbursement rates and readmission penalties for congestive heart failure (CHF) and joint replacement. While most of the risk-sharing agreements are one-off and confidential given their "experimental" nature, some have been made public. St. Jude Medical, for example, has stated its intent to pay hospitals a rebate of

45% of net price for cardiac resynchronization therapy (CRT) if a lead revision is required within a year of implantation as a result of a specific number of factors determined by the company. St. Jude has gone on record noting that this type of risk-sharing allows providers validation of the benefit of new technologies in improving patient outcomes.

Transition to Value-Based Payments

The transition to value-based payment arrangements by public and private payers is poised to accelerate. CMS's hospital value-based purchasing program, enacted into law in 2010, started quite modestly with rewards for doing things that hospitals should have been doing anyway. Over time, the measures are likely to move from activity tracking to actual outcomes achieved. CMS has committed to 50% of Medicare/Medicaid payment being attached to value-based contracts by 2018. A private multistakeholder task force has committed to receiving 75% of its business in value-based arrangements by 2020. Behind closed doors participants are quick to acknowledge that they are far from ready to assume up and down-side risk but want to prepare themselves for that eventuality. The key question for manufacturers is, "What does our organization stand to gain—or lose—from these arrangements with payers and providers?"

Use of Reference Pricing

The use of reference pricing is also likely to expand given the early success with it. Reference pricing isn't new; it's been around for years outside the United States as a primary mechanism of establishing a fair market value for new technology and reevaluating pricing for existing products. In the United States CalPERS has conducted a reference pricing pilot and reportedly saved over $5.5 million in 2 years. Essentially, the benefits provider set standard prices for hip and knee replacements and incented beneficiaries to select higher-value hospitals for the procedures, an approach not unlike Walmart's Centers of Excellence.

The price impact was stunning. Before the initiative. the average price was $42,000. The price fell to $27,148, within the first 9 months of operation in 2012, with CalPERS realizing a reduction of 26% in the 2 years the program was in existence. Based on their data, cost savings were realized by lower hospital costs, largely driven by negotiated rates on more standardized implants, and enrollee migration to high-value facilities.

Impact of Comparative Effectiveness on Medical Device Operations

The end of the "last version plus 5%" model will mean a radical change in the way that medical device companies develop products, manage their portfolios, and plan for the future.

In the past, this pricing/reimbursement model has often meant creating features that improve ease of use for surgeons, who would then effectively demand that payers reimburse the product. This model is failing as surgeons begin to accept responsibility for cost containment and as they lose power relative to payers. It has also been impacted by a more active Office of Inspector General/Department of Justice (OIG/DOJ), which is forcing companies to avoid the appearance of a cozy relationship with surgeons. This doesn't mean that surgeon-focused improvements are finished; they'll still have a place, but unless the surgeons themselves are willing to pay for them, they'll have to be of a nature that allows the cost to be passed through to payers, patients, or institutional providers.

For the most part, the incremental improvement model will be replaced, which means that product development will have to refocus on creating *substantial* differentiation between new products and older, competing ones. What's more, this differentiation will have to be along dimensions that matter to payers—CMS's interest in cost effectiveness being a primary example—or that matter to other parties who can supplement reimbursement payments out of their own pockets.

The most obvious examples are premium devices for specific patients who believe that such a device is appropriate for their specific circumstances—for example, the 80-year-old heart patient who can pay extra for a 50-year pacemaker and believes himself likely to take advantage of the extended product life, or the aging athlete who would benefit from a more advanced knee implant than his or her insurance will cover, or the young person who really needs a 60-year knee, or the elderly patient who would benefit from a knee that self-adjusts to help maintain balance.

There are other possibilities, however. Payment doesn't necessarily have to come from the patient—specialty hospitals, hospital systems, and surgical group practices might be willing to cover part of the cost of a device (or of related capital equipment) if doing so allowed them to be perceived as cutting edge, or if some features significantly shortened or simplified surgery or follow-up.

An example of this kind of improvement would be the ability to remotely monitor the performance of a joint implant—a potential up-sell opportunity to both the patient (who may be able to avoid the inconvenience and cost of follow-up visits) and the provider (who may be able to avoid the time and trouble of the visit). In part, the appeal of this kind of improvement depends on how reimbursement works. A return to a capitation-like system and focus on population health management make innovations, like remote monitoring, far more appealing to providers and payers.

Perhaps the most radical possibility is the development of *better than normal* devices: artificial joints, ligaments, and even sensory devices that enhance the capabilities of patients beyond what is natural. These *bionics* (in the 1980s sense of the term) could potentially appeal to younger, healthy patients willing to spend out of pocket to, effectively, upgrade their personal hardware.

The *last version plus 5%* model is already under significant pressure, but the most radical break with the past will come when CMS, in keeping with the actions of its global counterparts, demands evidence of clinical impact and cost effectiveness—in terms of patient-specific outcomes and raw dollars—of a new device as a precondition for reimbursement. This would require a change in the relevant legislation—changes that have been in the works and are likely to be realized in the next couple of years.

Given the potentially catastrophic impact this will have on the value of current product pipelines, it seems prudent to diversify away from this model immediately, as many leading global device manufacturers have begun to do.

Prudent Responses and Defensive Strategies for Medical Device Companies

Over the last several years, we've recommended that medical device companies pursue four key defensive responses:

- Adopt strategies suited to the new environment.
- Focus on reducing the cost of the procedure.
- Develop service wraps.
- Embrace the cost–functionality trade-off.

We stand by these recommendations as the market evolves.

Adopt Strategies Suited to the New Environment

Diversifying away from a business model that emphasizes incremental changes with the surgeon as primary customer to one that identifies and incorporates features that add significant value to payers, patients, and providers should continue to be an immediate concern for device manufacturers.

This requires (1) identifying what constitutes value for these distinct groups of stakeholders and understanding how these values vary within each, (2) refocusing research and licensing and acquisition licensing and acquisition (L&A) efforts on delivering value, (3) ensuring that evidence generation strategies result in a compelling demonstration of value, and (4) entering into risk-sharing agreements for specific products.

Device companies can also help themselves by taking a step back from a product-focused view of treatment, which tends to keep them locked into a pattern of creating the next version of the last product, in favor of a broader view of the disease state. Intervention after things reach the acute stage will give way, partly, to prevention and early intervention. With the right approach, device makers can be a part of that.

Focus on Reducing the Cost of the Procedure

To the extent that devices (or new designs) reduce surgical or procedural costs they will be more attractive relative to alternatives like drug therapy and no treatment. This should be a specific focus of device makers looking to develop new products.

Develop Service Wraps

To an even greater extent than for pharmaceutical companies, device companies can increase the value of their offerings by bundling them with well-designed services. The development of services that help to ensure that follow-up care goes well or that the additional health benefits made possible by a device (like the cardiovascular benefits that could accrue to a person with a joint replacement if he or she engaged in regular exercise) could add significant value to payers, providers, or patients. One illustrative example already seeing considerable activity is remote monitoring technology. To the extent that technology can report on the performance of a device and reduce the need for expensive interactions with providers (e.g., follow-up visits), it is likely to be codified into standard protocols for managing care.

Indeed, legislation passed in April 2015 as part of the sustainable growth rate "doc fix" specified that telehealth and remote patient monitoring are legitimate mechanisms to improve care and its coordination. This move is an acknowledgment by CMS that technology has advanced such that how and where services are performed will migrate outside the traditional hospital/ambulatory care setting.

Approaches that focus on providing rehabilitation services that are tailored to the needs of the individual may also play a role. By expanding the scope of the business to include things like sports medicine programs or support for those recovering from an injury, or rehabilitation services after surgery, the value proposition can be expanded.

Like pharmaceutical companies, device makers are likely to find that hospital systems and even surgical groups are willing partners in this development work, especially to the extent that developing a new standard of care that offers the wrapped services (a) helps to differentiate them from the competition, and (b) positions them favorably should the treatment protocol be adopted as the standard of care in the eventual guidelines.

Embrace the Cost–Functionality Trade-Off

Rather than always seeking to stay at the forefront of technology, medical device manufacturers should embrace the diversity of needs that exist globally. This means extending the life cycle of products that might otherwise have been retired to meet more basic needs and limited budgets of population segments across the globe. In addition, payers, providers, and patients globally are moving in the direction of cost–functionality trade-offs. With the massive consolidation occurring across healthcare delivery and the move to employ physicians or at least align incentives, issues of relative value will increasingly be in the forefront of product decision making.

Comparative Effectiveness: The Opportunity for Diagnostics

Unlike medical devices, diagnostics are in a great position to take advantage of the shift toward a cost-effectiveness orientation.[14] The ability of diagnostic tests to segment patients based on scientific criteria so that eligibility for various treatments can be restricted and sequenced represents an enormous opportunity. The transition won't be painless, however. The use of diagnostics will become subject to protocol and will need to be justified by demonstrating economic and clinical value.

The most important implications are expected to be reduced tolerance for redundant testing, a new commercial model, and the possibility of mass screening. Each of these is explored in the following sections.

Reduced Tolerance for Redundant Testing

The first impact of the comparative effectiveness dynamic on the diagnostic industry is likely to be restricted reimbursement for the use of tests to confirm a diagnosis already made on the basis of other tests. This application has been under attack for decades, but physicians—sometimes pressured by patients, sometimes responding to malpractice fears, and sometimes feeling a need for an added measure of certainty—have continued to order them.

This demand won't disappear, but CMS, other payers, and providers assuming risk for the total cost of care will increasingly create bureaucratic barriers to the use of multiple tests that target the same diagnosis, and this will rapidly reduce demand. As a result, diagnostics companies are likely to see a reduction in the number of tests performed. The impact will fall most heavily on those tests that purport to measure the same thing, such as markers of inflammation (e.g., erythrocyte sedimentation rate and C-reactive protein) or imaging techniques. This will force physicians to choose a preferred test, which will be the one they believe to be more diagnostically effective.

Eventually, these individual preferences will give way to specific guidance regarding the tests that are recommended in a particular situation, a decision that will be based on cost effectiveness rather than solely on diagnostic effectiveness.

Initial steps in this direction have already begun and are likely to accelerate as a function of consolidation and reimbursement pressure on delivery organizations. Even the American Medical Association (AMA) has weighed in, attempting to place bounds on the appropriate use of diagnostic imaging.

New Commercial Model

A new commercial model will become prevalent, as the customer changes radically. Currently, the focal customer for the diagnostics sales force is the lab director, with physicians a secondary target. In the future, two new groups will be the primary targets: payers and hospital executives. As standard (cost-effective) protocols come to dominate medical practice, inclusion of a diagnostic test in the protocol (on the basis of a compelling economic and clinical value argument) will be paramount.

We expect that there will be two sources of protocols in the United States: CMS and hospitals. CMS's interest will be in developing cost-effective ways to treat patients (primarily outpatients) who don't fall under the diagnosis-related group

(DRG) system, thus holding down its costs. This will tend to give license to administrators who want cost-effective guidelines developed and enforced within their hospitals to hold down costs of (primarily inpatient) treatment when there are fixed or at-risk payments.

This puts diagnostics makers in a position of having to demonstrate that the use of their tests as part of a treatment protocol leads to more cost-effective treatment. That means putting significantly more up-front effort into defining the value of possible new diagnostic tests from payer and administrator perspectives, selecting those that have a compelling potential value proposition, and demonstrating the value of the test prior to seeking reimbursement for it. The goal will be to get the new test incorporated into existing or new predictive care paths, as a standard element, as quickly as possible.

As lab directors and physicians become less important in the sales efforts, there will be a reprioritization of resources away from sales, and toward research and development, clinical trials, and health economics.

Possibility of Mass Screening

It's possible that some diagnostics companies will hit the jackpot if a proprietary test becomes standard (i.e., is incorporated into CMS guidelines) as a widely applicable, even population-wide, preventive screening measure.

In order to make this happen, diagnostics companies will have to focus on developing evidence that the test significantly improves the ability to distinguish people who would benefit from an intervention from those who won't. This may lead to partnerships or agreements with drug or device manufacturers, or with providers that have developed new treatment protocols, because identifying those people who would maximally benefit from their product or service increases their value propositions.

Personalized Medicine and Companion Diagnostics

The shift to new evidence requirements and a new commercial model will lead to a change in the way that diagnostic tests are developed, because more accurate determination of the probable success of the test in the marketplace will be possible. Hence, more thought and effort will go into determining what test should receive priority in the development process, and more effort will go into defining and conducting trials to support its value proposition.

Diagnostics companies need to begin the shift to a new commercial model immediately. Changes to the diagnostics market space so that guidelines effectively determine the success of a product mean that an effective economic and clinical value argument will be of paramount importance.

To the extent that guidelines make more distinctions regarding which patients should receive what treatment, testing (particularly genetic and biomarker testing that identifies optimal treatments) could play a much larger, more pivotal role. *This represents a significant opportunity for diagnostics makers.*

Given the lead time involved in product development and approval, those diagnostics companies that begin to put in place the infrastructure to successfully incorporate economic and clinical value into their decision making and to generate data in support of the economic and clinical value of current and next-generation products will be in a powerful position. Those that don't will be in a very weak one.

The potential blockbuster effect of a mass screening hit means that diagnostics companies should begin to take prudent steps toward developing such tests today.

In some cases, relatively inexpensive, primarily retroactive research may allow diagnostics companies to identify candidate drug or device partners (i.e., drug or device makers). The goal of such research would be to identify patients who have responded well to drug A (but not drug B), and to drug B (but not drug A), and apply the diagnostic test to see if it can discriminate between the two groups.

This may require an expansion of the clinical research group (or of the group that oversees clinical trials conducted externally), as well as up-front investment in developing partnerships with drug and device makers. It has the benefit, however, of identifying potential partners whose own products have a great deal to gain from the success of the diagnostic test. Many of these companies have the deep pockets necessary to support the research that will be required to create a compelling economic and clinical value argument for the use of the diagnostic test.

In "Theranostics: The Way Forward?"[17] we described the clinical and financial power of companion diagnostics. Theranostics can predict a response to treatment or clinical outcomes—for example, the HER2 gene amplification in breast cancer. The DakoCytomations Hercep Test based on HER2 is one of the best examples of a commercialized theranostic. The test is used to detect susceptible breast tumors and to target treatment to patients who might benefit from Genentech's Herceptin®.

The use of pharmacogenomics in theranostics is on the rise. Genetic polymorphisms are increasingly used to predict treatment efficacy or complications from oncology drugs. Going beyond cancer, single nucleotide polymorphisms (SNPs) are being studied to determine the outcome of treating patients with statins. Similarly, gene variants may predict the clinical response to the standard antiplatelet drug, Clopidogrel, indicated for cardiovascular disease.

Imagine a day in the not too distant future where personalized medicine is the norm, eliminating the costly and painful process of experimentation with drugs that may work for that statistical artifact—the "average" patient—but not for that particular individual. This will certainly challenge the blockbuster mass marketed approach that's been the recent hallmark of pharmaceutical companies, but it will be a breakthrough for individuals and better outcomes at lower cost.

Prudent Responses and Defensive Strategies for Diagnostics

As with device manufacturers, we've made recommendations to our diagnostics clients to pursue two key approaches: diversify the revenue base and begin to develop partnerships for custom diagnostics. We stand by these recommendations and discuss each in the following sections.

Diversify the Revenue Base

As with other segments of the healthcare industry, it will be important for diagnostics companies to look for sources of revenue beyond the formal, reimbursed setting. Many diagnostic tests are already sold over the counter, so this strategy isn't a foreign one. Still, it might be expanded by considering the market of those who "just want to be sure," either through a broader over-the-counter set of offerings or through retail clinics.

As an example of the former, blood glucose monitors might find an expanded niche by appealing to those who don't have diagnosed diabetes, but would like to make sure, perhaps because they have a family history of diabetes. A low-cost, limited-use test might offer a convenient way for such a person to put his or her mind at ease, while simultaneously reducing the burden on the healthcare system that would result if he or she went the traditional route.

Likewise, a test (or battery of tests) offered through a retail healthcare clinic that allowed a patient to determine his or her risk of developing significant heart disease would be likely to appeal to a reasonably large segment of the population. These clinics are typically staffed by medical professionals, who would be able to lend their clinical judgment to the interpretation of the results.

The point is that cost effectiveness as calculated by a large payer does not account well (if at all) for the value of factors like reduced anxiety or the increased sense of control a person may derive from having a diagnostic test performed. The result is that there will be a large number of people for whom the test would have significant value, but for whom the test will not be covered. Providing access to it in a retail setting has the potential to be very valuable.

Begin to Develop Partnerships for Custom Diagnostics

The development of custom diagnostics in support of personalized medicine presents an enormous opportunity, but it's one that would be best realized if diagnostics makers partner with drug or device makers, or with providers, to demonstrate the combined value of screening in association with the device or therapeutic agent. This will allow diagnostics companies to find partners for the high-powered trials required to convince a skeptical audience of the economic and clinical value of the diagnostic test.

Where a compelling argument can be made that a given diagnostic assay will successfully discriminate between individuals who will and will not be helped by a drug, device, or treatment protocol, it makes sense to begin to seek partnerships immediately. Even when there is no *single* diagnostic marker that seems likely to successfully discriminate the treatable from the untreatable, the possibility that a multivariate index assay will make that discrimination possible may be enough to support a partnership.

Where Do Medical Device and Diagnostics Companies Go from Here?

For companies that have relied on fast approval cycles and limited or no clinical data, the future will assuredly be far more demanding. They will be confronted with greater clinical data requirements—and associated expenses—and will need to develop an improved understanding of the clinical value of their products. As the FDA addresses its internal process issues, however, companies may benefit from the development of clearer standards that enable them to gain a better understanding of FDA expectations and requirements and, by extension, they will be able to anticipate hurdles to regulatory approval and plan appropriately.

In the long term, device and diagnostics companies should expect greater importance to be placed on health economics data as well. This will present a number of challenges for these companies. Even as the FDA deals with internal disputes about process, companies must be clear about the path they want to take, work with reviewers to make their case for comparison to a predicate very clear, and know the rules and regulations better than reviewers.

The commercial landscape will see accelerated pricing pressures globally that will go beyond reduced reimbursement rates. Since 2011 we have seen increasing attention to bundled pricing as organizations try to build on previous work done by centers such as Geisinger, Intermountain, and Kaiser. There will also be increased engagement of specialists in employment models and *accountability networks* in the United States continuing to dampen the role of individual surgeons in product decision making.

Focus on patient selection, outcomes, prevention, early diagnosis, and optimal intervention will continue and move the society from a sickness model of healthcare delivery to one of health maintenance and wellness over time. The role of the consumer in healthcare will continue to evolve, with efforts aimed at creating greater accountability. *Consumer Reports*, for example, launched a new division several years ago focused on the evaluation of healthcare delivery organizations and reported on cost, comparing alternative therapies.[18]

We can expect increased pressure for transparency in the United States. Global economic challenges will continue to accelerate cost cutting in the developed world, making the developing world a bigger opportunity *and* source of competitive threat. We expect that demand outside the United States (OUS) for less complex, less expensive products requiring support will migrate to the United States and that OUS competitors will begin to encroach on the U.S. market, causing technology gaps to close.

The dominant business model of this segment of the healthcare industry, like its counterpart segments, shows signs of entering the *decline* phase of its life cycle.

The definition of the *customer* has evolved and the relative importance of that customer in decision making will continue to change at an accelerated rate. It's harder and harder to differentiate among similar products, pressures toward commoditization are increasing, and market share changes slowly (despite hand-to-hand combat).

As stated earlier, in the United States, as CMS focuses increased attention on outcomes, private insurers are following suit and larger employers will fall in line. There will be increased concern over appropriate diagnosis, and choice of intervention for a given patient will become increasingly important with stringent guidelines (e.g., what drugs, including which cancer regimens, are likely to work for which types of tumors). These groups will also look for comparisons between drugs and classes of drugs (e.g., benefits of generics vs. newer, branded products), and nonsurgical intervention will become more salient as the evidence for operative success continues to be scrutinized (e.g., drugs vs. stents, drugs and physical therapy vs. surgery for lower back pain).

Physician customer loyalty has been a function of sales representative relationships, some product features (although most believe core products are interchangeable), and involvement in clinical studies and product development (which furthers physician identification with the product and profitability). *As a basis for differentiation, this is not sustainable going forward.*

CMS, working closely with the Agency for Healthcare Research and Quality (AHRQ) and the FDA in keeping with other developed markets, will continue to focus on the economic and clinical value of new products (i.e., cost effectiveness). This places the burden on medical device and diagnostics companies to *proactively* evaluate the value of their products (it's not just about *approval*, but it's also about reimbursement). Economic and clinical value considerations will have to be an integral part of research and development (R&D), business development, and commercial activity. It is imperative that these companies create products of real value to patients, providers, and payers. Economic and clinical value considerations must be considered early and will require a redefinition of roles and capabilities. Health economics must be integrated into market strategy. R&D, marketing, and clinical will need to be closely aligned to ensure cost effectiveness and product value *relative to existing treatment.*

Within the current paradigm, most manufacturers have focused on incremental product improvement to the exclusion of game-changing innovation. They've pursued the idea that some improvement is needed to ensure fundamental functionality and product performance. Additional features and functionality have been aimed at competitive positioning and delighting major customers. Yet, at some point, performance outstrips real need/value (manufacturers create more functionality than is required or can be legitimately paid for), the price-to-value ratio begins to shrink, and the stage is set for commoditization. The medical device and diagnostics industry is at a critical point where it is vulnerable to game-changing technology (and market disruption) that redefines price-to-value expectations.

Savvy medical device and diagnostics marketers have built their reputations and success focused on the surgeon-as-customer. Sales strategy and process have been defined on the premise that the surgeon was the only decision maker that counts because he or she defines patient needs, and that drives clinical choices. This has been a relatively simple sale, managed through a rep organization focused on building relationships with surgeons and providing them with the surgical liaison services they've come to expect.

Manufacturers and surgeons are now caught up in a reform environment focused on better health outcomes at lower cost. As argued throughout the book, this objective is putting tremendous pressure on *all* stakeholders—payers, providers, and manufacturers—to rethink their business models and challenge fundamental assumptions about their customers, their products and services, their prices, and how they go to market.

Amid this tumult, a new competitive landscape is rapidly emerging. The once-straightforward device and diagnostics purchase decision must now satisfy hospital and health system administrators faced with declining reimbursement, as well as surgeons. Building organizational capability to identify and meet the institutional needs of the hospital- or health system-as-customer is now a prerequisite for continued market success.

Hospital-as-Customer Requires a New Sales Model

The hospital–manufacturer relationship needs to be moved from a winner/loser price negotiation to a win/win/win partnership among hospital, surgeon, and manufacturer. The basis for this partnership is the shared interest in efficiency, margin, patient satisfaction, surgeon satisfaction, quality, and safety. The range of ways in which manufacturers can impact these objectives needs to be explored and explicitly understood.

This requires an executive-to-executive relationship. The manufacturer's representative must have the business acumen to surface nonobvious needs beyond the product itself and the ability to translate those opportunities into concrete action plans for the manufacturer and the hospital/health system.

With their focus on surgeon customers, traditional device and diagnostics reps haven't built strong relationships with hospital executives, and they are often not well positioned to do so. They lack credibility to explore strategic business issues because they are seen as transactional salespeople trying to preserve price. Institutional value requires a dialogue that should be outside the context of contract negotiations and focused on how the collective capability of the manufacturer can enhance service line growth, profitability, and outcomes.

Developing a capable hospital relationship management resource is just one part of the necessary new commercial model. Hospital-as-customer also implies more precise hospital targeting criteria by the manufacturer, focusing its value-creating relationship management resources on those hospitals most able to appreciate total value versus device cost.

Many hospitals aren't yet sophisticated enough to be looking for a total value proposition from a manufacturer relationship, but they're getting there. This can be accelerated by taking the lead in helping them recognize what they should be asking for.

The new winners in this market will be the first to establish and manage hospital executive relationships that collaboratively identify and implement a new business model and approach to care that deliver better outcomes at a lower cost.

Questions for Medical Device Manufacturers

- Does our product perform in the real-world as well as we say it does?
  - How strong is the economic and clinical value proposition of new products versus that for older products?
- How much product performance are stakeholders willing to pay for?

- How much representative support is my customer willing to pay for?
■ What data are we assembling to tell our value story?
  - Are we starting to capture it while we prepare for regulatory approval?
  - What is our message?
    • Will it resonate with a payer? Provider? Consumer?
  - Do we have an economic message?
    • Will it resonate with a payer? Provider? Consumer?
■ Have we considered a partnership with a pharmaceutical company? Another device or diagnostic company?
  - What would be the joint value in doing so?
■ Have we modified our sales approach to adapt to the evolving market?
  - Are we prepared to engage in discussions about care paths?
  - Do we know how these decisions are made?
  - Do we know who the critical players (decision makers) are within provider organizations?
    • If so, how strong is the relationship?
■ Are we prepared to engage in risk-based contracting discussions?
  - How well do we know how our products will perform?

Endnotes

1. Stephen E. Rothenberg and Jill E. Sackman. "Marketing a New Process in MX." *Medtech Executive.* December 2011. http://www.mddionline.com/article/mx-marketing-fresh-process.
2. US Food and Drug Administration. "Medical Device Recall Report, FY2003 to FY2012." http://www.fda.gov/downloads/AboutFDA/CentersOffices/OfficeofMedicalProductsandTobacco/CDRH/CDRHTransparency/UCM388442.pdf.

3. U.S. Food and Drug Administration. "CDRH Plan of Action for 510(k) and Science: Implementation of Recommendations from the 510(k) and Science Reports." http://www.fda.gov/AboutFDA /CentersOffices/OfficeofMedicalProductsandTobacco/CDRH /CDRHReports/ucm239448.htm.

4. U.S. Food and Drug Administration. "Draft Guidance for Industry and FDA Staff, 510(k) Device Modifications: Deciding When to Submit a 510(k) for a Change to an Existing Device." July 27, 2011. http://www.easconsultinggroup.com/EASeDocs/files /EASeDocs-MD050-11.pdf.

5. U.S. Food and Drug Administration. "Draft Guidance for Industry, Clinical Investigators, and Food and Drug Administration Staff, Design Considerations for Pivotal Clinical Investigations for Medical Devices." August 15, 2011. http:// www.fda.gov/RegulatoryInformation/Guidances/ucm373750.htm.

6. U.S. Food and Drug Administration. "Draft Guidance for Industry and Food and Drug Administration Staff, Factors to Consider When Making Benefit-Risk Determinations in Medical Device Premarket Review." August 15, 2011. http://www.fda .gov/downloads/medicaldevices/deviceregulationandguidance /guidancedocuments/ucm267872.pdf.

7. U.S. Food and Drug Administration. "Draft Guidance for Industry and Food and Drug Administration Staff, Procedures for Handling Section 522 Postmarket Surveillance Studies." August 16, 2011. http://www.fda.gov/RegulatoryInformation /Guidances/ucm268064.htm.

8. U.S. Food and Drug Administration. "Guidance for Industry, Oversight of Clinical Investigations—A Risk-Based Approach." August 2011. http://www.fda.gov/downloads/drugs/guidance complianceregulatoryinformation/guidances/ucm269919.pdf.

9. U.S. Food and Drug Administration. "Next Steps: 2013 Action Plan." February 2015. http://www.fda.gov/MedicalDevices/Safety /CDRHPostmarketSurveillance/ucm348796.htm.

10. U.S. Food and Drug Administration. "Unique Device Identification—UDI." March 2015. http://www.fda.gov/MedicalDevices /DeviceRegulationandGuidance/UniqueDeviceIdentification/.

11. U.S. Food and Drug Administration. "Benefits of a UDI System." September 2014. http://www.fda.gov/MedicalDevices /DeviceRegulationandGuidance/UniqueDeviceIdentification /BenefitsofaUDIsystem/default.htm.

12. U.S. Food and Drug Administration. "Compliance Dates for UDI Requirements." April 2015. http://www.fda.gov/MedicalDevices /DeviceRegulationandGuidance/UniqueDeviceIdentification /CompliancedatesforUDIRequirements/default.htm.
13. Alison Motluk. "The Wrong Tools for the Job?" *New Scientist.* December 2014. http://www.newscientist.com/article/dn26683 -the-wrong-tools-for-the-job.html#.VS_dAtLBwXA.
14. Rita E. Numerof. "The Impact of Comparative Effectiveness on the Healthcare Marketplace." Numerof & Associates, Inc. June 2009.
15. The FDA is in the process of moving to a more stringent defini- tion of what qualifies for 510(k) approval, independently of these considerations.
16. Jaimy Lee. "Device Makers Explore Risk Contracts with Hospi- tals." *Modern Healthcare.* December 2014. http://www.modern healthcare.com/article/20141206/MAGAZINE/312069964.
17. Rita E. Numerof. "Theranostics: The Way Forward?" Numerof & Associates, Inc. January 2013.
18. "Joint Replacement: 1001 Patients Tell You What Your Doctor Can't." *Consumer Reports* 71 (6): 15. 2006.

Chapter 10

Putting Value at the Center of Healthcare

What Is the Legitimate Role of Policy?

The drumbeat to *do healthcare reform* culminated in 2010 with passage of landmark legislation whose 2,700 pages purported to "fix the system." While the effectiveness and implementation of this watershed policy have been debated in public opinion, legislative circles, and even the Supreme Court, one thing is for certain: the healthcare industry needs reform, and policy makers have an important role in enabling that to happen.

While we agree that *healthcare reform* is an incredibly important topic and needs to be addressed, it means many different things to different people; it's complex, the problem didn't just emerge, and we need to be mindful of what exactly we're reforming. There are always unintended consequences to any action, no matter how well intended. Once in place, it is very difficult to dismantle legislation and the bureaucracy put in place to realize it. The primary rule of medicine is probably worth remembering: *First, do no harm.*

It's possible to have too much of a good thing. As we have discussed, having more of the latest and greatest medical procedures and treatments does not guarantee improved patient outcomes. In the case of healthcare policy, as well, too many prescribed details can be detrimental to successfully reducing costs and improving quality.

While the reform efforts are well-intentioned, in reality they have established a bureaucratic labyrinth of new organizational structures, regulations, and incentives. Rather than developing the capabilities and culture needed to accelerate the move toward better outcomes at lower cost, providers and payers are compelled to invest in new staff and technologies to comply with new regulations and maneuver the new system.

There is no shortage of examples of the unintended consequences of inadequate policy. For instance, the health insurance exchanges are so complex that the Centers for Medicare & Medicaid Services (CMS) has recently offered $201 million in grants to support "marketplace navigators," adding to the bloat of healthcare spending that's a direct result of an overly complex policy.[1]

An example that is close to the heart of any physician, clinician, or healthcare administrator is the rush to adopt electronic medical records systems after the Health Information Technology for Economic and Clinical Health (HITECH) Act was passed as part of the 2009 economic stimulus package. HITECH pushed providers to adopt new health IT systems with the stated goals of improving patient care coordination and reducing unnecessary or duplicate tests. But instead of linking funding to the adoption of new systems that make it easy for providers to share patient data and facilitate better care coordination, the policy prescribed the minute details of how a provider should use the systems—and how the provider would prove that it was "meaningful." The so-called "meaningful use" policy has prompted years of bureaucratic headache for those trying to incorporate IT into their daily practice,[2] all while funneling more than $30 billion tax-payer dollars into the electronic medical record (EMR) industry.[3] Healthcare providers now have expensive software suites that they're using to satisfy federal guidelines, but they still rank patient coordination as one of their chief challenges when it comes to managing variation in cost and quality.

Another example of policy falling flat is tying physician performance incentives to activities that should be considered the standard of care, such as monitoring hemoglobin A1C in diabetes patients. If the desired goal is to improve complex medical management of challenging patients that often have multiple comorbidities, creating a bureaucratic framework for documenting routine care in exchange for a chance for increased earnings is not the answer!

There is a role for health policy in creating a patient-centric, transparent, accountable healthcare system. Healthcare reform should be about creating cultural changes within the industry, and behavioral changes within individuals, to produce predictable and improved costs and outcomes. Well-designed policy can help to define agreed-upon goals and establish standards that support those goals.

Policy must also define accountabilities. Providing carrots alone won't lead to change—there must be accountability for non-performance! In this respect, one of the most important events to spur healthcare reform was CMS 2008 decision to stop paying for medical errors that should never happen, or "never events."[4] This was not an act of law and there was no public debate or outcry, but it demonstrated that poor performance would no longer be reimbursed, setting the stage for improved quality control initiatives nationwide.

In short, healthcare reform wasn't well enough defined to act on despite the vote on March 23, 2010. And although it was framed as an effort to reform the insurance sector, payers have ironically profited handsomely with new exchange customers, increased prices, and government subsidies—a predictable "surprise" given the concessions made in the legislation to buy the sector's support. As we noted in Chapter 2, healthcare is big business, and every component has an agenda to pursue and a stake in the outcome. All need to change. What it means in many quarters is understood only in relatively vague terms: for example, affordable insurance, better outcomes for our dollar, and higher quality at lower costs. In our experience, organizations that lack precision in what they're trying to do always fail.

While it's generally recognized that there are three parts to any type of serious healthcare reform—insurance coverage, delivery, and payment—the initial legislation really only addressed the first part and did so at great cost and complexity. Incentives for care delivery innovation have had marginal impacts for a variety of reasons and have come at great cost.

Access to care has frequently been cited as another issue that healthcare reform needed to address. The population that didn't have access is often poorly defined, and there are many examples of subsidized clinics that have offered free care for years that hasn't been used—appointments aren't kept and sometimes aren't even made, and the general issues of health habits and adherence that plague mainstream society crop up here, too.

Without a clear, coherent, and relatively simple strategy defining the underlying issues that we're solving for, piecemeal solutions will only continue to aggravate the problems that we have today. We have already spent resources we can't afford, and we risk spending more without correcting the inefficiencies in the system as it is structured today. We need to be sure that people understand how we got to the situation we have (which clearly isn't working), what keeps the current system in place, and the myriad options that could help to resolve gaps.

Once we have this "diagnosis," and we understand how the component parts reinforce a status quo that most would agree isn't optimal, we can define a set of principles to guide innovations to improve the situation. These can be implemented in a "reasonable" time period with interventions that are staged, sustainable, and effectively coordinated and that achieve a simple goal: improved patient outcomes at reduced cost.

One could argue that once we deal with insurance sector–specific problems related to coverage restrictions for preexisting conditions, continuity, transparency, choice, and service, healthcare delivery is at the heart of real reform. All the other sectors we've discussed in earlier chapters feed into healthcare delivery—selling products and services directly or indirectly to consumers who engage with providers and delivery organizations to attempt to get better health outcomes at lower cost. Because reform of healthcare delivery is so central in this equation, it is a major focus of this chapter. The legislation outlined experiments to change delivery and payment models, followed by complex administrative rule writing. These efforts have been wholly inadequate. They have also spawned a flood of consolidation with healthcare delivery systems buying or affiliating with other systems, and physicians seeking refuge in employment from proliferating bureaucracy. The real danger we face as a nation is that these systems become too big to fail... and, more importantly, too big to care.

Recent Legislative Solutions and Why They Won't Work

As we discussed earlier in this book, the Patient Protection and Affordable Care Act (PPACA) is the most recent effort to address the problems of the healthcare system. The legislation attempted to address the high and unsustainable costs of the system and provide greater access to care for the uninsured. Yet, while these goals are noble, the solution PPACA offered is fundamentally flawed. The requirements outlined in PPACA have created administrative behemoths that have limited individual choice, increased bureaucracy, and will ultimately drive up costs!

Two of the central, and ironically most onerous, provisions enacted by PPACA are accountable care organizations (ACOs) and state insurance exchanges. The intent of these efforts was well meaning, but the resulting regulations have served to increase bureaucracy, fragmentation, and costs without improving outcomes. Let's discuss these in more detail.

Accountability for Care Is a Good Concept

ACOs: Their Original Purpose

Accountability for care is not a new concept.[5] It entered the spotlight in the 1990s through such programs as *pay for performance* and various managed care initiatives that were intended to create "greater accountability on the part of providers for their performance."[6] In this context, the locus for accountability was limited to individual providers and did not address the need for integrated delivery of quality care.[6] In order to address the need for provider accountability across an integrated care continuum, a new model, the accountable care organization, was proposed. The ACO model developed as a way of addressing accountability of both healthcare providers and the delivery systems in which they practice, collaborate, and interact.[7]

ACOs were offered as a solution to the "serious gaps in quality and widespread waste" within the healthcare system.[6] The underlying intent of the ACO model was to address the lack of financial incentives for reducing costs while improving quality, coordination, and consistency of care.[7]

Evolving Concept

The ACO concept has evolved since its inception several years ago. Most proponents of ACOs agree that they should, at a minimum, offer services across the continuum of care and in various institutional settings, be able to budget and forecast resource needs, and be *large enough* to sustain reliable and universal performance measurements.[7] By working with local providers already centered around and connected to one or more hospitals, it's presumed that physicians and hospitals can create an "organized system" that payers could then hold accountable for improvements in quality of care and costs.[8]

At the conceptual level, the incentive for ACOs would be to increase efficiency and avoid overuse and duplication of services, resources, and facilities. In this model, ACO provider members would share in the savings resulting from the increased coordination of care.

Nowhere in these discussions was there an attempt to enable a simplified market-based solution that puts patients at the center, requires transparency of cost and outcomes, and ensures that primary care physicians would play the critical role of healthcare quarterback on behalf of their patients.

ACOs: Their Role in PPACA

PPACA mandated a shared savings program among health-care providers, which generally follows the ACO model discussed previously, but did not include provisions to test real-world feasibility in a controlled way. In effect, the legislation has been an experiment. Through this program, ACOs are awarded their portion of the shared savings if they sufficiently reduce costs and simultaneously improve quality. The ACOs are tasked with distributing savings among participating providers, who have continued to be reimbursed on a fee-for-service (FFS) basis. Aside from retaining the current FFS reimbursement system, PPACA did not indicate how savings should be divided among participants.[9] This situation creates a moral hazard, as providers will be incented to do less for patients, perhaps waiting before authorizing needed tests or withholding treatments longer than might be optimal. They would essentially be replaying the experience of health maintenance organizations (HMOs) in the 1980s, a topic covered in the next section.

PPACA describes ACOs as provider groups that accept responsibility for the cost and quality of care delivered to a specific population of patients cared for by the groups' participating clinicians. The legislative intent is that these groups will have an incentive to invest in infrastructure and redesigned care for high-quality and efficient delivery of services. From an organizational standpoint, however, PPACA defines ACOs only loosely, and eligibility requirements are vague.

An ACO may include different participating groups, such as physician groups and hospitals, which are to coordinate their services. Eligible organizations must have a formal legal structure, must include enough primary care providers for 5,000 Medicare FFS beneficiaries, and must contract or employ any additional providers that their patient population requires. They must be prepared not only to meet specified performance standards, but also to measure and report quality outcomes in a uniform manner as required by CMS, using highly integrated information systems.[9]

While steps to improve quality performance by standardizing metrics and reporting requirements are mandated in PPACA, requirements in the legislation are still largely ambiguous, as performance standards and metrics are a moving target. The specifics continue to be determined by the Department of Health and Human Services (HHS) and include areas such as clinical processes and care, patient experience, and the amounts and rates of services rendered.

As developed in PPACA, ACOs were designed to create what are, in effect, *virtual organizations* composed of local hospitals and affiliated providers covering groups of patients.[6] There are still no enrollment requirements for patients, who are assigned to ACOs based on which provider they visit most frequently and may not even be aware of the ACO's existence. The performance standards that ACOs are expected to meet use data collected from uniform information systems, which the ACOs themselves are required to implement. ACO spending is measured against a comparable national target (historic data for the same or a similar patient population). If an ACO meets its performance and quality standards (which remain largely undefined), the ACO shares in any savings.[9] While CMS has recognized issues with its existing program and announced a "next generation" model in early 2015,[10] the core issues largely remain with over 500 pages of new rules.

Government-Sponsored Payment and Delivery Systems

Given the enormous size of the Medicare program, Medicare policy changes have a profound influence on private-sector health insurance practices, including payment systems.[11] Congressional leaders have long attempted to improve quality and lower costs by developing complex payment and delivery systems intended to increase accountability.

In the 1980s, Congress created a prospective payment system (PPS) for Medicare in an effort to control rising healthcare costs in hospitals.[12] Under this new system, hospitals were reimbursed a predetermined amount for each diagnosis-related group (DRG) (category of inpatient cases).

This new strategy was intended to place pressure on organizations to increase efficiency and minimize unnecessary spending, as they would only be reimbursed a set amount for each case. To give organizations a way of monitoring provider efficiency by DRG category, resource-based relative-value units (RBRVUs) were introduced. RBRVUs, however, continued to reimburse providers on an FFS basis and reflected a highly complex set of calculations.[13]

Since they were paid for each service they provide, not for the outcomes they help patients achieve, providers continued to have a profit-based motive not to ensure the quality and efficiency of patient care, but rather to increase volume at the service code level. As a result, these changes did not ultimately translate to lower spending. In fact, they resulted in more spending, reduced the quality of care, empowered specialists to deliver more nonintegrated and perhaps unnecessary care, and diminished the core role of primary care providers as "quarterbacks" or "gatekeepers" responsible for managing, coordinating, and directing patient care in the most efficient way possible. Fee-for-service, activity-based provider payment creates no incentive for providers to increase efficiency and acts as a disincentive for those who take more time to coordinate care, because they don't get paid for time not spent with the patient.

With the Health Maintenance Organization Act of 1973, Congress directly promoted the growth of managed care arrangements in the private sector. In the 1990s, private organizations and employers sponsored HMOs, PPOs, and physician–hospital organizations (PHOs) as part of their managed care efforts to reduce costs by eliminating provider incentives for inappropriate care and excess productivity.[14]

These *managed care organizations* would often enter into capitated arrangements with contracted providers, where these providers would receive a fixed amount per patient member of the organization that chose to seek care through that provider. Capitated payments were determined based on historic FFS data. These efforts were intended to emphasize primary care as central to improving healthcare and keeping hospital costs under the capitated amount.

Yet capitation created a new profit motive that was equally, if not more, detrimental to patients than productivity incentives created by FFS plans. Because (again) payment was not tied to outcomes, capitation encouraged providers to cut spending *without* sufficient concern for patient welfare.[15] We anticipate a similar scenario unfolding with ACOs as attempts to define outcomes connected to payment have been watered down under industry pressure. In fact executives in leading healthcare systems across the country have told us again and again that the incentives for changes are "tepid," but "without meaningful use and related bonus opportunities for compliance we would never have taken this trip." While they have complained publicly about the burden of change, they are also quite surprised *that so little has been asked of them in terms of accountability for real improvement in quality and cost.* There's another side to this, reflected in the comments of one physician as he describes the challenges of value-based payment:

> While SGR is gone, the "value based payments" loom. There is no yardstick yet that says what the measurements of "value" are. The yardstick will probably be a bungee cord, stretched and bent around various obstacles, whose marks move at the whim of government.

Top-Down Approach to Complex Health Policy Problems

Past healthcare initiatives that have relied on organizational structure to address the complex challenge of delivering higher quality at lower cost have not succeeded in improving either efficiency or performance. In fact, they have largely exacerbated the problems they were intended to address. Neither DRGs nor HMOs created a shared goal for all parties. In both cases, provider profit motives lacked the counter-pressure of consumer demand to preserve quality while minimizing cost. While DRGs and RBRVUs encouraged providers to focus on production without consequences for unnecessary interventions, HMOs and other managed care organizations encouraged providers to minimize intervention, regardless of whether doing so could hinder the quality or completeness of patient care. Outside the HMO model, providers had the perverse incentive to fix the quality problems that they frequently created.

In most industries, consumer demand drives service providers and product manufacturers to improve quality while maximizing efficiency. In healthcare, patients are not direct consumers when they don't pay for their care directly. So, providers don't face pressure from the *consumer* to provide high-quality and affordable care. Generally, patients seek care from providers and organizations that are covered under their insurance plan, which, quite often, is selected by their employers. Providers and healthcare organizations negotiate the most favorable rates with payers to protect their revenue stream, without an incentive to increase efficiency or improve quality.

Past attempts at manipulating organizational structure to reduce cost (and implicitly improve outcomes) ignore the underlying problem: the minimal role that consumer (patient) demand plays in driving market competition among providers and organizations. Instead, these efforts have decreased accountability for and quality of care by:

- Preserving FFS provider reimbursement, which encourages volume-driven production, not outcomes
- Favoring large players who consolidate or monopolize the market, thereby reducing competition
- Reducing the role of primary care providers, whose logical role is to be the "quarterback" of patient care
- Failing to create accountability that extends across a continuum of care
- Failing to require transparency of cost and quality outcomes in order for consumers to make informed choices and create effective competition in the market

ACOs: Key Deficiencies

As noted, ACOs were introduced to remedy the inadequate accountability for excess spending and quality of patient care. Under PPACA, however, as we predicted in 2010, ACOs will likely fail to ensure accountability. We stand by that prediction. Specifically, PPACA provisions have the three flaws discussed in the following sections.

PPACA Does Not Empower Consumers to Be Stakeholders in Their Own Care

The PPACA provisions are obviously not a market-based set of solutions; they do not allow consumers to make fully informed choices about their coverage and care.

Consumer-driven markets do not need to create artificial incentives to improve quality and performance because competitors are constantly working to improve their products, attract consumers, and ultimately increase market share. Except for certain services—cosmetic dermatology and Lasik eye surgery, for instance—the healthcare market does not operate this way. Since employers contract with insurers who enter into arrangements with providers, competition is limited, and the *real* consumer—the patient—has no part in driving that competition. The result has been a lack of transparency and a lack of incentives for healthcare providers to offer quality "products."

Instead of remedying this problem and increasing competition among payers and providers by treating patients as informed consumers, PPACA includes vague requirements for performance measurement and fails to address underlying issues driving cost.

Ironically, many physicians are reluctant to assume accountability for patient outcomes since they recognize that much of the outcome is directly under the behavioral control (and thus accountability) of the patient-consumer. Taking the patient-consumer out of the equation undermines any attempt at creating true accountability for healthcare decisions.

PPACA Does Not Encourage Provider Accountability

Though it seems that provider buy-in would be integral to an ACO's success in the shared savings program, providers continue to be paid for each service they perform. Given the uncertainties and practical complications of distributing savings, the fundamental incentive to provide a service and receive a fee remains in place.

Even with the possibility of a bonus from shared savings, maintaining the FFS system encourages providers to continue delivering excess services so that they can maximize their return. By creating incentives for each provider to increase his or her own productivity, FFS payment undermines the importance of provider collaboration across the continuum of care. Providers have an incentive to *intervene* and *do something* as opposed to engaging in thoughtful discourse and collaboration with patients. Faced with the choice between generating a fee for themselves now or sharing some future possible savings with the entire set of providers, many will opt for the former course of action.

PPACA Creates an Unfair Competitive Advantage for Large Organizations

The mandated program centers on a single, untested, and vague model that is largely hospital centric. Eligibility requirements, while vague and ambiguous, collectively suggest that larger, more complex organizations have an implicit advantage. Groups of independent practitioners as well as other types of small- and mid-sized practices may lack the infrastructure, technology, or other resources needed to qualify and succeed on their own. Also, smaller, entrepreneurial organizations that want to venture alone may find themselves competing against similar physician practices that have joined ACOs or been acquired by larger organizations and, as a result, will be under less financial and clinical pressure to improve efficiency and quality.

Large delivery systems are, once again, able to claim or consolidate their hold on substantial portions of their markets, resulting in less competition. Large systems may become "too big to fail" and will have increased leverage with payers. Without effective competition, they might have little incentive to reduce spending or improve quality of care. Ironically, the most significant costs relate to end-of-life care, hospital inefficiency, and hospitals' inability to manage *never events*. Why continue to reward the very institutions that failed to lead the industry in transformation?

PPACA's Pioneers: Lessons from the Field

The pioneer ACO program launched with 32 member organizations in January 2012. These "pioneers" were selected because they'd already made progress in building the infrastructure and capabilities required to coordinate care, reduce costs, and manage risk; if any organizations could be successful at providing accountable care, these were the ones! But the headlines suggested a problem, as 9 of the original 32 health systems dropped out after the first year, and four more dropped out in year 2.

Despite the mass exodus of nearly a third of the original participants, some first year headlines heralded success. Aggregate gross savings totaled $87.6 million, with $96 million in year 2.[16] Most organizations improved on the quality metrics in place. But results at the individual level varied: While approximately a dozen organizations met the shared savings threshold, several ended up owing CMS millions.[17]

With only 19 participants remaining as of this writing, the question is what went wrong for those who dropped out. Ironically, the biggest problem the pioneer dropouts had wasn't their lack of performance, but rather how CMS measured their improvements and tied them to penalties and rewards.

The pioneer model requires organizations to reduce spending based on national benchmarks, which proved to be untenable for providers that were already operating more efficiently and at lower cost than providers in other regions of the country.[16,18,19] One of the original pioneers to drop out, Presbyterian Healthcare Services (New Mexico), noted the biggest problem with the program: When you're in a geographic area that already has low-cost and low-utilization, there's not a lot of waste to cut.[16]

After 2 years, it appears that the program rewards ACOs that operate in markets with above-average health spending and penalizes ACOs that were ahead of the game in providing quality care at lower costs. Pioneer participants have also expressed serious concerns about program design, including its administrative complexity, the weakness of financial incentives relative to penalties, and the inability to manage beneficiaries' outcomes and costs when they aren't permanently assigned to the ACO or limited to ACO providers.[10,20,21] Not surprisingly, these are the very issues we identified before the program launched.

One additional point of context bears mention. In year 1, 19 organizations on average saved $89.6 million—a little over $4 million each. However, these figures don't take into account the enormous administrative costs to manage the program—for the government or for participating systems. In contrast, many large healthcare systems have embarked on significant cost reduction programs on their own in anticipation of shrinking reimbursement. Many of these established savings targets of over $100 million over 2–3 years. The message is clear. When performance really matters, organizations do change.

Recommendations for Policy Makers: Healthcare Delivery

Throughout this book we've tried to provide some illustrations in a number of key areas to demonstrate concretely why we continue to believe that there is enough money in the system to address issues of access, broader coverage, and so on. Our contention is that business models need to change and it is unlikely that they will unless there is some outside intervention—again, focused on specific principles. Industries and specific organizations, like individuals, frequently don't change until and unless forced to do so. We need to be careful about what we ask them to do or we risk crippling the economy and a healthcare system that, while uneven, still delivers some of the best care in the world. We do need to get costs under control and have hard conversations about what we're willing to pay for.

We need a market-based model that would encourage accountability in the healthcare delivery system and stimulate change across the industry, as opposed to relying on an institution to funnel accountability down to the various types of providers. We stand by the recommendations we made 6 years ago.[22] Such a new organizational model for enterprising provider groups would:

1. *Require accountability from primary care providers and patients for prevention, health maintenance, health education, and primary care.* Primary care providers and patients are the foundation for this model, driving accountability across all four tiers. Primary care providers will be responsible for educating the patient and facilitating prevention, health maintenance, health education, and primary care. They will also be responsible for resuming their traditional role as coordinators of patient care by collaborating with providers in other tiers, ensuring mutual accountability, and emphasizing prevention and primary care.

2. *Require accountability from specialists focused on the care continuum, cost efficiency, and increased quality of* needed *services.* Specialists who demonstrate a commitment to management of care across the care continuum, an emphasis on primary care and prevention, cost efficiency, and increased quality of *needed* services will comprise the second tier of this model. Under this new system, specialists will not be rewarded for the number of services they deliver, but rather for their contribution to

effective, efficient, and tightly integrated delivery of quality care. This requires interdisciplinary communication, collaboration, and a commitment to each patient's best interests.

3. *Require institutional accountability, focused on delivering better outcomes at lower cost, coordinated by primary care physicians.* Hospitals and specialty care organizations will serve as the third tier in this model and will focus on delivering better outcomes at lower costs. They will be responsible for monitoring and managing progress by setting goals, assessing individual performance, and creating internal initiatives to promote collaboration and good practices. Rather than trying to force accountability among providers, organizations will simply serve as vehicles for integrating providers that have already demonstrated accountability. Again, primary care providers will be integral to coordinating and facilitating these organizational changes.

4. *Promote coordination across community agencies, reinforcing prevention, health maintenance, and disease management.* Responsibility for health and healthcare should not be confined to hospitals and physician practices. In order to truly empower consumers as stakeholders in their own health, concepts like prevention, health maintenance, and disease management should be reinforced at the community level. Private-sector success will spill over into the public sector, and policy makers will be encouraged to hold social service agencies, nursing homes, home health organizations, and other community agencies accountable for continued patient education, support, and advocacy. Public and private entrepreneurs can begin to ensure that prevention, awareness, and accountability become part of a lifestyle that consumers embrace and the healthcare industry is required to sustain.

In theory, ACOs provide financial incentives to organizations that, by encouraging providers to work under a common organizational umbrella, can reduce costs and improve outcomes. In reality, given the complexity of the existing system, such a strategy will not only fail—it will most likely exacerbate the very problems it was designed to fix. ACOs will concentrate more and more power in fewer and fewer organizations, allowing them to become too large to fail. Such a system will undermine competition and entrepreneurship, the bedrock of innovation and job growth in this country. Thus, PPACA creates the potential for increased bureaucracy, fragmentation, and costs without improving outcomes.

There is no evidence that supports the use of untested, complex organizational structures to improve quality of care and reduce costs. Indeed, the evidence suggests the opposite. Only by systematically changing the underlying payment model, enabling competition, and introducing transparency in cost and outcomes will the goals of healthcare reform be achieved. Creating incentives that focus on achieving quality outcomes, providing choice, and allowing real competition are what will transform healthcare delivery to a system that provides higher quality healthcare at lower costs.

In the midst of reform debates, the subject of tort reform is often the focus. The argument goes as follows. Physicians, out of fear of legal action, frequently order more tests and prescribe more drugs than they themselves would argue are medically necessary. One rationale is that patients are pressuring them to do the "latest" just to be sure that the diagnosis is accurate. Since most patients aren't paying anyway, the issue of cost doesn't often come up. So, after the patient rejects an initial suggestion by the doctor that the test isn't really needed, most physicians go ahead and order the test. In the absence of guidelines, physicians are in the awkward position of arguing with the patient.

Under pressure of time, the path of least resistance—ordering the test—seems rational. Given that physicians are increasingly evaluated on patient satisfaction measures that may not reflect adequacy of care, appeasement may seem a more desirable path. Until there are more specific guidelines and care paths defining what is optimal for a given condition, this situation is unlikely to change. Indeed, physicians who follow clinical guidelines could be given safe harbor in the event of a subsequent lawsuit.

Enabling Markets to Create Access to Care

As we described in the prior section on ACOs, the same bureaucratic approach characterizes another core element of PPACA: state-based health insurance exchanges. One element of the insurance piece of the puzzle has been determining how to expand the number of people who have affordable healthcare coverage. The answer offered by PPACA was to mandate that the uninsured and everyone else purchase coverage, choosing either an employer-offered program, if available, or from a limited range of subsidized and heavily regulated health plans offered via healthcare insurance exchanges that must be created, managed, and funded by each state. The controversy surrounding this has continued since passage, all the way up to the Supreme Court. Despite the ruling upholding subsidies for state and federal exchanges, the controversy over them continues.

Although the goal of extending healthcare coverage to more of the population is a noble one, the solution PPACA offers is fundamentally flawed and unsustainable. The requirements outlined in PPACA have resulted in the creation of bureaucratic structures that will continue to limit individual choice and drive up costs. States still have an opportunity to define how they will address their specific needs.

A market-based approach would accomplish the goal of making coverage more affordable and more widely held, but would preserve flexibility for states, preserve choice for consumers and insurers, and avoid the creation of another expensive bureaucracy. A market-based approach is more likely to lead to better health outcomes at lower cost.

Creating Access to Affordable Health Coverage

Almost everyone can agree that the high cost of healthcare in the United States is a barrier to access; who among us could afford to pay *full list price* for every drug, office visit, or procedure? Almost everyone can also agree that expanding access to care, assuming fundamental changes are made in payment and delivery, would not only be a moral good for society, but would also lower healthcare costs over the long term. With greater access to care, individuals would be more likely to seek treatment earlier, when it is generally cheaper to be treated, and would be less likely to wait until they experience an emergency. Likewise, with greater access to care, individuals would also have greater access to prevention and wellness programs, and education about health behaviors that could positively influence health outcomes.[23]

There is general agreement that coverage through a health plan increases access to care, and that coverage options have become unattractive due to their high cost, complexity, and other limitations. Those with mid to high incomes generally enroll in employer-sponsored health plans, where available, which pool risk and share costs in order to gain access to care. Coverage through taxpayer-funded assistance programs (e.g., Medicaid and Medicare) also increases access to care for those with low incomes and for those over 65.[24] Those who don't qualify for assistance programs or who don't have health plan coverage through their employers, have been forced to do without, hope for the best, wait until they have a health emergency, or elect to purchase coverage on their own.

What everyone doesn't agree on is the best way to increase coverage or, more specifically, enrollment in health plans and assistance programs. PPACA's solution is to combine a personal mandate with state-run exchanges, forcing consumers to choose from a limited slate of commoditized health plans, funded in large part by federal subsidies.

Five years ago we predicted that PPACA's solution would limit choice, create new bureaucracies, and cost more, putting additional burdens on the states. As of 2015, nearly half of the 17 exchanges established by states and the District of Columbia are facing serious financial challenges related to surging technology costs and lower than expected enrollment rates. Some of these exchanges are dealing with major funding shortfalls, and it's unclear when—or even if—they'll ever become self-sustaining. For example, officials in Hawaii estimate that the state exchange will need an additional $28 million to fund operations through 2022.[25]

There is an alternative: States can create market-based solutions that leverage the laws of supply and demand to enable greater access to more affordable health coverage options.

Recommendations for Policy Makers: Access to Care

As we've discussed, health insurance exchanges will accelerate healthcare spending, but ironically, not on healthcare services aimed at improving health. Instead, they will continue to create more bureaucracy and place more burdens on states already strapped for cash. States should take this unique opportunity to focus on their own insurance markets to find out why they don't operate as effectively and efficiently as they should.

Like anything else, state insurance markets evolve over time and are sometimes loaded down with last decade's concerns, or with provisions that just aren't effective, so it's important to review market performance and give the regulatory environment a thorough scrubbing, keeping what works, and discarding what doesn't. State governments shouldn't have to spend a penny more on market regulation, but should "rightsize" and align regulations so that the market can accomplish the desired outcomes of greater access to care by providing more affordable insurance coverage options.

What is the legitimate role for state governments in enabling more efficient markets? Generally, states should look to accomplish the four goals discussed in the following sections.

Ensure Legitimacy of Participating Businesses

States have a clear role to play in registering businesses and making sure that market participants are following the rules. For insurers specifically, appropriate consideration must be given to preventing use of inadequate health plan documentation and misleading marketing materials, as well as ensuring reserves so that insurers will maintain sufficient financial assets to cover health plan obligations. Healthcare coverage is so complex that insurers can take advantage of consumers through use of industry jargon, medical terminology, or claims about financial strength.

Aggressively Prosecute Fraudulent, Negligent, and Abusive Business Practices

For markets to function efficiently, a neutral party like a state regulatory agency can hold market participants accountable to standards of good business practices. Regulators go too far, however, when they try to protect consumers from themselves, attempting to prevent consumers from making unwise or risky choices. Consumers should be free to purchase more or less coverage than the government thinks they need and take responsibility for their decisions.

Some states may need to play a greater role in monitoring and censuring unfair business practices such as denial of claims to stretch out cash flows, changing policies without telling members, or unfairly weeding out sicker members.

Remove Legislative Barriers to Competition and Consumer Choice

In highly efficient markets, sellers compete to develop products that consumers demand. How efficient is the local insurance market at matching consumers with affordable health coverage? A review of local markets will likely reveal significant gaps, some of which are due to specific regulations that could be loosened or removed.

One common barrier to competition is the proliferation of coverage mandates, requirements that all plans offer coverage for a specific disease or treatment. The number of coverage mandates has risen from nearly 1,000 in 1997 to over 2,250 in 2012.[26,27] Coverage mandates put the government in the role of second-guessing consumers, and each mandate adds cost to all plans for all subscribers when some may not need or want that particular coverage.

Estimates suggest that the cumulative effect of coverage mandates adds 20%–30% to the cost of premiums.[28] In other words, basic health coverage would be 20%–30% cheaper without expensive mandates. States could relax legislative demands on coverage and rely on consumer demand and competition instead: insurers that won't offer the "right" types of coverage will lose market share to those that will, but only if markets operate more efficiently.

Closely related to this idea is the need to enable personalization of health plans. States should remove any barriers to offering a basic catastrophic coverage plan with a menu of additional coverage options.[29] This may require some changes to regulations regarding risk pools so that insurers have more flexibility to spread the cost of unusual coverage needs over a wider population of members to keep coverage costs down.

Barriers to competition often exist in the types of organizations that are allowed to offer self-funded plans. Legislators might ask, "Can chambers of commerce or affinity groups form risk pools for self-insured coverage plans?" If not, why not? In Missouri, the Regional Chamber and Growth Association (RCGA) formed a trust over 30 years ago so that employers could join together to create a larger entity with greater bargaining power, enabling small- and mid-sized employers to have group coverage options that would typically be available only to large employers.[30]

Promote Transparency So That Consumers Know What They're Getting

For healthcare insurance markets to function more efficiently, consumers need greater transparency about what they are trying to purchase. Legislators should find out what's preventing consumers from making more detailed cost comparisons for health plans.

Currently, it is difficult for consumers to compare available health plans and the insurance companies that offer them. Ideally, consumers would have easy access to useful and relevant data so that they could determine which insurers have, for example, the highest member satisfaction, the lowest frequency of serious complaints, the fastest and most accurate claims processing, or the highest medical loss ratios (MLRs). Regulators in some states may need to require expanded public disclosure of essential data so that private-sector firms can offer them to the public in a timely and convenient manner.

Similarly, consumers need better tools to understand the mechanics of health plans, especially how health status and lifestyle choices impact premiums. Consumers should be able to answer simple questions like, "How much would I save if I lost 20 pounds?" or "Which plan offers the best discounts to diabetics like me who comply with health management programs?" Unfortunately, the current rules and process of enrollment are not consumer friendly, even for otherwise capable people. It is a sad commentary that college educated, accomplished business people have spent days trying to sort out eligibility for coverage and subsidies on the federal exchange, even with the help of exchange navigators! The fact that the rules are so complex and inconsistent is a clear sign that things are quite broken and need to be fixed.

You'll recall that in Chapter 1 we noted that in every other industry, advancing technology has generally resulted in lower costs and improved products and services. Until we create a true market-based approach to the healthcare industry, we won't be able to crack rising costs and improved outcomes in any meaningful way. Transparency, increased accountability, and competition are the core components of a market-based model for healthcare and will be necessary to achieve the goal of better health outcomes at lower cost.

Supporting Innovation: Finding the Right Balance at the Food and Drug Administration

We've spent the bulk of this chapter with a focus on PPACA and its implications for policy makers going forward in their efforts to support market-based solutions for healthcare delivery. Most of our discussion centered on two major elements of the legislation: ACOs and state-based insurance exchanges. In Chapter 4 we talked about the role of data and comparative effectiveness research (CER) and how it translates to healthcare delivery and the manufacturers who sell critical products into the sector to support positive health outcomes—namely, pharmaceutical, medical device, and diagnostics companies.

We would be remiss if we did not spend at least some focused discussion on the role of the Food and Drug Administration (FDA) as it is the gatekeeper for new products coming into the market, and increasingly, for products staying in the market. Despite intense controversy surrounding the agency—with critics lambasting it for either too little or too much oversight, processes that remain opaque or contradictory, and decisions that are made too fast or too slowly—the FDA is in an extraordinarily difficult position, compounded with problems of staffing and staff capability in light of complex, emerging technology and combination products (i.e., drug–device products). Keeping current in this milieu is extraordinarily challenging and raises important questions about the structure and role of the agency—questions that are beyond the scope of this book.

No agency or organization is without flaws and neither is the FDA. The agency regulates the products coming to and staying in the U.S. market. It does so through formal guidance that typically follows scientific method and requires evidence of the safety and efficacy of the products it reviews. As we noted in Chapter 4, the mandate of the agency is in transition. It has begun to openly engage in discussions around cost with CMS, and we expect cost considerations to be taken into account in reviewing product evidence going forward. Thus, issues concerning the relative "value" of a given product will be considered as part of the regulatory approval process (e.g., does product X, which costs more than product Y, deliver superior outcomes to warrant bringing it to market? Does product A, which is similar to product B but costs much less, provide market value warranting its approval?).

In a nutshell, this dynamic is at the heart of discussions concerning accelerated approval for biosimilars and generics on the pharmaceutical side, as well as 510(k) devices. Pressure has mounted against the approval of "me-too" products, and there is more scrutiny regarding the rigor of evidence being brought forward—not just for reimbursement, but also for regulatory approval. See Chapter 8 for coverage of these topics.

These dynamics are very important as we think about the underlying objective of healthcare reform: better outcomes at lower cost. And the FDA clearly plays an important role in this whole dynamic.

Regulation's Impact on Innovation: A Two-Edged Sword

The extent to which the pharmaceutical and medical device industries are regulated has consistently increased over the years.[31] This trend is, at least in part, responsible for the decline in innovative new products (as measured by the number of approved new molecular entities and original premarket approvals). And in the current environment of activist government, the movement toward more regulation and more stringent enforcement seems certain to accelerate.

But there is one aspect of increasing regulation that has the potential to trump all others in terms of its potential impact on innovation: comparative effectiveness research.

Why is this likely to have a tremendous impact on innovation? There are two reasons. First, despite assurances to the contrary, comparative effectiveness has the potential to be used to evaluate the cost effectiveness of alternative treatments. Even if comparative cost data are not collected in the course of research, the outcomes that are measured can be associated with costs after the fact, and given the near-desperate desire of CMS to control the cost of healthcare, it's difficult to envision this move being a long time in coming. That would have a profound impact on the relative risk of innovative and derivative products, and hence on the extent to which innovation occurs.

Second, this represents only the first foray by the U.S. government into comparative effectiveness research. Going forward we expect to see increasing effort in this arena, because it does, in fact, pay off. The ability of the UK's National Health Service (NHS) to control costs relies heavily on guidance issued by the National Institute for Health and Clinical Excellence (NICE). This guidance is based on explicit evaluation of the costs and benefits of competing treatments—in other words, on comparative effectiveness research with costs worked into the mix, with the goal of getting the most bang for the pound. And despite the myriad complaints lodged by the British people against NHS, in this respect it has been extremely successful; it currently spends about $3,600 per person per year, compared to about $9,100 per person per year spent on healthcare in the United States.[32]

If the rise of comparative effectiveness research results in the adoption of a set of NICE-style guidelines by CMS, there will be significant negative impacts on innovation. The United States is the largest market in the world for innovative treatments, largely because there is a willingness to pay for them. If CMS starts to weigh cost into its approval process, there will be significantly less willingness to pay.

That translates into increased risk for the developers of innovative new treatments because it presents a new hurdle to market success: A product no longer has to be merely safe, effective, and appealing to physicians and their patients; now it has to be cost effective as well. Within the NHS, this frequently means that new treatments are rejected or are considered appropriate only under very restricted circumstances. The United Kingdom is a large market for healthcare services, but the United States is much larger; receiving payment at full market price within the United States is extremely important if the developers are to cover the full costs of developing the drug or device, which include the costs of the multiple failures that are typically required before a successful new product comes to market.

By their nature, innovative drugs and devices present more risk of failure than derivative products do, and raising the bar not only increases the chances that any given product will fail, but also increases the number of failures that each success has to "cover" for the company to maintain profitability. What's more, "successful" products may become less so, on average; strong restrictions on the population for which a product is approved and the circumstances under which it can be used, extremely common in NICE guidelines, greatly reduce the size of the potential market. This makes it even more difficult to recover these costs.

This puts pharmaceutical and medical device companies in a very difficult situation. They need to develop new drugs and devices—that's what they do—but innovative products would become exceptionally risky and uneconomical. Their rational response might be to become high-throughput producers of derivative products, dropping their pursuit of the big innovations, and focusing on products that can make money at a low price point. This implies a bias toward products that can be developed quickly and cheaply, that are likely to have safety profiles similar to currently marketed drugs and devices, and that can find a niche among those who are less-than-perfect candidates for other available options. It creates impetus for innovation in manufacturing processes, rather than products. This is valuable work, but it isn't the kind of innovation that pushes the frontiers of medical treatment.

And it should be noted that this effect applies not only to established companies, but also to startups. These companies may not rely on profits to fund their research, but they do rely on investors to support their attempts to develop innovative new products. Reducing the expected return on those investments decreases the capital that will be available and the number of small research and development (R&D)-focused firms that can be supported. One of the most active sources of innovative new products will be significantly impaired.

On the other hand, there is also danger in focusing solely on derivative products. By their nature, they will generally justify only incremental additional reimbursement and, in some cases, may not justify additional reimbursement at all. This is especially likely if government decides that there isn't enough "real innovation" going on or if budgets get very tight.

Companies might respond in two ways. Following the lead of regulators, they will rush to engage in innovation where it is perceived that reimbursement policies are more rewarding. This is likely to be in select product areas where it is difficult for regulators to "just say no" without significant push-back from patient advocacy groups.

Alternately, efforts will turn with even more strength than today toward ways to reduce the risk of highly innovative development efforts—toward finding better ways of screening drugs (perhaps through biomarkers), of modeling the durability and performance of devices, and of the interaction of products with the body. This would mean better health outcomes on any budget and would represent an increase in truly valuable innovations. If it succeeds spectacularly, it would usher in a new era of lower cost innovation in drug and device firms.

The question is, can regulators—through cost-effectiveness research—find the "sweet spot" that encourages increased productivity in the industry? It seems unlikely. The more that cost-containment policy is effective, the more disincentives there are to innovate. Over the long term, as wealthy societies in the United States and Europe age, there will undoubtedly be a backlash against such policies. But in the short and medium term, there are likely to be waves of consolidation and a steep reduction in innovation as the pharmaceutical and medical device industries contract to deal with the government's monopsonic pricing power. As in other highly regulated industries, the reduction in competition provides another disincentive to innovate.

The world values innovative new drugs and devices, but it does not value them infinitely, and we are now coming up against the unwillingness of even the most generous public payers to bear their costs. Clinical effectiveness research and the regulation that is likely to follow it are the first step in their systematic plan for saying "no." Depending on how these data are used, this may result in more focus on real economic and clinical value. It may also create a strong disincentive to product innovation of all kinds. It's a two-edged sword that cuts both ways, but will certainly cut deeply.

The only other alternative, which is only hinted at in Europe and some programs in the United States (like Medicare Part D drug coverage for seniors), is to create more market-based incentives that allow consumers to choose between more expensive (but innovative) products and cheaper generics. Wealthier segments of society could also be asked to pay more for healthcare innovations that, over time, become less expensive as they lose patent protection and become more widely adopted. This type of differential pricing strategy has the potential to reconcile the twin goals of cost containment and innovation at a market-clearing price.

Making the Rules Clearer, More Transparent, and Simpler

This is a country of law, of rules. What's at issue in the recent debate over the proper role of the FDA is how far those rules have gone to basically undermine innovation. If you start with the premise that people (and therefore business) can't be trusted, then your goal is to prescribe, in infinite detail, what can and can't be done and then delineate the penalties for noncompliance. Even in Soviet Russia under communist/socialist rule and the real threat of severe penalties, people found ways around rules, with people often paying officials large sums to enable special treatment (in Soviet Russia corruption was widespread). Not that we're suggesting our federal government has become an entirely socialist system—yet. But the move in recent years toward more rules is quite alarming, and it carries with it the real possibility of stifling the very innovation and entrepreneurship that has made this country great.

Too much structure (i.e., rules) stifles freedom and creativity. Too little structure can breed chaos and corruption. We are unfortunately becoming a nation of people watching people to make sure that others don't violate the rules. But often the rules that we do have are not enforced. The solution is not, as some would suggest, to layer on more rules. The solution, ironically, may be to make the rules clearer, more transparent, and simpler.

Some people in general and some people in business will focus on finding the loopholes to give themselves an advantage. Nothing can be so ironclad as to prevent people from finding ways around onerous rules. So finding the minimally necessary structure or the right level of guidance to balance competing interests and maintain innovation and safety is really what the doctor ordered. Effectively applying this principle to the challenges facing the FDA as it confronts the Prescription Drug User Fee Act (PDUFA) and Medical Device User Fee Act (MDUFA) will be critical to success.

Government has a responsibility to protect its citizens from harm—whether the threat comes from abroad or within. The removal of bureaucratic rules that keep potentially life-saving innovations from reaching their intended audiences is clearly in the spirit of protecting citizens from harm. So, it is in that spirit that we look favorably on recent efforts within the FDA to accelerate the new-drug approval process.

Real-Life Example

The FDA's removal of Avastin's indication for breast cancer is a lagging indicator. The FDA was just picking up on what the market had already realized. One could even argue that the revoked approval was redundant, since the market had responded to postapproval studies, as indicated by the fact that use of the drug for treating metastatic breast cancer had plummeted as more data about the drug's limitations became available.

The ability of the market to self-correct supports the case for expanding the accelerated approval process to other therapeutic areas. But herein is the dilemma: Which therapeutic areas get to be a part of the accelerated process?

Who is the government to decide that one drug for, say, Alzheimer's disease has any more right to get to market more quickly than a drug for diabetes? And if the market is this responsive to available data, why don't we start utilizing accelerated approval for every drug? If the accelerated approval process is a good enough indicator of safety and efficacy for certain products, then why is it not sufficient for others?

It's pretty clear that there is a political upside to making approval requirements less onerous. The question becomes whether or not the government should get to decide which areas deserve research the most.

If the accelerated approval process were normative, manufacturers could design clinical studies that rely on data reflecting a real-world evidence approach and modeling, rather than the traditional, large-scale, randomized (placebo-controlled) clinical trials (RCTs) with their associated inclusion/exclusion issues. Instead of waiting years for an actual clinical outcome from RCTs, manufacturers could use a *surrogate end point* (like tumor shrinkage, in the case of cancer drugs) to establish an event that can reasonably predict increased survival rate. Drugs would reach the market more quickly and give many patients who might otherwise die the opportunity to try a progressive drug.

Additional confirmatory studies would provide longitudinal evidence that the drug either does or does not provide clinical benefits for specific sets of patients, allowing the FDA to react accordingly. Given trends toward personalized medicine, focused clinical studies for narrower patient populations seem more appropriate.

Utilizing accelerated approval could reduce development costs, and pharmaceutical companies could focus their attention on innovating new life-saving therapies, rather than having to funnel all their resources to getting one drug approved. This could revolutionize the industry as we know it.

Patent Life: Shooting Ourselves in the Foot

When you think about the industries where the United States has been preeminent, it's mostly a list of has-beens—steel, autos, and heavy equipment. Those few industries where the United States is still a world leader include pharmaceuticals and medical devices. But this is changing.

As described in Chapter 8, pharmaceutical and medical device manufacturers have 17 years from the date of patent issuance to make their investment pay off. But having a patent is not the same as having a product. First you need FDA approval.

That's when the real work begins. Experts estimate that it costs over $1 billion and 10 years to bring a new drug to market. Lots of patents never see the commercial light of day. In the earliest stages of discovery, side effects may prove to be problematic, so development stops. Some molecules may fail to perform. Drugs that make it to market have to recoup the costs for all the products that failed before them. Finally, CMS must agree to reimburse the product or its potential may be limited.

Given the substantial time and financial commitments required to bring a new drug to market, congressional and public pressure to further reduce the length of patent protection represents a major challenge for the U.S. medical products industry. What most people don't realize is that this very pressure puts at risk one of our few remaining industrial jewels.[33] The argument put forth in support of more limited protection is the opportunity to bring generics to market faster and at a significantly lower cost than branded pharmaceuticals.

That generics come at a cheaper price should come as no surprise to anyone. Generic manufacturers don't have to invest in risky R&D, don't bear the brunt of regulatory approval, and don't have the same commercialization costs to bear. But the focus on bringing generics out faster to lower overall healthcare costs misses one critical point. Pharmaceuticals, while highly visible, represent only about 10% of the cost of healthcare in the United States. And they enable greater productivity on the part of people taking them for the most part! If we're serious about lowering healthcare costs, then we need to look elsewhere.

Finally, increased regulation in this country makes it more difficult to get drugs approved in the first place—so much so that venture capitalists, in evaluating investment opportunities, commonly reject proposals from start-ups that want to launch their new products first in the United States. They regard such plans as reflecting business naiveté.

If the risk to innovation and access to life-saving new compounds isn't significant enough, consider this: Six million jobs—good jobs—are connected to the pharmaceutical and medical device industry. There was never a time we could afford to put six million jobs at risk—and certainly not now.

Questions for Policy Makers

- Are policies in place that will ensure transparency, accountability, and consumer choice?
- Does the policy create a framework and guidance to ensure that accountability and ensure the delivery apparatus is appropriately held accountable by consumers and other key stakeholders?
- Are there regulations in place to allow small businesses to take advantage of some of the same scale opportunities afforded to large businesses?
- Do the rules have sufficient "teeth" to ensure that accountability and transparency are in place?

Endnotes

1. Timothy Jost. "Implementing Health Reform: Navigator Grants, Another ACA Challenge Rejected, and More." *Health Affairs* blog. April 2015. http://healthaffairs.org/blog/2015/04/16 /implementing-health-reform-navigator-grants-another-aca -challenge-rejected-and-more/.
2. Centers for Medicare & Medicaid Services (CMS). "An Introduction to the Medicare EHR Incentive Program for Eligible Professionals." Department for Health & Human Services. http://www.cms.gov/Regulations-and-Guidance /Legislation/EHRIncentivePrograms/downloads/Beginners _Guide.pdf.

3. Eric Whitney. "Sharing Patient Records Is Still a Digital Dilemma for Doctors." NPR. March 2015. http:// www.npr.org/blogs/health/2015/03/06/388999602/sharing -patient-records-is-still-a-digital-dilemma-for-doctors.

4. Centers for Medicare & Medicaid Services. "State Medicaid Director Letter." Department of Health & Human Services. July 2008. http:// downloads.cms.gov/cmsgov/archived-downloads/SMDL/down loads/SMD073108.pdf.

5. Rita E. Numerof. "Why Accountable Care Organizations Won't Deliver Better Health Care—And Market Innovation Will." The Heritage Foundation. April 2011. http://www.heritage.org /research/reports/2011/04/why-accountable-care-organizations -wont-deliver-better-health-care-and-market-innovation-will.

6. Elliott S. Fisher, Douglas O. Staiger, Julie P. W. Bynum, and Daniel J. Gottlieb. "Creating Accountable Care Organizations: The Extended Hospital Medical Staff." *Health Affairs* 26 (1:) 44–57. 2007. http://content.healthaffairs.org/content/26/1/w44 .full.pdf+html.

7. Kelly J. Devers and Robert A. Berenson. "Can Accountable Care Organizations Improve the Value of Health Care by Solving the Cost and Quality Quandaries?" Urban Institute and Robert Wood Johnson Foundation. October 2009. http://www.urban .org/research/publication/can-accountable-care-organizations -improve-value-health-care-solving-cost-and and http://www .rwjf.org/en/library/research/2009/10/can-accountable-care -organizations-improve-the-value-of-health-c.html.

8. Mark Merlis. "Health Policy Brief: Accountable Care Organizations." *Health Affairs*. July 2010. http://www.health affairs.org/healthpolicybriefs/brief.php?brief_id=20.

9. One Hundred Eleventh Congress of the United States of America. "Medicare Shared Savings Program." Patient Protection and Affordable Care Act, H. R. 3590, Sec. 3022. January 2010.

10. Joshua Zeitlin. "More to the Story: A Look at ACOs under the ACA." *American Health Line*. October 2014. http://www .americanhealthline.com/analysis-and-insight/features/more -to-the-story.

11. This influence is not necessarily benign. "The size and power of Medicare are such as to easily distort the healthcare market-place, the consequences of which will ultimately be harmful

to everyone." (Harry Cain, "The Medicare Menace." *Harvard Health Policy Review* 2 (1): 20, 2001. http://www.hcs.harvard .edu/~epihc/currentissue/spring2001/cain.html).

12. Tim Brady and Barbie Robinson. "Medicare Hospital Prospective Payment System: How DRG Rates Are Calculated and Updated." U.S. Department of Health and Human Services, Office of Inspector General, Office of Evaluation and Inspections. August 2001. http://oig.hhs.gov/oei/reports/oei-09 -00-00200.pdf.

13. Louise J. Sargent and Renwyck Elder. "Overview of Medicare for Managed Care Professionals." *Journal of Managed Care Pharmacy* 2 (2): 165–167. 1996. http://www.amcp.org/data /jmcp/Update_165-172.pdf.

14. Harry A. Sultz and Kristina M. Young. "Financing Health Care." In *Health Care USA: Understanding Its Organization and Delivery*, 6th ed. Burlington, MA: Jones & Bartlett Learning, pp. 240–242. 2009.

15. Katherine Swartz and Troyen A. Brennan. "Integrated Health Care, Capitated Payment, and Quality: The Role of Regulation." *Annals of Internal Medicine* 124 (4): 443–444. 1996.

16. Jenny Gold. "9 Pioneer ACOs Jump Ship after First Year." *WebMD.* July 2013. http://www.webmd.com/health-insurance /20130716/9-pioneer-acos-jump-ship-after-first-year?page=2.

17. Melinda Beck. "A Medicare Program Loses More Health-Care Providers." *Wall Street Journal.* September 2014. http://www .wsj.com/articles/a-medicare-program-loses-more-health-care -providers-1411685388.

18. Bob Herman. "Sharp HealthCare ACO Drops out of Medicare's Pioneer Program." *Modern Healthcare.* August 2014. http://www.modernhealthcare.com/article/20140826 /NEWS/308269963.

19. Melanie Evans. "Medicare's Pioneer Program Down to 19 ACOs after Three More Exit." *Modern Healthcare.* September 2014. http://www.modernhealthcare.com/article/20140925 /NEWS/309259938.

20. Bruce Japsen. "White House Launches 'Next Generation ACO' with High-Touch Value-Based Care." *Forbes.* March 2015. http:// www.forbes.com/sites/brucejapsen/2015/03/10/obama-admin istration-launches-next-generation-of-value-based-care-a-high -touch-aco/.

21. U.S. Department of Health & Human Services. "Affordable Care Act Payment Model Saves More Than $384 Million in Two Years, Meets Criteria for First-Ever Expansion." May 2015. http://www.hhs.gov/news/press/2015pres/05/20150504a.html.

22. Rita E. Numerof and Michael N. Abrams. *Healthcare at a Turning Point: A Roadmap for Change.* Boca Raton, FL: CRC Press. 2013.

23. Rita E. Numerof. "What's Wrong with Healthcare Insurance Exchanges…" Galen Institute. May 2012. http://www.galen.org/assets/WhatsWrongWithExchanges.pdf.

24. The Congressional Budget Office (CBO) has estimated enrollment in Medicaid programs will expand from nearly 68.7 million in 2013 to 90.1 million in 2017. (Congressional Budget Office, "The Budget and Economic Outlook: Fiscal Years 2012 to 2022." Congress of the United States, January 2012, http://www.cbo.gov/sites/default/files/01-31-2012_Outlook.pdf).

25. Lena H. Sun and Niraj Chokshi. "Almost Half of Obamacare Exchanges Face Financial Struggles in the Future." *Washington Post.* May 2015. http://www.washingtonpost.com/national/health-science/almost-half-of-obamacare-exchanges-are-struggling-over-their-future/2015/05/01/f32eeea2-ea03-11e4-aae1-d642717d8afa_story.html.

26. There were "only seven state-mandated benefits in 1965 [and in 1997] there are nearly 1,000." (John C. Goodman and Merrill Matthews, Jr. "The Cost of Health Insurance Mandates." National Center for Policy Analysis, brief analysis no. 237. August 1997. http://www.ncpa.org/pub/ba237).

27. There were 2,271 mandates reported in 2012. (Victoria C. Bunce, "Health Insurance Mandates in the States 2012: Executive Summary." The Council for Affordable Health Insurance. April 2013. http://www.cahi.org/cahi_contents/resources/pdf/Mandatesinthestates2012Execsumm.pdf).

28. Victoria C. Bunce and J. P. Wieske. "Health Insurance Mandates in the States 2010." Council for Affordable Health Insurance. October 2010. http://www.cahi.org/cahi_contents/newsroom/article.asp?id=1037.

29. Catastrophic coverage plans operate more like other types of insurance (e.g., auto, home, life, or personal liability). However, comprehensive coverage plans have become something entirely different: They are used to pay for less expensive, run-of-the-mill expenses for which consumers can plan, such as regular

check-ups, vaccinations, and elective procedures. If auto insurance worked this way, claims would have to be filed, verified, and reimbursed to pay for oil changes or to replace a flat tire. If Americans would rethink the purpose of healthcare insurance, enormous cost could be pulled out of the system. High-deductible health plans and health savings accounts are encouraging more savvy consumer decisions in the purchase of healthcare services.

30. St. Louis Regional Chamber and Growth Association. http://www.stlregionalchamber.com/.
31. Rita E. Numerof. "Regulation's Impact on Innovation: A Two-Edged Sword." *Medical Progress Today.* May 2009. http://www.medicalprogresstoday.com/spotlight/spotlight_indarchive.php?id=1804.
32. The World Bank Group. "Health Expenditure per Capita (Current US$)." 2013. http://data.worldbank.org/indicator/SH.XPD.PCAP.
33. Rita E. Numerof. "Shooting Ourselves in the Foot." *Medical Progress Today.* January 2012. http://www.medicalprogresstoday.com/2012/01/shooting-ourselves-in-the-foot.php.

Chapter 11

Creating a Roadmap for Change

Revisiting the Challenge of Industry Transition

As we have argued throughout this book, the healthcare industry is clearly an industry in transition. Like other industries that have traveled this route before, healthcare faces unprecedented change. However, unlike others, the assaults are coming simultaneously from all four of the factors that create transition in any industry: significant changes in the regulatory environment, a dynamic and rapidly changing competitive landscape, shifts in technology, and changing market expectations. In the face of this, all industry players must challenge fundamental assumptions about their business models, how they go to market, the types of products and services they offer, the nature of their customer base, and the competencies that will be critical to continued success.

Even under normal circumstances, managing through this set of changes is hard. When all four forces descend at once, successful navigation becomes that much harder. Not surprisingly, there is enormous resistance to the needed changes. On the face of it, the resistance makes sense. Organizations have built infrastructure to support their current business model, and staff have been rewarded and promoted on the basis of it. Investments in the model have generally paid off. To make things harder, the current business model is still throwing off cash. So the challenge comes down to building the new amid uncertainty and general turbulence, while generating revenue from the old.

Despite the warning signs that the road ahead is "out" and a detour needs to be taken quickly, there is so much momentum behind the current way of doing business that it's going to be hard for many to avoid going over the cliff.

We have needed healthcare reform in this country. For the reasons we've outlined, the industry sectors didn't take needed action to fix serious problems when they could. In the face of the Patient Protection and Affordable Care Act (PPACA) they have been forced to. And the dust hasn't yet begun to settle. As one industry executive recently put it,

> PPACA was a gun to my head...Our entire industry had opportunity after opportunity to fix the problems facing us—lack of customer responsiveness, lack of transparency, lack of efficiency, lack of service integration, lack of meaningful choice—and we essentially chose to do nothing about it. Our future survival depends on our ability to reinvent ourselves...and some of us are unlikely to make it.

A sobering thought—one we hear expressed often from industry executives behind closed doors. PPACA, regardless of the view one has of the legislation, has created enormous disruption, and with it comes enormous opportunity as well as risk.

Unfortunately, we have proven ourselves capable of only suboptimal solutions to date. Without real clarity on the goal and an overarching, integrated strategy for how to realize it, with lots of choice in the process, we won't get the result we need. PPACA is both too prescriptive and not sufficiently strategic. It's a Rube Goldberg contraption that essentially doesn't work.

The intense debate around the constitutionality of the individual mandate really concerned fundamental issues regarding the legitimate role of government in our society. At one level, PPACA compels people to enter into a contract that's not necessarily in their own self-interest in order to subsidize others. It is a classic case of wealth transfer: confiscating individuals' earned assets or prerogatives by the government to redistribute them to those deemed more worthy. As David Brooks (columnist for the *New York Times*) pointed out, the law represents another step toward centralization of power in the federal government.[1]

He suggested that the government could have defined the overall goal and then left it to the states and individuals to figure out how to get there. This is exactly the position we've been arguing for years.

Most people in this country would agree that providing some form of basic coverage for all in need is the mark of a good society. In other countries, government provides a base level of coverage for all of its citizens, with private insurance coverage layering options on top. What's included in that base has been hotly debated in the United States. Even though the country is a meritocracy, there are progressive threads that find the idea of a multitiered system abhorrent. Some have the view that "everyone among us deserves the same" and that anything else is unfair. With unlimited dollars, this approach might be desirable. However, as we've pointed out, we don't have unlimited dollars, and with the "silver tsunami" forming, we don't have much time to fix the problem.

Establishing the central goal might have worked if the Centers for Medicare & Medicaid Services (CMS) had said years ago, "We're not going to pay for never events; we're going to tie payment to outcomes." They had the authority to do it, but for the reasons discussed here, didn't. PPACA gave them the political cover to do it, but ironically, any real teeth have been taken out.

Part of the dilution has come from pressure from the delivery sector and a lack of real spine on the part of the political establishment. The political reality of healthcare delivery and how money flows deserves comment here. In many communities, hospitals are the largest employers and large campaign contributors. People are dependent on these employers for jobs and, as importantly, for their well-being as healthcare providers when they're sick. So, the idea of applying real pressure for fundamental change is a tricky proposition. The irony is that in many of these organizations, people at the top are paid richly and their organizations receive substantial subsidies from the government, while at the same time they decry the lack of reimbursement and their inability to redesign their business models.

Understanding the money flow helps to inform a productive dialogue, allowing consumers to be more thoughtful in their utilization, and business leaders to be wiser in their purchase of services. Clearly, delivery organizations alone can't mount the changes that are needed. The basis for payment needs to change, and they own one key part of the puzzle. Real solutions will require collaboration among industry players in local markets. We're all part of the problem, and we all need to be part of the solution. Unfortunately, the dominant moves in the industry have been consistent with the current business model.

Safety in Size? The Rush to Affiliation

As has been true in years past, industry consolidation and attempts to leverage size and scale have been used to stave off competitive threat and to generate enough scale to extract concessions from suppliers and payers. In the 1990s, hospitals embarked on massive affiliations and buying sprees. Hospitals scooped up primary care practices, often as a defensive maneuver to protect the referral base for lucrative specialty services. A great many of those ventures didn't pan out as expected. Some hospital systems overpaid for the assets they bought. Still others couldn't get the productivity gains they'd envisioned, learning the hard way that employed physicians aren't the same as private practice doctors, and that managing small businesses required a nimbleness and focus that most large, siloed bureaucratic institutions couldn't master. Not unlike other mergers or acquisitions across industries, the failure rate was quite high, frequently due to cultural incompatibility.

We're likely to see a repeat of the 1990s in the next 5 years unless better discipline is applied to the hard work of merger and acquisition integration. We're already seeing physicians exiting private practices in droves to become hospital employees. But remember that getting the deal inked is typically the easy part.

What most healthcare systems, payers, and manufacturers don't realize, however, is that the real threat comes from not-in-kind competition, as we've described earlier. So scale and competitive consolidation that rely on the current business model will offer only temporary respite from the real disruptive innovation lurking around the corner. As we described in Chapter 1, new entrants have begun to sell insurance and offer retail healthcare services. Even supermarkets are dipping their toes into the healthcare business, capitalizing on convenience, price, choice, and ease of use.

These major retailers represent a threat to the way things have been. They've successfully shaken up prescription drug pricing by offering generics at very low prices. They understand negotiation in a way that insurers and hospitals don't. They understand outcomes and move quickly in response to market needs. The problems of unpredictable costs and inefficient management of chronic illness could be the very problems firms like these are ready to tackle. What happens when retail chains jump into the mix and start offering health insurance or when Progressive's model for car insurance changes the dynamics for this insurance market?

It is likely that in the short run hospitals will join forces and use their size as a competitive deterrent. Smaller stand-alone hospital groups find affiliations with larger, better financed organizations attractive in the face of increasing regulation and changes in how hospitals will be paid. Whereas size has historically been used to extract higher payments from insurers, that's unlikely to be the case today. Hospitals must become more efficient in the face of reduced reimbursement from Medicare and other insurers must become more transparent and more consumer centered. They must also demonstrate the economic and clinical value of what they offer compared to alternatives and answer the question as to why should anyone should come to their institution?

Insurers have dipped their toes in the water and acquired healthcare delivery organizations; health and disease management companies; research, IT, and health outcomes organizations; and pharmacy benefit managers (PBMs). As one example on the delivery side, UnitedHealth Group (UHG) went on a buying spree in 2011, which continues. Some of the systems it has purchased include Monarch Healthcare, Memorial, and AppleCare, all California-based delivery groups, and Southwest Medical Associates, based in Nevada. A driving force behind this is the exercise of more control over practice patterns and ultimately cost.

One of the real concerns this raises in the short run is the massive consolidation of power in a few very large players, limiting choice and accountability. Similarly, it raises the question of whether they are getting too big to fail, or worse yet, too big to care. Private equity firms have also entered the game. Oak Hill Capital Partners established a partnership with St. Louis-based Ascension Health to buy Catholic hospitals around the country. Others who are looking to get into the market are sitting on the sidelines, evaluating how these new arrangements perform financially.

Consolidation and the Challenge for Manufacturers

These moves will have significant and likely negative implications for manufacturers selling into the delivery sector. With size comes greater purchasing power and the ability to extract price concessions from manufacturers wanting to sell their goods and services into these organizations. Increasingly, we expect to see downward price pressure, accelerated consolidation, and fewer suppliers serving specific markets—a trend that began in earnest in 2010. Unless manufacturers can demonstrate the economic and clinical value of their product in relation to alternative products and therapeutic options, the commoditization trend will accelerate.

Some industry observers have seen these shifts as good for the industry, suggesting that insurers need to start thinking about themselves as one-stop shops. These kinds of moves, they argue, can enable greater competitiveness as they look to create networks of hospitals and doctors responsible for delivering and coordinating care in large communities. It sounds a lot like the government's plan for accountable care organizations (ACOs), which we discussed in Chapter 10. Unlike the government's plan, this one is being initiated by the market and is insurer driven rather than provider driven. Like the government plan, it erroneously assumes that bigger will be more efficient and effective. But none of the players has created a new business model, so it's unlikely that consolidation will result in a better solution. In fact, such consolidation will present fewer choices to patients in any given market, but might result in a stronger system financially. That strength, in turn, *could* deliver better quality at lower cost. Given past history, however, that's unlikely.

The problem with this approach is the consolidation of power in some of the very institutions that have brought us to the brink. Insurers have not been patient centered, let alone consumer centered. Large delivery organizations have not been efficient, integrated, or consumer centered. They have been guilty of upcoding, being opaque in their charges, and adding unnecessary services. Moreover, their service processes haven't generally centered on the patient/consumer. Ownership by insurers, who are committed to reducing unneeded services, has the potential to address cost, but only if the fundamental business model of both sectors changes. So far we haven't seen demonstrations of such leadership.

Those large healthcare delivery organizations that have successfully mastered the challenge of managing variation in cost and quality—like Kaiser, Intermountain, Cleveland Clinic, and Geisinger, among others—have invested millions of dollars annually in building the IT infrastructure, but more importantly have committed to compliance to agreed-upon care paths across a broader continuum of care approach. Such change is not for the faint of heart or conflict avoidant among us.

In some respects, creating an ACO to achieve clinical and financial integration is naïve. No one told Microsoft to acquire companies and combine under one umbrella, or Johnson & Johnson to become a diverse holding company with products ranging from baby shampoo and Band-Aids to complex medical devices, diagnostics, and pharmaceutical and biotech agents. Nor was Boeing directed to make all of the components of its new aircraft itself. Indeed, in every market, successful companies have engaged selectively and strategically with partners that shared a common vision. Their strategic alliances, strategic partnerships, or joint ventures succeeded or failed on the clarity of the vision, the rigor of execution, the commitment to a common purpose and shared culture. None was successful because it was legally *mandated*.

Additional Challenges for Manufacturers

Manufacturers not only have to figure out how to address their changing customer base, but they are also under significant pressure in light of a hostile business environment. The pharmaceutical industry, in particular, has been the common target of a convenient alliance of media, government, and academia, each with its own agenda. It has been accused of, among other things, influencing physicians for purely commercial reasons—in some cases bringing products with dubious value to market, creating demand for drugs to treat conditions of questionable medical need, withholding clinical data that would position products in a less than optimal light, and using continuing medical education (CME) for commercial promotion as opposed to balanced objective education. The general lack of real evidence behind many of the accusations, the tendency to generalize from specific incidents to the whole industry, and a generally nonscientific approach to the underlying controversy have had the continuing feel of a political witch hunt gathering momentum.

As an example, a vocal academic minority believes that industry can never add value to CME and should be out of the business altogether, except for its "obligation" to pay for CME (and related grants) through an undifferentiated common pool of funds that others would administer. But let's face it: Every sector, every professional, every individual has a bias.

Critics make the assumption that any commercial interest in the mix taints objectivity and negates any legitimate value. The further assumption that commercial interests are the only source of bias is simplistic. Many of the actors in the health-care debate have underlying agendas related to control of power and resources, and some of the extreme positions taken reflect a broader antibusiness orientation that is increasingly common in the current political dialogue.

In any case the business model for manufacturers will certainly change. The days of getting paid for products, regardless of whether or not they work for a given patient, will come to a close with a move to more personalized medicine and greater diagnostic precision. As one pharmaceutical executive said to us recently, "In what other industry can you get paid a premium price for administering products you know only work less than 20% of the time? We need to get used to the fact that we had a great business model, and it's on its way out."

Creating Collaborations to Develop Lifetime Value

Collaborations are where the opportunity lies. It will be up to manufacturers to design—on the basis of a rich understanding of the interactions between disease states, lifestyle variables, and the characteristics of their products—interventions that provide maximum clinical and economic value over the lifetime of a patient. These interventions are likely to incorporate service wraps and other inherently differentiating features that boost the effectiveness of the core products and enhance their value.

Demonstrating this enhanced value will require studies that take into account the expected downstream impacts of an intervention and allow quantification of these benefits in a comprehensive fashion. Their focus will be longer term and the outcome measures more complex than are common today. There are implications for the scope of interventions as well; for example, a monitored, structured lifestyle change program might be necessary to maximize the lifetime value of an intervention, which would effectively render it a part of a manufacturer's offering.

It will also fall to manufacturers to shape the understanding of insurers, patients, and physicians regarding this approach. Ultimately, the case that manufacturers would like to make is that the entirety of benefits accruing to an intervention should be reflected in the valuation of that intervention and weighed against its costs. This would justify premium pricing and help to avoid what might otherwise become the default position for payers and, increasingly, a position being taken by large provider organizations—a preference for the least expensive intervention that alleviates the currently salient problem, an approach that could well be "penny wise and pound foolish."

The good news is that payers, physicians, and patients are primed to accept a lifetime value orientation; they've been saying for more than 20 years that prevention is less costly than treatment, so they can hardly object to the idea that downstream impacts are important. The bad news is that this imposes a heavy burden of proof on manufacturers. Outcome studies are risky endeavors with large uncertainties regarding the size of the economic and quality-of-life impacts that can be expected downstream. The burden may be too heavy to bear unless patients, physicians and, especially, payers make commitments to collaboration.

Manufacturers, however, have something of value that can be traded: the ability to focus their efforts on the development of supremely cost-effective treatments. That key point of leverage needs to be used to convince other parties that requiring absolute proof of the lifetime benefits of an intervention before approving payment is not in anyone's best interests because it will stifle the development of these ultimately more cost-effective and innovative approaches. Instead, manufacturers should support efforts based on agreed-upon methods for estimating those downstream impacts, with the true value to be determined over time as actual patient records become available, essentially elevating the importance of postmarket studies.

Many insurers already have systems for tracking patient outcomes in place (Kaiser Permanente is perhaps the most advanced on this front) and are well positioned to aid in these efforts. With its focus on long-term outcomes, CMS would be another logical initial partner, as would large nationalized or seminationalized healthcare systems in the United Kingdom, Australia, and Canada.

For manufacturers, the approach will be to devise a set of quantitative models that represent best estimates regarding the downstream impacts. These models, which would capture the causal pathways linking disease states, lifestyle, and treatment variables, would serve as the basis for estimating the full economic and clinical impacts of an intervention and could also help to guide the search for evidence by specifying the outcome measures of primary interest. These models would be vetted with payers, which would agree to value a limited number of interventions prospectively on the basis of the predicted downstream benefits.

Why Now?

The lifetime value approach is simple—almost obvious—but it hasn't made major inroads yet because the pressure required to move the various elements of the healthcare industry toward it simply didn't exist. Today, however, the pressure is on, and it continues to mount. The time is right for manufacturers and insurers to make the leap.

The approach is entirely ethical; it is a pure attempt to deliver better health outcomes with maximum efficiency. The end result will be sustainable differentiation of interventions, a more efficient, cost-effective healthcare system, and improved outcomes when viewed from the perspective of the continuum of care. It's a powerful case to make—one that needs to be made today.

Reprising the Consumer

From our perspective, much of the resistance to real healthcare reform in this country stems from the reluctance of market players to envision another world in which the consumer—not the insurer, not the physician, and not the hospital—is at the center. As the business model shifts to a consumer orientation, those players who have long dominated the healthcare marketplace will be challenged by market leaders that are more nimble and retail savvy. We anticipate that over the next several years, despite PPACA's attempt to define comprehensive, universal health benefits as an entitlement, the move to a defined contribution—by both employers and government subsidies—will encourage more personal choice. The market will move from a wholesale model to a retail model, the former focused on the employer/corporation and the latter on the individual consumer.

With this shift will come a change in core competencies. As we discussed in prior chapters, real customer service will become king, characterized by availability, 24/7 access support, broad choice, and customized services to meet the unique needs of specific customer segments.

Power of Choice

One general strategy for producing net positive value to physicians, patients, or payers is to provide them with choices. Presumably, people will pick the option with greater value— at least that's what economists tell us; thus, if hospitals add service no one is worse off, and some people are better off. As a practical matter, of course, there may be additional costs associated with providing extra options, and this may even make both options more expensive, but the general principle is still sound. Offering choices generally increases the value you provide.

But what kinds of choices can hospitals offer? A number of hospitals and hospital systems (such as Alegent in Omaha, Nebraska and Memorial Health System in South Bend, Indiana) have decided that one choice they can offer is *where* patients engage with medical services. They have opened walk-in clinics in places like drug stores, grocery stores, and other locations. Easily accessible and offering extended hours, these clinics give patients a way to have simple diagnostic tests performed on their own schedule. They give worried parents of ailing children an alternative to phone tag with on-call doctors and "can you come in at 2:00 tomorrow afternoon?" and give those without a primary care physician an alternative to appearing at the emergency room door for a sore throat, pinkeye, or common earache. Those who use them love them, and many happily forgo coverage under their insurance for the convenience the clinics provide (though many such clinics do accept insurance). They aren't for everyone, but then, no one has to use them. That's the beauty of choice.

But choice doesn't have to be limited to where people seek care. *How* hospitals provide care and *what kind* of care they provide can also be points of differentiation. Would patients be willing to pay more out of pocket for a single room? Some of them would, a point that hasn't been lost on U.S. hospitals for many years. A hospital in Canada, by way of example, takes the idea a step further. Toronto East General Hospital, in Ontario, offers patients the option to upgrade from standard rooms to semiprivate, private, or private deluxe rooms, and posts the nightly charge on its website. It's a relatively easy thing for Toronto East to do because virtually every patient has the same coverage, but the calculations that would be required to offer similar options in the United States are hardly prohibitive. And room upgrades are just the beginning; the opportunities for premium services are virtually unlimited. Premium food, bedside Internet access, frequent visits by friendly faces might all prove popular with patients, and all have the potential to be very profitable.

For those concerned about an increase in enforced cost effectiveness, whether from consumer-directed healthcare, reinvigorated managed care plans, or a desperate CMS, creating choices now will help in two ways. First, it will provide a source of revenue independent of reimbursement: The less the consumer pays for, the more opportunities there are to offer premium services. In the longer term, by getting into the game of providing "by choice" premium services directly to patients, hospitals will be situated to take advantage of premium private insurance plans (like those that have sprung up around other nationalized healthcare systems).

Increase Perceived Quality

Another way to increase value is to increase perceived quality of care. Hospitals might, for example, select a set of highly salient outcome measures, work to become world class on those measures, and market their outcomes. Metrics might include recovery times, complication rates, and rates of hospital-contracted infections. Volume within a given diagnosis can be a differentiator, because experience is associated with competence; a similar argument can be made for the creation and marketing of *super teams* within a specialty.

Efforts to increase the perceived quality of offerings can also be directed at patients. There may, for example, be opportunities to restructure, or simply re-explain, care delivery so that it makes sense to them. The ability to tell a coherent story about *why* a service works the way it does is a major differentiator of successful firms in most service-providing industries. When auto rental companies advertise that they'll pick people up so that renters don't have to figure out a way to get to the rental office, or financial services firms explain that they provide personal financial planning services to ensure that their clients' investments are structured to meet their needs, they create a reason for customers to voluntarily choose them despite a price premium. If hospitals can tell a similar story about cardiovascular care—a "we'll do these tests and you'll talk to these people because..." story—they can also increase the perception of quality and command a premium. This is especially true for the first hospital to create such a coherent story.

As is the case with offering increased choice, increasing the perceived quality of services positions healthcare systems to thrive in a world that is increasingly concerned with cost effectiveness. At the very least it creates a compelling argument that their treatment is worth a premium.

Competing on value may be more difficult than competing on cost, but it offers opportunities for sustainable differentiation, improved relations with others in the healthcare community (including patients), new revenue streams, and better margins. And it is being done today, in many places, in many ways. Ultimately, the value provided by hospitals (and other healthcare providers) goes beyond standardized care at the lowest cost. It means finding ways to provide more. More choice, better service, and increased convenience are the first places to look.

Creating and Sustaining a New Business Model

It's hard for any organization to conceptualize a new business model, especially when meeting the current plan is getting increasingly difficult in a dynamic market. This is the work of executive leaders. Only they can envision a different future and make the difficult decisions required to reconfigure their organization to achieve its new vision. This cannot be accomplished over the course of a few weeks of focused planning meetings. It's ongoing executive leadership work that must remain a top priority, even while these same leaders are also running their current business which they are still expected to grow and keep profitable.

Once envisioned, a new business model must be embedded into the organization. This is an equally difficult aspect of creating and sustaining a new business model. A company is reliant on its managers for such change, and they are steeped in the old business model. Managers are usually promoted on the basis of strong technical skills and the ability to execute efficiently within the existing structure and business model. As a result, many managers are likely to lack the managerial skills that allow them to drive change through the organization, and they are often exceptionally resistant to changing the system that has worked so well for them.

True managers need an understanding of their role in the organization that goes beyond technical expertise to encompass things like strategy-directed corporate stewardship. They need to understand where the organization is going and what their role will be in getting there. Without redefining the role of management, and providing the training and tools to support it, most current managers will never reach that point. As healthcare industry leaders act to change their business models, they need to give more attention to the management infrastructure necessary to implement and sustain it.

Harnessing Consumer Choice and Competition to Ensure Accountability: Final Thoughts for Policy Makers

As we've discussed throughout this book, initiatives that rely on complex organizational experiments to build accountability are not only likely to fail, but also likely to increase costs. Instead, policy makers should establish market conditions where innovative accountable organizations can flourish in a competitive environment, driven by consumer choice. It's easy to imagine how, in such an environment, organizations that are responsive and accountable to patients could flourish. They can focus on prevention, cost efficiency, and improved outcomes and rely on market incentives to enhance accountability across the care continuum.

Imagining a New Market

While PPACA provides health insurance for Americans who previously lacked coverage, it has done so at enormous cost and will continue to exacerbate the trend of provider consolidation, thereby reducing competition, and leading to greater inefficiency, less innovation, and, ultimately, less access to healthcare for consumers. Achieving better health outcomes at lower cost can be accomplished by eliminating perverse financial incentives and unnecessary bureaucracy. Modifying PPACA with enabling legislation that would provide robust free-market choice and real competition would transform the delivery of healthcare. Market pressures would stimulate organizations to deliver better health outcomes at lower cost.

In a free market for health plans and providers, competing organizations will have powerful incentives to pay for healthcare delivery that reflects predictive care paths and evidence-based medicine. Providers *and* healthcare delivery organizations would be required to demonstrate that their services deliver economic and clinical value. To create accountability, healthcare delivery organizations would address variation in treatment practices and inefficiencies in care delivery. Establishing predictive care paths and effectively using evidence-based medicine would help providers and organizations achieve better quality and cost-effective health outcomes.

Properly used, clinical effectiveness research would be integral to assessing the value of various procedures, care paths, and strategies. Providers and the organizations with which they are affiliated would need to provide evidence to support the value of the care they deliver before they can expect to be reimbursed for their services.

Using predictive care paths and evidence-based medicine would lead to effective treatment approaches that are good for all stakeholders—patients, physicians, and organizations. These policies would help improve outcomes, establish efficiencies, reduce variations in treatment patterns, and create baselines for determining effectiveness. Instead of the standard top-down administrative payment arrangements modeled on Medicare, primary care physicians would replace resource-based relative-value units (RBRVUs) with a time-based and outcome-based approach that reflects real prices, market value, and transparency.

Securing better healthcare at lower cost will involve changing the wrong-headed financial incentives and bureaucracy characterizing the present third-party payment system that dominates both the public and private sectors.

Within every organization in a competitive and transparent environment, financial incentives that reward outcomes will be critical to improving quality of care and gaining market share. Primary care physicians would be able to take a leadership role in ensuring accountability for care, to spend the time required to accurately diagnose patients, and to focus on achieving better outcomes. The incentive to subject patients to tests or other procedures that may not be helpful is removed. This approach will also remove the incentives that drive specialists to conduct unnecessary medical procedures; creating counterincentives to work across the care continuum to achieve improved healthcare will be essential.

The rapid evolution of the current system toward these types of organizational arrangements will not take place until federal and state policy makers eliminate the existing barriers to private health insurance competition and create a truly competitive marketplace by giving patient-consumers direct control of both healthcare dollars and decisions. In a transparent, information-driven environment, doctors would need to compete for patients, and those who follow predictive care paths and use evidence-based medicine to provide quality care in a cost-effective and transparent manner should succeed.

A truly competitive space provides smaller businesses with the same opportunity to flourish and achieve market share that large organizations have. Each must be able to demonstrate accountability for its role in delivering integrated and coordinated care.

In order to achieve such a level playing field, policy makers must break down the barriers to private insurance competition by increasing transparency, accessibility to market information and data, and consumer education, while preventing patient discrimination. Doing so empowers the *real* consumers—patients—to make informed decisions about the healthcare for which they are ultimately paying. Informing patients and letting them shop around for the coverage that best meets their needs will ultimately lead to increased demand for better outcomes, an emphasis on prevention and health maintenance, and lower premiums.

End Game

At its most basic level, adapting to a changing landscape means a shift in thinking from simply controlling costs to actively seeking growth *by doing business differently.* Competing in this market is a new game. It will take a redefinition of customers, products, and value propositions. And it will require the development of competencies and management infrastructure to create and sustain an environment where entrepreneurial activity can flourish.

The end game is better health outcomes at lower cost. It will only happen if consumers are empowered to make better choices and incented to do so. Twenty-first-century solutions to healthcare will reflect collaboration and innovation in the business models of each sector. Most importantly a new healthcare future will require a level of integration and coordination among disparate, previously siloed players in the industry—manufacturers, payers, and healthcare delivery providers working in concert with savvy consumers. This is reflected in the intersection of the Venn diagram in Figure 11.1.

The end game can't be prescribed by governments at either the state or federal level. Government can help enable this process but it can't mandate it. It can establish the goals and create powerful incentives for change. Success requires every one of us to drive real change. If we do, we'll all be winners. The model of healthcare tomorrow is highly connected, highly integrated, information rich and technology enabled. And it is the consumer who ultimately will determine the outcome.

Creating a twenty-first-century model for healthcare means creating value in healthcare—achieving better health outcomes at lower cost—and it requires transparency and greater consistency in reporting outcomes. But transparency and outcomes

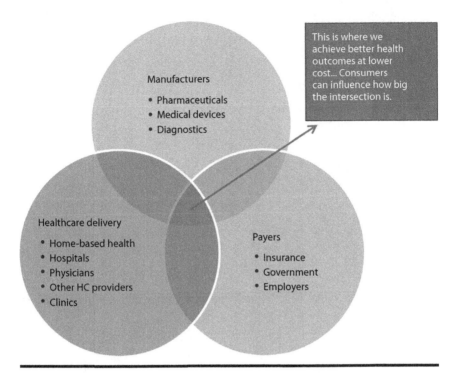

Figure 11.1 The twenty-first century model for healthcare. (Courtesy of Numerof & Associates, Inc.)

have to be tied to financial incentives for better performance. We are all in this together. Improving quality of care, reducing error, fostering prevention, and ensuring efficient treatment will require the engagement of all stakeholders in a new partnership for better health.

The future is possible.

Endnote

1. Savannah Guthrie. *Meet the Press*, NBC. April 2012. http://www .nbcnews.com/id/46915274/ns/meet_the_press-transcripts/t /meet-press-transcript-april/#.VYgaZvlVhHw.

Index

building the value narrative for
consumers, employers, and
insurers, 132–135
    emerging market
requirements, 132
    traveling for care, 133
    who is making the transition,
133–135
bundled price, competing with,
131–132
delivering value tomorrow,
124–131
    bundled pricing, case study
of, 130–131
    consumer expectations, 125
    cost transparency, 128
    fee-for-service environment,
129
    foundation for population
health and bundled pricing,
124
    medical education, 126
    proactive approach to market
in transition, 131
    rationalizing failure, 129
    steps, 127–128
future of rural hospitals, 138–140
    commercial entities, 140
    intersection of rural hospitals
and retail medicine, 139
    low-hanging fruit, 140
how hospitals and health systems
should change, 135–136
how value is defined, 136–137
questions for delivery
organizations, 140
NHS, *see* National Health Service (UK)
Niche busters, 195
NMDP, *see* National Marrow Donor
Program
Not-in-kind competition, 281
NP, *see* Nurse practitioner
Nurse practitioner (NP), 61

O

Oak Hill Capital Partners, 282
Obesity, treatment of, 184
ODD, *see* Orphan drug designation
Office of Inspector General (OIG),
86, 217
OIG, *see* Office of Inspector
General
Orphan drug designation (ODD),
195
Outcome studies, 287
Over-the-counter (OTC) products, 3

P

Patient-Centered Outcomes
Research Institute (PCORI),
83
Patient-powered research networks
(PPRNs), 84
Patient Protection and Affordable
Care Act (PPACA), 241
additional regulations since
introduction of, 30
administrative behemoths
created by, 241
alternative payment mechanisms
authorized by, 121
disruption created by, 278
issues not addressed by, 249
legislation, 7
lessons from the field, 251–252
mandates emanating from, 246
Medicaid expansion through,
79
modifying of, 293–294
provider accountability under,
249–250
role of ACOs in, 243–245
unfair competitive advantage
under, 250–251
unsustainability of, 256

About the Authors

Rita E. Numerof, PhD, president of Numerof & Associates, Inc., is an internationally recognized consultant and author with more than 25 years of experience in the field of strategy development and execution, business model design, and market analysis.

Her clients have included Fortune 500 companies such as Johnson & Johnson, Eli Lilly, Pfizer, Westinghouse, AstraZeneca, Merck, Abbott Laboratories, major healthcare institutions, payers, and government agencies. The focus of her consulting addresses the challenges of maintaining competitive advantage in highly dynamic and regulated markets.

Dr. Numerof has been a consistent advocate for the importance of strategic differentiation; organizational alignment of structure, competencies, and metrics to ensure effective implementation; and anticipating rather than reacting to industry trends. She's been a pioneer in the area of economic and clinical value, anticipating the impact of changing global payer attitudes on the fundamental business model of the healthcare industry. Her work across the entire healthcare spectrum gives her a unique perspective on the challenges and needs of manufacturers, physicians, payers, and healthcare delivery institutions.

Under her leadership, Dr. Numerof has developed proprietary approaches that provide precise insight and practical solutions to some of the industry's most complex business challenges. Taking a systemic approach, Dr. Numerof has addressed such diverse issues as population health management, comparative effectiveness research, accountable care, bundled pricing, consumer engagement, operationalizing compliance and transparency, portfolio management, the identification of growth platforms that provide sustainable differentiation through economic and clinical value, and effective commercialization based on value propositions that matter to key constituencies.

Dr. Numerof is widely published in business journals and has authored six books. She has served as an advisor to members of Congress on healthcare reform and comparative effectiveness research and to the Centers for Medicare & Medicaid Services on innovation. She was a senior advisor with the Center for Health Transformation, a regular contributor to the Manhattan Institute, and wrote the Heritage Foundation's policy paper, *Why Accountable Care Organizations Won't Deliver Better Health Care—and Market Innovation Will.* She led a tripartisan, cross-industry work group on payment reform and developed recommendations for new payment models that incent better health outcomes at lower cost. In addition, Dr. Numerof provides guidance to policy organizations and agencies on the relationship between innovation and regulation, working to support innovation and ensure responsive regulatory oversight.

Dr. Numerof graduated magna cum laude from the Honors College, Syracuse University, and received her MSS and PhD from Bryn Mawr College.

Michael N. Abrams, MA, cofounder and managing partner of Numerof & Associates, Inc., has served as an internal and external consultant to Fortune 50 corporations, major pharmaceutical and medical device companies, healthcare delivery institutions, the financial services industry, and government agencies for over 25 years. He has worked extensively in the areas of strategic planning and implementation, product strategy and portfolio development, market analysis, consumer engagement, and operational improvement.

Abrams is well known for his expertise in the design and implementation of strategies for building competitive differentiation, defining sustainable value, identifying market influence mechanisms, and translating white space analysis into the creation of innovative solutions to meet unmet needs. His ability to identify market opportunities and to effectively improve organizational performance has been an invaluable resource to client companies on a global basis across industries.

Abrams has structured and managed innovative programs to evaluate care delivery and payment models, thereby defining the internal change processes necessary to translate business opportunities into effective market position, operations, product portfolio management, and new product design consistent with changing regulatory requirements. He has provided solutions to healthcare delivery systems to improve the management of care transitions, thereby reducing unnecessary hospitalizations; and reduced length of stay by identifying and managing factors causing extended stays, changing admissions and patient care management processes, and managing across the continuum of care while maintaining or improving clinical outcomes and reducing costs.

He is experienced in the design and execution of econometric modeling and analysis and decision support systems for a variety of science-driven industries and applications. He has designed technology solutions to meet a wide range of needs, including strategic account planning and management, thought leader interface, and key opinion leader management. His ability to manage the process of technology integration to support business objectives across multiple business environments ensures return on investment.

Abrams has written extensively on economic and clinical value creation and the need for integrated, systemic solutions to the challenges facing the global healthcare industry. His articles have appeared in more than a dozen leading business journals, and he coauthored the books *Healthcare at a Turning Point: A Roadmap for Change* and *Employee Retention: Solving the Healthcare Crisis*. As an adjunct faculty member of Washington University, St. Louis and LaSalle College, School of Business Administration in Philadelphia, Abrams has taught MBA courses in strategic management, product planning and evaluation, quantitative decision making, and market analysis.

Abrams completed his doctoral work in business policy at St. Louis University. He received his MA from George Washington University in Washington, DC.

About Numerof & Associates

Numerof & Associates guides businesses across the global healthcare sector to compete and win. Bringing cross-industry expertise and a tailored approach, we develop and operationalize strategies that help clients define, demonstrate, and deliver value.

For more than 25 years, our rigorous, structured approach has solved complex strategic and operational problems in a range of industries in transition. We've served as trusted advisors to clients across the healthcare sector, from healthcare delivery organizations and major payers to global pharmaceutical, medical device, and diagnostics companies.

Our work across the entire healthcare value chain enables us to anticipate challenges from the perspectives of the patient, physician, supplier, payer, and healthcare delivery institution. We understand how policy, demographic, and technology drivers have shaped the current environment and will drive future change. To serve our clients, we have developed proprietary approaches that provide precise insight and practical solutions to some of the sector's most complex business challenges.

Dr. Numerof's seasoned team members work side by side with clients to bring strategy to life. We facilitate cultural shifts, build competencies, and enhance competitive differentiation based on economic and clinical value. We challenge thinking about approaches, provide guidance on how to navigate unfamiliar territories, and help ensure successful implementation.

Our clients trust us to tell them what they need to hear, driving out risk and capturing value in the process. In every challenge, we see the opportunity to help clients take the lead. Our work with manufacturers such as Johnson & Johnson, Merck, Medtronic, Bristol-Myers Squibb, Pfizer, and Eli Lilly; payers like UnitedHealthcare; and leading healthcare delivery systems provides a unique perspective on the continuum and the challenges that complex organizations face.